H 572

Dyslexia and Literacy

D1056470

LB1050.5 D93 2002

Hjelmquist, Erland, 1948-

Dyslexia and literacy

The Publishers wish to express their thanks to the Swedish Council for Working Life and Social Research for their generous support of this publication.

Dyslexia and Literacy

Edited by

ERLAND HJELMQUIST

Department of Psychology, Göteborg University, Göteborg, Sweden

and

CURT VON EULER

Karolinska Institutet, Stockholm, Sweden

Consultant in Dyslexia

MARGARET SNOWLING

University of York

Arrendale Library
Piedmont College
1021 Central Avenue
P.O. Box 40
Demorest, GA 30535

W
WHURR PUBLISHERS
LONDON AND PHILADELPHIA

© 2002 Whurr Publishers Ltd
First published 2002
by Whurr Publishers Ltd
19b Compton Terrace, London N1 2UN, England and
325 Chestnut Street, Philadelphia PA 19106, USA

All rights reserved. No part of this publication may be
reproduced, stored in a retrieval system, or transmitted in any
form or by any means, electronic, mechanical, photocopying,
recording or otherwise, without the prior permission of
Whurr Publishers Limited.

This publication is sold subject to the conditions that it shall
not, by way of trade or otherwise, be lent, resold, hired out, or
otherwise circulated without the publisher's prior consent in
any form of binding or cover other than that in which it is
published and without a similar condition including this
condition being imposed upon any subsequent purchaser.

British Library Cataloguing in Publication Data

A catalogue record for this book
is available from the British Library.

ISBN: 1 86156 316 7

Printed and bound in the UK by Athenaeum Press Ltd,
Gateshead, Tyne & Wear.

Contents

List of contributors

Elisabeth Arnbak, Department of Educational Psychology, University of Education, Copenhagen, Denmark

Carsten Elbro, Department of General and Applied Linguistics, University of Copenhagen, Copenhagen, Denmark

Curt von Euler, Karolinska Institutet, Stockholm, Sweden

Uta Frith, Institute of Cognitive Neuroscience and Department of Psychology, University College London, UK

Päivi Helenius, Brain Research Unit, Low Temperature Laboratory, Helsinki University of Technology, Espoo, Finland

Erland Hjelmquist, Department of Psychology, Göteborg University, Göteborg, Sweden

Torleiv Høien, The Dyslexia Research Foundation, Stavanger, Norway

Che Kan Leong, Department of Educational Psychology and Special Education, University of Saskatchewan, Saskatoon, Saskatchewan, Canada

Ingvar Lundberg, Department of Psychology, Göteborg University, Göteborg, Sweden

Heinz Mayringer, Department of Psychology, University of Salzburg, Salzburg, Austria

Pekka Niemi, Department of Psychology, University of Turku, Turku, Finland and Stavanger University College, Stavanger, Norway

Lars-Göran Nilsson, Department of Psychology, Stockholm University, Stockholm, Sweden

Åke Olofsson, Centre for Reading Research, Stavanger University College, Stavanger, Norway

David R. Olson, Unit of Applied Cognitive Psychology, Ontario Institute for Studies in Education, University of Toronto, Toronto, Canada

Richard, K. Olson, Department of Psychology, University of Colorado, Boulder, Colorado, USA

Elisa Poskiparta, Department of Psychology, University of Turku, Turku, Finland

Riitta Salmelin, Brain Research Unit, Low Temperature Laboratory, Helsinki University of Technology, Espoo, Finland

Stefan Samuelsson, Centre for Reading Research, Stavanger University College, Norway and Department of Education and Psychology, Linköping University, Linköping, Sweden

Li Hai Tan, Cognitive Science Program, University of Hong Kong, Pokfulam, Hong Kong

Heinz Wimmer, Department of Psychology, University of Salzburg, Salzburg, Austria

Preface

At the turn of a millennium, it is a time to look back and a time to look forward, and also a time to look at the contemporary scene. This book is the result of a symposium in honour of Professor Ingvar Lundberg on the occasion of his 65th birthday. The age of 65 is the year of formal retirement in Sweden. As it happens, Ingvar Lundberg's 65th birthday was in 1999. However, he had already taken early retirement a few years earlier. As there is, in Ingvar Lundberg's case, no connection between retirement, whether early or at the expected age, and research activities and accomplishments, the year 2000 seemed a proper springboard for his future contributions. This volume is in honour of a man who took early retirement to be able to do more research, close to his loved one. We are grateful for funding of the symposium from the Swedish Council for Social Research and the Swedish Council for Research in the Humanities and Social Sciences. Printing support was provided by the Swedish Council for Working Life and Social Research.

Erland Hjelmquist and Curt von Euler
Göteborg and Stockholm, May 2001

Tragically, Professor Curt von Euler died later in May 2001, untimely and unexpectedly, at an old age but with a young, eager and curious mind. He will be remembered as a friend and colleague of unique qualities.

EH

Ingvar Lundberg

With some awe, I write this introduction to Professor Ingvar Lundberg's contributions to academia. It would be easy to fall into the panegyric mood, being a friend as well as a younger colleague of Ingvar. I will therefore be brief, following a Gricean maxim for logic and conversation.

Lundberg was born in Stockholm in 1934 and was educated in the same city. He was originally trained as a schoolteacher and served in the inner city schools of Stockholm. However, he soon turned to academia and worked with Professors Carl Ivar Sandström and Gösta Ekman at the Department of Psychology in Stockholm. He was active in fields varying from sex differences to psychophysics (Sandström and Lundberg, 1956; Ekman and Lundberg, 1965). The psychophysical air at the department in Stockholm was theoretical, cool, clean and well disciplined. In the 1960s, Ingvar left Stockholm for Umeå, in the north of Sweden, and a newly established university, the fifth in Sweden. The opening of a university in Umeå was an exercise in regional planning and educational politics. Ingvar presented his PhD thesis at the Department of Psychology in Umeå. The thesis concerned a fundamental issue in perceptual and cognitive psychology – the processing of order information (Lundberg, 1971). Umeå University turned out to be a success story, as did Ingvar's research. The barren landscape and the lack of a distracting urban environment in Umeå seemed to be very favourable to the production of high-quality research, and Ingvar became a Professor of Developmental Psychology and stayed there until 1995, when he moved to Göteborg and the Department of Psychology at Göteborg University. Luckily, the move to the south of Sweden was not detrimental to Ingvar's scientific contributions.

Ingvar's thesis on processing of order information soon locked into psycholinguistics and the psychology of language, in particular alphabetic reading and writing, and developmental dyslexia. In a sense, Ingvar was of course true to his schoolteacher's training. After all, alphabetic script was perhaps the first human artefact demanding formal schooling and principles of instruction. He published his early ideas on reading, writing and dyslexia in 1978 in Swedish (e.g. Lundberg, 1978b) and in English (e.g. Lundberg, 1978a). These early writings were not immediately well received in all quarters, nor on the domestic or international scene. The ideas were too challenging to many of the then prevailing conceptions of dyslexia. The first papers were conceptualised within the 'linguistic awareness' framework, and the phoneme was identified by Ingvar as a crucial construct within that framework from the very beginning. As a pioneer in the field of phoneme awareness and its predictive value for later reading development, Ingvar used his skills as an experimenter, applying his rigorous training at Ekman's department. However, unlike many of his Stockholm colleagues, Ingvar broadened his methodological repertoire to include practically all tools in the toolbox, not least of which was keeping up with the latest development in various fields, including multidimensional analyses and brain imaging.

Although mainly a researcher in a quantitative tradition, Ingvar has used qualitative methods when suitable, e.g. letting pupils and adults with dyslexic problems describe their experiences in interviews. Ingvar Lundberg is in essence a very unorthodox researcher, looking for the means that can help him make empirical what has first been identified as theoretical and conceptual issues within the very practical problem of dyslexia (e.g. Lundberg, 1999). Thereby, he has shown that it is possible to combine the fuzzy world of human problems with high-quality, theoretically based, behavioural research. A landmark paper was published in 1988 (Lundberg, Frost and Petersen, 1988). This training study included the whole apparatus, from theoretical and conceptual analysis to implementation of preventive methods in a pre-school environment. Recently, his feelings for 'the really pressing problems' (Kuhn, 1996, p. 36) took a new direction when he turned to the question of whether prison inmates and juvenile delinquents have a higher frequency of dyslexia than expected (Svensson, Lundberg and Jacobsson, 2001).

Numerous (hundreds) of papers and dozens of books have been published by Ingvar and collaborators on the issues of dyslexia, its theoretical explanation and possible remediations. Ingvar has also served on a number of committees, boards and research councils, too many to list. Let it just be mentioned that he has been a member of the task force involved in the international comparisons of reading and literacy within the IEA Study of Reading Literacy involving 32 countries (e.g. Lundberg and Linnakylä, 1992); he is a member of the Rodin Academy of Remediation, a member of the Society for the Scientific Study of Reading, a member of the International Dyslexia Foundation, a Fellow of Academia Europea, one of the founders of the Swedish Dyslexia Foundation, organiser of the International Congress of Psychology in Stockholm 2000, and on the editorial board of several scientific journals. In brief, his international collaboration and network are formidable, ranging all over the globe.

Ingvar is a reading researcher, but his eloquence as a lecturer has made him a frequently invited speaker in all possible habitats, be it a small rural school in Sweden, talking to pre-school teachers, lecturing to university students, prison inmates or giving the T.R. Miles lecture in Bangor, UK in 2001, key note speeches at international conferences or saluting the Åbo Akademi, Finland, when awarded an honorary doctorate there in 1999. His verbal entertainment has often been accompanied by pictures from the world of art, illustrating the universe of reading, both inner and outer. Ingvar Lundberg has been singularly successful in putting literacy and dyslexia in its cultural and historical context, blowing life into dead letters and creating a tempting landscape of colours and fragrance. Recently, the relationship between artistic talent and dyslexia was to be found on Ingvar's scientific agenda (Wolff and Lundberg, 2002), as well as bilingualism and dyslexia (Miller Guron and Lundberg, 2000). Stockholm certainly lost a very ambitious schoolteacher, but the world of literacy, reading and dyslexia research won one of its most outstanding scholars.

Erland Hjelmquist

References

Ekman, G. and Lundberg, I. (1965). Über Theorie und Messung in der Psychologie. *Enzyklopedie der geisteswissenschaftlichen Arbeitsmethoden*. Munich: R. Oldenburg Verlag.

Kuhn, T.S. (1996). *The Structure of Scientific Revolutions*, 3rd edn. Chicago: University of Chicago Press.

Lundberg, I. (1971). The processing of order information. Experimental studies of scanning and selection of spatio-temporal relations in rapid input sequences. Doctoral thesis, Department of Psychology, University of Umeå.

Lundberg, I. (1978a). Aspects of linguistic awareness related to reading. In: Sinclair, A., Jarvella, R.J. and Levelt, W.J.M. (eds), *The Child's Conception of Language*. New York: Springer Verlag. pp. 83-96.

Lundberg, I. (1978b). Kognitionspsykologiska aspekter på den första läsinlärningen. I: Hjelmquist, E., Sjöberg, L. and Montgomery, H. (eds), *Undervisningspsykologi*. Stockholm: AWE/Gebers. pp. 146-70.

Lundberg, I. (1999). Towards a sharper definition of dyslexia. In: Lundberg, I., Tönnessen, F.E. and Austad, I. (eds), *Dyslexia. Advances in theory and practice*. Dordrecht, The Netherlands: Kluwer. pp. 21-52.

Lundberg, I. and Linnakylä, P. (1992). *The Teaching of Reading around the World*. The Hague: IEA.

Lundberg, I., Frost, J. and Petersen, O.-P. (1988). Effects of an extensive program for stimulating phonological awareness in preschool children. *Reading Research Quarterly* **33**: 263-284.

Miller Guron, L. and Lundberg, I. (2000). Dyslexia and second language reading. A second bite of the apple? *Reading and Writing. An Interdisciplinary Journal* **12**: 41-61.

Sandström, C.I. and Lundberg, I. (1956). A genetic approach to sex differences in localization. *Acta Psychologica* **12**: 247-253.

Svensson, I., Lundberg, I. and Jacobsson, C. (2001). The prevalence of reading and spelling difficulties among inmates of institutions for compulsory care of juvenile delinquents. *Dyslexia*, 7, 62-76.

Wolff, U. and Lundberg, I. (2002). The prevalence of dyslexia among art students. *Dyslexia: An International Journal of Research and Practice* 8: 34-42.

Introduction

The contents of this book testify to the success and prosperity of research on literacy from a cultural, societal and individual perspective. The focus of the book is on obstacles to successful acquisition of literacy skills, or developmental dyslexia. The use of reading and writing is a late innovation in the history of humankind. It is a cultural phenomenon, as is dyslexia. Humans are meant for talking and listening, and to look at each other while doing this, not to be on their own, bent over texts or writing utensils. In illiterate societies, there are no dyslexic people, although particular perceptual and cognitive functions related to dyslexic problems are to be found in illiterate populations.

The chapters of the book include issues related to biological, cultural and societal perspectives on literacy. Literacy is put in the perspective of externalisation and storing of human experience in general. The way in which literacy was first a tool for authority with its use restricted to élite groups, in contrast to its widespread use in the current IT infrastructure, is also discussed. Learning of reading and writing has consequences for brain functions and structure and these consequences are different for different languages and, more specifically, there is emerging evidence that dyslexia is correlated to specific brain activation patterns. Closely related to this fascinating line of research is that dyslexia has very different manifestations in different languages. This brings us to some core questions: what is dyslexia, what is the role of environmental factors and genetics, and what is the interaction between the environment and genes like? A common suggestion has been to define dyslexia as a specific and unexpected difficulty in relation to a child's age-adequate education, chronological age and general mental abilities, often construed as IQ. This is still the definition, a 'discrepancy' definition, used in the *Diagnostic and Statistical Manual of Mental Disorders* (DSM-IV – American Psychiatric Association, 1994) (where 'reading disorder' and 'writing disorder' are used rather than 'dyslexia'). This view has been challenged. In this book we find chapters that elaborate and extend this discussion.

One theme of the book is the more promising theoretically motivated definition of dyslexia, namely the phonological deficit hypothesis. This is also the field where Professor Lundberg made perhaps his most significant contribution, in the sense that in the 1970s he proposed a framework (Lundberg, 1978) that, in 1988 (Lundberg, Frost and Petersen, 1988), was used in a much-cited paper on training of phonological skills and its consequences for development of reading and writing skills. However, the role of phonological skills and phonological training for the success of developing reading and writing skills is not settled. Several chapters of the book demonstrate the complexity of the issue, alerting us to care about conclusions. Another key question is whether different scripts are related to fundamentally different reading and writing processes. Dyslexia research started from the perspective of alphabetic scripts, and most of the published research is still based on alphabetic writing systems. However, morphosyllabic scripts, such as Chinese, have attracted research, providing intriguing results, some of which are presented in this volume.

In Chapter 1, Hjelmquist argues that script and literacy should be understood as particular types of externalisation of human experiences. The first type of symbolic artefacts, dating back some 40 000 years, were representations of visual information, animals and human beings. The second type of representation, script, and in particular alphabetic systems, referred to auditory information. The most recent type of representation using computer models refers to thought processes. Representational systems have thus evolved to take care of human experiences from vision, hearing and thinking.

Chapter 2, by von Euler, is an overview of the start of how specific reading and writing problems were identified and named by neurologists during the nineteenth century. Analogous to other disability conditions, dyslexia was used to refer to some remaining literacy skills, whereas alexia meant a total loss of reading ability (and agraphia a loss of writing skill). Dyslexia was thus originally defined as an acquired disability, although soon enough children with specific reading and writing deficiencies were also described in case files. During the twentieth century, in particular during the last 30 years, we have seen how dyslexia has become recognised as a developmental disability. Already during the nineteenth century, the left hemisphere 'language' areas were suggested as being implicated in dyslexia conditions.

In Chapter 3, David R. Olson draws attention to the fact that the recent millennium shift was accompanied by deep changes in readership and uses of literacy. Literacy has largely been a tool for social organisation used by élite groups for record-keeping purposes of various kinds, and it has reached a position of authority and autonomy, although recently it has become a necessity for everyone in IT societies in the new millennium. Olson, in effect, then agues against the discrepancy notion of dyslexia, from an 'institutional category' point of view, rather than a 'phonological deficit' point of view, and the conclusion is that we are in much need of a theoretical understanding of 'human diversity'. He warns against education based on large-scale group data in the individual case.

Samuelsson summarises in Chapter 4 research that seems to indicate that there are no differences between dyslexic people and 'ordinary poor readers' on reading subskills or reading-related cognitive skills. The concept of 'ordinary poor readers' refers to generally learning-disabled readers, i.e. those who on the basis of IQ could be expected to score low on reading tests. In a study of very-low-birthweight children, Samuelsson finds further support for the similarities between dyslexic children and generally learning-disabled readers in the domain of phonological skills. A conclusion of relevance for special education is that generally these readers run the risk of not receiving proper support and help because they are not thought of as having dyslexic problems.

Chapter 5 focuses on a basic unit in reading, at least in certain alphabetic scripts – the word. Høien articulates the view that automatic recognition of words is a prerequisite, although insufficient, for good reading. Automatic recognition means in essence that an orthographic reading strategy is used, i.e. the spelling gives direct information about the word. A phonological reading strategy is the poor reader's strategy where one has to reconstruct the sound form of the word by pronouncing it. Høien provides further evidence for the validity of this pattern of reading processes. Nevertheless, the orthographic strategy could be used in a compensatory way by older, less-skilled readers. The results together point to the complex interaction between orthographic and phonological components of reading at different ages.

In Chapter 6, Elbro and Arnbak also tackled the definition of reading efficiency and reading problems. In their case it was empirically studied by analysing the predictive value of reading comprehension in respect of successful education. Below a certain reading level, educational achievement was at a low level. It was also shown that the component of reading that implies an open mind and an ability to consider unexpected facts and reasoning was a predictor of educational achievement among adults and young adults.

In Chapter 7, Niemi and Poskiparta present results from a 3-year longitudinal study, starting at pre-school. A 13-week training of phonological awareness of children with the lowest phonological awareness scores at the beginning of grade 1 showed no remaining positive effects on reading-related scores at the end of grade 3. Also, a group of pre-schoolers who had good phonological skills and could be predicted to show a successful reading development during the first school years, unexpectedly turned out to be poor readers. The results are challenging and the authors interpret them in a framework of perceptual–cognitive, linguistic and motivational aspects of development and skill acquisition, with the motivational factors emerging as a possibly important explanatory variable.

Chapter 8 by Richard K. Olson gives further evidence for the importance of phoneme awareness in reading development. He emphasises the bi-directional relationship between learning to read and phoneme awareness. Olson also contributes data and arguments that complicate the role of phoneme awareness for the long-term development of literacy skills and text comprehension. He offers a number of explanations for the weak relationship between successful early phoneme awareness training and later reading achievement. These explanations point in the direction of more abstract, and differentiated, learning mechanisms than usually taken into account in early intervention studies.

Wimmer and Mayringer demonstrate in Chapter 9 the importance of orthography for understanding dyslexia. They show that, in German – a language with a highly regular orthography compared with English – reading speed rather than reading accuracy is a relevant measure of dyslexic problems. Lexical and sublexical reading routes differentiated between slow and normal readers, indicating that sublexical processes are part of the slow readers' problems, although not the lexical processes. In the German language, dyslexia thus seems not to be a 'surface' problem, but rather characterised by speed problems of accessing and assembling phonological structures at the sublexical level.

In Chapter 10, Che Kan Leong and Li Hai Tan give a concrete example of the importance of the script, namely Chinese, for understanding literacy, and poor literacy, in different cultures. By studying children who read Chinese as well as English as a second language, it was possible to show that phonological processing is also important in Chinese, otherwise a largely meaning-based morphosyllabic writing system. Orthographic processes were also implied in the results. Equally important, it was shown that pseudo-word reading in the two languages was differently predicted by different phonological tasks. When reading Chinese, the importance of syllable and morpheme levels was demonstrated, whereas processing of onset and in particular rime was important when reading English. These patterns can be ascribed to the paradigmatic and tonal character of Chinese word reading.

Chapter 11 by Olofsson highlights research on adults with persisting problems of phoneme awareness but normal reading skills. A number of studies have identified such readers who somehow have developed compensating reading techniques. Revisiting an old sample of poor readers, Olofsson found not only persisting phonological problems, but also deficits in advanced orthographic processing. A group of dyslexic university students had very similar test results compared with a group of dyslexic people not qualified for university studies, with the exception of one phonological test, in which university students performed better. The results point to the intricate processes involved in the development of compensating reading strategies.

In Chapter 12, Helenius and Salmelin demonstrate how magnetoencephalography (MEG) can be used to trace differences in cortical activities between dyslexic and normal readers. Their results indicated similarities between the two groups at the stage of visual feature analysis. However, at the prelexical orthographic stage and the semantic stage, differences emerged, showing no cortical activation, or delayed activation, among the dyslexic people compared with normal readers.

In Chapter 13, Frith scrutinises the definitional problems of dyslexia. She uses a three-level framework – brain, mind and behaviour – for analysing the apparent contradictory findings in dyslexia research and the appalling lack of a coherent definition of dyslexia. Combining this framework with brain-imaging techniques, she suggests that it is possible to go beneath the behavioural level to look at the commonalities and differences between poor readers and dyslexic individuals of different languages. She shows that it is possible to have a theoretically based definition of dyslexia, which accounts for the behavioural variation of reading patterns related to different orthographies, regular versus irregular.

In Chapter 14, Nilsson gives an example of how genetic studies can be used for understanding complex cognitive processes, in this case memory. This line of research was inspired by earlier studies of the genetics of dyslexia together with Lundberg. Although the chapter does not directly address literacy issues, it brings to the front a precondition for efficient reading and writing. Long-term memory is of course implied in both the successful acquisition of literacy and its maintenance in adult age. Therefore, dementia is a highly relevant aspect of literacy research. In old age, preserved cognitive resources that enable reading and writing are consequently of great importance for successful ageing. The moral of the efforts to relate genetic markers to memory performance is that such a complex function is probably regulated by multiple genes in complex interactions with the environment. It is a good guess that the same holds true for such complex, and culturally created, skills as reading and writing.

In Chapter 15, Lundberg gives a personal account of the development of dyslexia research. As he has had the advantage of being an active researcher both before and after the 'cognitive revolution', he can give inside information on the way studies of reading and writing emerged as a field of theoretical as well as applied importance. Retrospectively, it could be described as a happy marriage between new theoretical approaches and a societal request for 'useful' research. In a way it was the *Zeitgeist* in academia, as well as in society, that paved the way for a better understanding of dyslexia. This, in its turn, allowed for a theoretical definition of dyslexia, based on perceptual, cognitive and biological constructs. Nevertheless, as dyslexia is only manifest (at least in its palpable form) in particular social settings, it requires a framework also encompassing motivational, social psychological, societal and cultural factors.

References

American Psychiatric Association (1994). *Diagnostic and Statistical Manual of Mental Disorders*, 4th edn revised. Washington, DC: American Psychiatric Press.

Lundberg, I. (1978). Aspects of linguistic awareness related to reading. In: Sinclair, A., Jarvella, R.J. and Levelt, W.J.M. (eds), *The Child's Conception of Language*. Berlin: Springer-Verlag, pp. 83-96.

Lundberg, I., Frost, J. and Petersen, O. (1988). Long term effects of a preschool training program in phonological awareness. *Reading Research Quarterly* **28**: 263-284.

CHAPTER 1

Beyond literacy

ERLAND HJELMQUIST

Phonological skills are put to use for the cooperation and coordination of activities among humans. Cooperation and coordination appeared, first, without speech and eventually involved 'mind reading' (see Byrne and Whiten, 1988, for more on the history of mind reading). Somewhere between 150 000 and 35 000 years ago, *Homo sapiens* started to communicate with spoken language. Since then, text reading and dyslexia have been a potential problem, but only in relation to certain types of text reading and therefore only during the most recent millennia. The path from mind reading to text reading has indeed been a long one. Seminal studies of the development of literacy and writing systems were presented by Gelb (1965), Goody (1986), Goody and Watt (1963), Olson (1994) and Street (1984). The emergence of literacy and literate cultures must be understood in its social and historical contexts, but here the focus is on psychological concepts and processes that seem to recur in the history of human communication and text reading. Of necessity, there are similarities between the view presented here and other theories and suggestions about the emergence of human communication and language and the role of speech. Lieberman (1991) and Corballis (1992, 1999) are both inclined to equate the appearance of modern humans some 150 000 years ago with the emergence of speech and language, although Corballis suggested that language could have existed long before that as a manual modality. Bickerton (1995) believes in a sudden biological change, about the time of the appearance of anatomically modern humans, giving rise to language or, more precisely, syntax.

There is by now a convincing amount of research to show that the perception of sounds, including speech sounds, is a skill that is available to species quite remote from human beings. Kluender, Diehl and Killeen (1987) showed that Japanese quails could be trained to discriminate phonetic categories. Recently, Ramus et al. (2000) demonstrated that cotton-top tamarin monkeys, a new-world monkey, can discriminate between the prosodic features of Japanese and Dutch much like human newborns, i.e. a discrimination ability at sentence level, not the phonemic level typically used in other studies of animal auditory perception. It adds further strength to the idea that speech perception among humans relies on quite specific structures that have a long evolutionary history. One classic study on the early emergence of categorical perception among human newborns is of course that of Eimas et al. (1971), in which it was shown that 4-week-old infants could perceive phonemes categorically.

It thus seems that, somehow, the capacity to analyse speech endowed on the human mind via a long ancestral link has only recently been put to use for communicative purposes. This slumbering talent was activated at some point in time and came to be a part of the language system. From this perspective it makes sense to speculate whether a phonological module is 'something of a luxury' (Frith and Frith, 1998). The most radical question is perhaps: why speak at all? If speech is not necessary for language, as shown by the sign languages of deaf people, maybe spoken language is a result of the utilisation of an ancient skill - speech analysis - for symbolic communication, which developed much earlier. Goldin-Meadow and McNeill (1999) have an interesting hypothesis about why language is typically spoken rather than signed. The idea is essentially that the oral and manual modality has divided the work involved in language production. Speech in the oral modality is only capable of handling segmental, categorical encoding, whereas the manual modality can handle not only segmental, categorical encoding, but also what Goldin-Meadow and McNeill (1999) and Donald (1991) called the 'mimetic' encoding, i.e. iconic and holistic manual expressions. The division of work implied that the oral modality was given responsibility for what it is good at – segmental, categorical, combinatorial encoding – whereas the manual modality had to take care of the communicative encoding that only it could handle, i.e. that carrying mimetic information. However, as speaking is the preferred mode of language, and deafness is a rare condition, speaking must have been advantageous in the long, evolutionary, run.

It is commonly suggested that the freeing of hands for purposes other than language production was important for the development of speech. Also the possibility for speaker-listeners communicating without seeing each other, such as in darkness or thick vegetation, or by shouting over long distances, etc., is supposed to have been formative in the reliance of *Homo sapiens* on the spoken rather than the manual modality (Lieberman, 1991; Bickerton, 1995; Corballis, 1999).

Interestingly, a quite different advantage that is of great relevance for speaking is the relative ease with which abstract models of speech, i.e.

scripts, were developed. Alphabetic and phonemic writing systems are very effective models of speech, and thereby of language, involving crossing the boundary between visually and auditorily transmitted information. Evolution could not of course foresee this advantage of speech made obvious only in specific cultural contexts. Sign language seems to meet with great difficulties when it comes to developing an analogue with the relationship between speech and script (Bergman, 1977). An unexpected advantage of speaking rather than signing is possibly its amenability to being modelled by technically simple but conceptually very complex artefacts. When speech was silenced and put on permanent records the real work on the development of new varieties and possibilities of mind reading got started (Olson, 1994). This advantage of speech (and hearing) is there only in relation to the visually encoded (and decoded) information. It might be that parallel usage of both modalities, although not necessary, at the very least promotes the development of permanent models of language, i.e. scripts. As sign language has the same segmental and combinatorial power as spoken language (Goldin-Meadow, McNeill and Singleton, 1996), the lack of scripts for sign languages cannot be sought in their formal characteristics. Rather, reliance on one modality, with no possibility for relating to another modality, might hinder the creation of an effective external model of sign language. There are of course other modalities (touch and taste) but the experience of efforts to develop tactual alternatives of text and pictures for blind people has demonstrated the difficulties for cross-modal representations outside the realm of sight and hearing.

Even though, or perhaps because, the origins of auditory processing skill were not aspects of linguistic communication in the first place, this shows a remarkable resilience to a range of other obstacles and dysfunctions that have not been identified as dyslexia. Frith and Frith (1998) summarised the evidence from studies of reading and phonological awareness among children with Down's syndrome and with autism; this indicated largely preserved phonological awareness among the latter and at least basic and implicit awareness among the former. Quite another disability – cerebral palsy – has been studied by our research group in respect of phonological awareness and literacy skills (Dahlgren Sandberg and Hjelmquist, 1996a, 1996b, 1997; Hjelmquist and Dahlgren Sandberg, 1996). In a group of 27 children and adolescents, ranging in age between 8.5 and 19.8 years, 21 had no or unintelligible speech from birth, whereas 6 had moderately or hardly intelligible speech. In comparison to two groups without cerebral palsy, one matched for mental age and one matched for mental and chronological age, there were no differences on phonological awareness tasks, however. These results are evidence in favour of the extraordinary resilience of the phonological processing skills despite severe, or total, restrictions on the articulation of speech. The non-vocal people had picked up relevant phonological distinctions by listening to others. The final and even more surprising aspect of the results was that their development of phonological awareness could hardly have been promoted by literacy skills because they scored lower on reading and writing tests than the comparison groups and 17 of them had very low performance. The results are in line with what Bishop (1985), Bishop and Adams (1990), Bishop, Byers Brown and Robson (1990) and Bishop and Robson (1989a, 1989b) have found, who also showed that phonological awareness can develop despite severe language production problems. The phonological analysis has thus proved to work efficiently despite a number of other severe restrictions on linguistic communication.

Bishop (1985) showed that anarthric individuals were good at spelling, at variance with our own results (Dahlgren Sandberg and Hjelmquist, 1996a, 1996b, 1997). However, spelling and reading tests were not comparable in the two sets. Most important, Bishop did not include reading tests for anarthric children and, in the studies by Dahlgren Sandberg and Hjelmquist, the results on the spelling tests tended to be on a higher level than the reading tests. The good results on spelling tests shown by Bishop (1989) are compatible with the notion that spelling might be easier than reading for non-vocal children. As reading is the goal for a person striving to become literate, the lack of the expected step from phonological awareness to reading skills is noteworthy. Phonological awareness and formal reading and writing training at school, the case for a number of participants in the study of Dahlgren Sandberg and Hjelmquist, are not sufficient for developing literacy skills. The functioning of working memory is probably one important factor in explaining this pattern of results (see Gathercole et al., 1999).

Reading and writing systems are technologies, or *technologies of mind*, invented by humans. Specific difficulties with phonological analysis, often described as dyslexia, are therefore not surprising. If phonological analysis is a specific skill, perhaps modularised, it must of course be at risk of being damaged for one reason or another. Technological artefacts, or writing systems, are not the consequences of biological evolution. Rather, the variation and development of artefacts must be explained as a function of learning and culture: learning, because the individual changes are a consequence of experiences, and culture, because *what* is learned varies among different groups of people (Goody and Watt, 1963; Goody, 1986; White, 1989). The aim in this chapter is to discuss what psychological processes and concepts are common to this variation in space and time.

To start this analysis, we must first decide what is legitimate evidence for technologies of mind. As late as 1989, it was still noteworthy that findings in archaeology and palaeontology had challenged the common wisdom of the time that *Homo sapiens* appeared about 35 000 years ago, which coincided with the first rich records of non-utilitarian tools (White, 1989). Utilitarian tools have a longer history (White, 1989) and are used for gathering and preparing food; they can be found far down in the hierarchy of species. Some birds use stones to break eggs (Lawick-Goodall and van Lawick, 1966) and primates use a variety of utilitarian tools (Lawick-Goodall, 1968; de Waal, 1998). In disciplines as diverse as archaeology and biology, use of tools and tool making have thus been a focus of interest and an object of explanation.

On the other hand, in the behavioural sciences, not least in psychology, the use of tools has often been taken for granted rather than being posed as a problem. The use of tools has been regarded as a natural output of the intellectual capacity of the human mind, i.e. non-utilitarian tools are supposed to be an aspect of *Homo sapiens* – human beings and non-utilitarian tools come in the same package. Rarely has there been a discussion of types of tools, such as utilitarian versus non-utilitarian ones (for a notable exception, see Gregory, 1981).

As our interests are psychological, a definition of utilitarian versus non-utilitarian tools, which makes sense from a psychological perspective, should be formulated. One psychological process is indicative of non-utilitarian tool use, namely *externalisation* of conceptions of the world. Such externalisations first appeared when two-dimensional and three-dimensional 'objects' with a concrete resemblance to the world were manufactured. This took place about 35 000 to 40 000 years ago. As pointed out by Knecht, Pike-Tay and White (1993) and White (1989), the appearance at this particular time of non-utilitarian objects is highly remarkable and intriguing because, according to the latest archaeological analyses, *Homo sapiens* appeared some 100 000 years ago, i.e. much earlier than previously suggested (Vandermeersch, 1995), or maybe even 150 000 years ago (Corballis, 1999). If these relatively new perspectives on the emergence of human beings turn out to be reliable, they would unequivocally show that such things as the production of images depicting the external world of human beings is not biologically determined, but reflects a cultural development. If so, for a period of at least 60 000 years, *Homo sapiens* did not produce any artefacts that externalised their conceptions of the world around them in the form of depictions. The psychological processes involved in putting the world outside oneself were thus not exercised until relatively late in the history of the human being.

A key concept of cognitive psychology, and cognitive science, is *representation*, i.e. the idea that the human mind works on something that is systematically and veridically related to the outer world, and that enables effective interaction with this outer world. What anthropologists and archaeologists call 'objects of a symbolic nature' (White, 1989, p. 74), are of course external representations, in the case of nature, and more precisely the *visible*, concrete, natural objects, such as mammoths, fish and human beings. This kind of representation implies two other concepts, namely *preservation* and *interpretation*. It was now possible to freeze experiences and thereby turn them into external objects of thought, individually and collectively. Preservation in its turn implies interpretation. The fact that today we can see that a 35 000-year-old object 'is' a mammoth shows that the representation was good enough to enable successful interpretation, despite the time gap between the production of the representation and the interpretation process that takes place each time the object is recognised by a human being as a mammoth. Human beings might have produced externalised representations of nature much earlier than 35 000 years ago, but in ways that escape our interpretation. This is a possibility, but it is hard to find any reason why representations of nature should not resemble it in the way that pictures resemble what they depict, as long as we assume that biologically we are the same today as 150 000 to 200 000 years ago. A more reasonable qualm is the possibility that earlier representations have been destroyed and are not to be found in the archaeological records.

Finally, biological changes crucial to the development of externalisational functions could take place without accompanying changes in the palaeontological and archeological remains, which is the point of view taken here. For the purpose of this chapter, we rely on the fact that no discernible positive evidence has been found in favour of biological changes related to symbolic or intellectual abilities of *Homo sapiens* over the last 150 000 years, if we do not take the emergence of symbolic artefacts as evidence for such biological changes (see McManus, 1999). A converse hypothesis is that language developed around 40 000 years ago as a consequence of increasing social complexity, putting to work long existing biological structures and functions that enable the creation of symbolic objects (Lock, 1999). In relation to the second hypothesis, the contention here is that humans could well have been using languages of a 'modern' complexity for 150 000 years without creating social structures associated with the non-utilitarian artefacts emerging 40 000 years ago. The arguments are of two kinds. First, it is difficult to understand why the present enormous diversity over the globe of social organisations on different levels – family, tribe, society, nation, .com, etc., should have no essential impact on the natural languages (6000–7000 in number) of the world. Instead all natural languages are equally good at representing the entire universe of human experience (e.g. Bickerton, 1995). From this perspective there are no primitive languages. If social organisation does not matter now for the basic design features of language, why should it have mattered 40 000 years ago? The suggestion that 40 000 years ago there was a qualitative change in social organisation, which demanded new forms of communication not inherent in later changes, begs the question. It seems more parsimonious that people were talking much like we do now 100 000 or 200 000 years ago, although they did not produce non-utilitarian artefacts. Lieberman (1998) has no reservations about modern humans and speech arriving in the same package.

The hypothesis suggested here is that it is as likely that humans talked without carving figures out of mammoth ivory or painting rocks as it is that people started to talk, carve and paint 40 000 years ago, but did not invent script until 5000 years ago. There seems to be no big controversy over the hypothesis that people actually did talk 40 000 years ago. The development from then up to the first indications of script in the Middle East area is as much in need of analysis as is the time lapse between 200 000 and 35 000 BC.

A framework is suggested for summarising the essential components of this development. The main claim is that modern humans, *Homo sapiens*, have the ability to externalise experiences, making the inner world an outer world. Examples of such externalisations are non-utilitarian artefacts, scripts and computer programs. This conceptualisation reminds us, of course, of Donald's (1991) 'externalisation of memory'. The perspective is different, however. The focus is on the externalisation of subjective experiences and, as it were, their sequential emergence related to the perceptual processes of seeing and hearing, and the experience of thinking.

We thus have three concepts: externalisation, preservation and interpretation, which all are different aspects of one and the same process, namely the development of non-utilitarian tools or representations of a particular kind. It is suggested that these three aspects can account for what is specific about human tool use, ranging from two- and three-dimensional manifestations of the external visible world, representations of speech, to representations of conceptual content in a computer. Together they form integral parts of what can be called 'technologies of representation'. These technologies are all 'tools of mind' (Gregory, 1981, p. 48). Gregory (1981) has given an excellent overview of the development of human technology, and the way that it represents extensions of unaided psychological functions. What is contributed here is a way of structuring these extensions of the human mind through the three concepts mentioned above, referring to three different processes. It is the unique combination of the three, and the application to specific domains – described below – that has accomplished the particular forms of communication across time and distance associated with human beings. The specific manifestations of these processes are culturally determined and not 'natural' consequences of the human mind. They depend on learning and teaching – the transmission of culture.

Representation of nature and social structure

The outline of the frame of reference to be used in the following is first applied to the earliest evidence of representations, referring to nature and social structure.

Technology of representation

Psychological processes	Represented phenomenon	Manifestation
Externalisation and preservation and interpretation	Nature	Visual images

A technology of representation is the output or product of a number of very specific mental processes which are prerequisites for the material manifestation of the phenomenon represented. As seen below, the character and quality of these mental processes change and are applied to new domains of externalisation. It could be argued that a progression relates the processes. Externalisation and preservation come before interpretation, in a sense, although externalisation is of course dependent on a continuous interpretation, in the way that carving a sculpture is dependent on efficient interpretation of the successive stages of the carving. Evidently, human beings have always interpreted the world around them, but the kind of interpretation process involved in the non-utilitarian tool making is qualitatively different from 'interpreting' the visual information of an animal as an animal, because interpretation of a non-utilitarian tool requires not just recognition, but also externalisation and preservation of a model of the world. We could characterise the externalisation process in terms of development of learning to represent and interpret.

Externalisation is at work in the invention of artificial artefacts with a perceptual resemblance to the *visible* world. As it is a representation, it captures *aspects* of what it represents – it is not identical to it. However, the earliest of these artefacts also relate to social identity and social structure (White, 1989). As these aspects of human relations do not have any simple visual manifestations, an arbitrary relationship between what is represented and the form of the representation is already present at this early stage of the development of externalisation. The very earliest externalisation has an iconic relationship to what is represented. As soon as the principle of externalisation is introduced, however, it allows a more abstract relationship between the form of the representation, e.g. beads, and what is represented, e.g. social relationships.

The particular character of the mental conception embodied in externalisation should be contrasted with the kind of mental conception that is involved in creating utilitarian tools used for such things as digging in the soil and making fire. The simple but crucial difference is that utilitarian tools have no representational function in relation to the 'natural' world. However, they undoubtedly reflect the human being's ability to adapt efficiently to the environmental demands and to change the environment, and in this way indirectly demonstrate complex conceptions of the world. The non-utilitarian tools, by definition, are not developed to meet such environmental demands, and therefore are very peculiar types of artefacts, although the use of artefacts for marking social relationships serves a practical purpose. Therefore, it is the origin of the tools, their psychological history, that differentiates the human tools originating about 40 000 years ago from other human tools, and from tools used by other species. The aesthetic and practical aspects of tools of the mind went hand in hand once the principle of externalisation was applied to human experience.

The earliest technologies of mind were thus used in two different domains of human experience: to represent nature and social relationships. These technologies preserved experiences in numerous ways: the astonishingly beautiful spearheads carved as seals, the mammoth sculptures of such thrilling quality, and the rock paintings of striking vividness and aesthetic effect, to mention but a few of the remarkable accomplishments of early technologies of mind.

One important aspect of the creation of such artefacts is that human experience was decontextualised and could be contemplated outside the natural habitat of such experience. From now on, decontextualisation will be a recurrent and crucial theme in the development of human conceptions of the world.

Representation of human communication

The next remarkable step in the development of externalised representation implied a change of the domain of represented phenomena. It was no longer only the concrete objects and events that were externalised, but also human communication and language. This is the beginning of reading and writing. The development of reading and writing systems was a slow and diverse process, which lasted for millennia. As we know through the research of scholars such as Gelb (1965) and Schmandt-Besserat (1986), the first means of externalising and preserving communication actually depicted nature on clay, with iconic signs or with clay moulded into a three-dimensional shape. Therefore it might seem as though there were no important changes in the externalisation process. However, the crucial step taken was in terms of *what* was externalised, namely human communication. The direct face-to-face oral communication was gradually augmented by preserved signs of communication, functioning outside their original social context. Ultimately, this meant that aspects of the ephemeral spoken communication, i.e. sounds, were preserved. Unlike mammoths, seals and deer, sounds appear and vanish continuously and they are not preserved in any external form. A deer can actually be touched, but sounds of speech cannot, and they are preserved only in the memory of people. Human oral communication is in that sense a very abstract process, and it resisted externalisation for a very long time. With the introduction and refinement of writing, not least alphabetic systems modelling the phoneme level of speech, first in Greece (consonants *and* vocals) and later in other cultural centres, the practice of externalisation, preservation and interpretation became routine, and the concepts of externalisation, preservation and interpretation became a *sine qua non* for characterising what writing is.

The general psychological operations involved in externalising communication are the same as was necessary for the externalisation of nature. But the phenomena to which these operations apply change. Rather than externalising the nature *seen*, one must externalise the linguistic sound form *heard* or, more precisely, aspects of what is heard. Just like sculptures that are not identical to what they depict, the alphabet is not a copy of what is heard but represents aspects of it. The interpretation of an alphabetic text requires the ability to decode the script into sounds, letters, words, phrases, etc., and it is well known that some individuals have great problems with these processes, even if they have no difficulties when interpreting the picture of a flower as a flower and no general intelligence deficits (Lundberg, 1991). Although it is true, then, that the nature of the processes involved in interpretation are similar in principle, the content – represented, preserved and interpreted – changes importantly from one perceptual world, *vision*, to another, *hearing*. The content and structure represented might in turn require, and bring about, new qualities of the psychological processes involved in the representation.

The conceptual scheme can now be repeated within a new domain.

Psychological Processes	Represented Phenomenon	Manifestation
Externalisation and Preservation and Interpretation	Human Communication, Speech	Script

The way this general principle took on a special character is well illustrated when the tools of externalisation changed to the domain of human communication, i.e. when writing systems started to develop and had reached an advanced level, as in the case of hieroglyphs, cuneiform and alphabetic systems. Interpretation now had to become a highly explicit activity in the sense that learning to read means learning how to recover meaning from a text, a form of learning that requires explicit instruction. The qualitative change brought about by the peculiar kind of externalisation, preservation and interpretation processes inherent in writing systems can hardly be overestimated. At one level, the externalisation of human communication repeats what happened earlier when visible nature was externalised, at the same time as it adds a new dimension to the awareness and explicitness of concepts. Mastery of a script system requires a learning process where attention is also deliberately focused on the *form* of cultural knowledge, not just on the *contents* conveyed. This type of representation system is no longer dependent on, or possible to learn, through everyday experiences of the 'natural' world. Abstraction *from* everyday experience – decontextualisation – becomes the keyword rather than dependence on such experience. This is a qualitatively new kind of conception of the world. It goes hand in hand with the development of logic, i.e. formal reasoning of an Aristotelian kind during the centuries before the common era. In a classic paper, Goody and Watt (1963) discussed the emergence of alphabetic script, logic and other formal notation systems. More specifically, their contention was that literacy promoted the development of other symbolic systems. What has happened since the development of alphabetic systems is spread to various domains of the symbolic principle. As described by different scholars (Street, 1984; Goody, 1986; Ong, 1982; Olson, 1994), the introduction of reading and writing affected the individual mind as well as the societal structure of institutions, but also vice versa.

Representation of human thought

Recently a new application of the three basic psychological principles of externalisation, preservation and interpretation has taken place in the development of 'technologies of the mind', namely technologising thought. Ong (1982) talked about 'technologising the word', which was the aspect of tools of mind discussed above, i.e. the development of writing systems. In a way, technologising the word is technologising thought to the extent that written text can be said to embody thoughts. The new development is the attempt to technologise thought explicitly. To enable technologising thought, however, one needs something more abstract than a script. Logic had of course been available since Aristotle, but it was not until the idea of an automaton of general symbol handling was developed by Turing (1950) that technologisation of thought, or more correctly *aspects of thought*, became a distinct possibility. As pointed out by Gregory (1981), tools of mind had been used thousands of years before Turing, although Turing's invention was an all-purpose machine in which any rational procedure could be embodied. Aspects of human thought could be externalised and made an object of interpretation. We can thus repeat the scheme above accordingly:

Psychological processes	Represented phenomenon	Manifestation
Externalisation and Preservation and Interpretation	Thought	Machines and programs

We thus have a progression of the objects of externalisation: *what is seen*, *what is heard*, *what is thought*. Although at the general level presented in the schemes above the concepts used are common to all three, there are differences at other levels. It seems plausible that the interpretation processes used when handling and looking at externalisations of nature were acquired and applied implicitly. The psychological processes involved were close to the 'natural' perceptual and cognitive abilities of daily life. Interpretation was mainly an implicit activity that required no specific methods for transmitting the relevant operations between generations.

However, once interpretation was tied to externalisation, it became increasingly explicit. The process implied a successive elaboration of rules for understanding. These rules, or guides for interpretation, were orally transmitted and connected to concrete activities. We know little about what these activities actually involved (although talk about hunting is one likely candidate – Whiten, 1999), but the mere fact that everyday life contained artefacts – pictures, sculptures, etc. – made explanations, comments and descriptive utterances a natural part of the discourse. In the context of child rearing such activities are ubiquitous, and among adults the activities of daily life make discourse of that kind a natural ingredient. In any case, the main means available for transmitting this kind of information was skill learning and oral discourse. The context dependence in these interpretation processes is a *sine qua non* for its efficiency.

As indicated above, externalising human communication in the form of script is in a sense externalising thought. As acquisition of literacy required interpretation, teaching of these skills also became a distinct activity with specific social institutions, i.e. schools, not withstanding that the form of the teaching of literacy took on many different shapes over the centuries, varying from professional teachers to skilled laymen practising reading in the home environment of children. In all cases, however, the focus was on the peculiar type of interpretation necessary for handling script in its dependence on explicitness and awareness, an interpretation totally different from that involved in understanding pictures and sculptures. However, these qualitatively different principles do not exclude, actually they cannot exclude, closely related but more abstract psychological principles being applied in each interpretive case. The founding principle is very simple. When humans externalise an experience, there is something new to be learnt from this externalisation. The artefact brings new aspects, not relevant before, to the focus of attention and consciousness. This means concept formation, implicit and explicit, of *seeing*, *hearing* and *thinking*, and practice of skills. It so happens that some aspects of the relationship between artefacts for externalising and processing speech, and speech itself, are difficult for some people to conceptualise and practise to a high skill level to the end that reading and writing can become a problem.

Acknowledgement

This study was supported by grants from the Swedish Council for Research in the Humanities and Social Sciences and the Swedish Council for Social Research.

References

Bergman, B. (1977). *Signed Swedish*. Stockholm: National Swedish Board of Education.
Bickerton, D. (1995). *Language and Human Behavior*. Seattle, WA: University of Washington Press.
Bishop, D.V.M. (1985). Spelling ability in congenital dysarthria: Evidence against articulatory coding in translating between graphemes and phonemes. *Cognitive Neuropsychology* 2: 220–251.
Bishop, D.V.M. and Adams, C. (1990). A prospective study of the relationship between specific language impairment, phonological disorders and reading retardation. *Journal of Child Psychology and Psychiatry* 31: 1027–1050.
Bishop, D.V.M. and Robson, J. (1989a). Accurate non-word spelling despite congenital inability to speak: Phoneme–grapheme conversion does not require subvocal articulation. *British Journal of Psychology* 80: 1–13.
Bishop, D.V.M. and Robson, J. (1989b). Unimpaired short-term memory and rhyme judgment in congenitally speechless individuals: Implications for the notion of 'articulatory coding'. *Quarterly Journal of Experimental Psychology* 41A: 124–140.
Bishop, D.V.M., Byers Brown, B. and Robson, J. (1990). The relationship between phoneme discrimination, speech production and language comprehension in cerebral-palsied individuals. *Journal of Speech and Hearing Research* 33: 210–219.
Byrne, R. and Whiten, A., eds (1988). *Machiavellian Intelligence*. Oxford: Clarendon Press.
Corballis, M.C. (1992). On the evolution of language and generativity. *Cognition* 44: 197–226.
Corballis, M.C. (1999). Phylogeny from apes to humans. In: Corballis, M.C. and Lea, S.E.G. (eds), *The Descent of Mind. Psychological perspectives on hominid evolution*. Oxford: Oxford University Press, pp. 40–70.

Dahlgren Sandberg, A. and Hjelmquist, E. (1996a). A comparative, descriptive study of reading and writing skills among nonspeaking persons – a preliminary study. *European Journal of Disorders of Communication* **31**: 289–308.

Dahlgren Sandberg, A. and Hjelmquist, E. (1996b). Phonological awareness and literacy in nonspeaking, nonretarded preschool children with cerebral palsy. *Augmentative and Alternative Communication* **12**: 138–153.

Dahlgren Sandberg, A. and Hjelmquist, E. (1997). Language and literacy in nonvocal children with cerebral palsy. *Reading and Writing: An Interdisciplinary Journal* **9**: 107–133.

Donald, M. (1991). *Origins of the Modern Mind: Three stages in the evolution of culture and cognition*. Cambridge, MA: Harvard University Press.

Eimas, P.D., Siqueland, E.R., Jusczyk, P. and Vigorito, J. (1971). Speech perception in infants. *Science* **171**: 303–306.

Frith, U. and Frith, C. (1998). Modularity of mind and phonological deficit. In: von Euler, C., Lundberg, I. and Llinás, R. (eds), *Basic Mechanisms in Cognition and Language*. Amsterdam: Elsevier, pp. 3–17.

Gathercole, S., Service, E., Hitch, G. J., Adams, A.-M. and Martin, A. J. (1999). Phonological short-term memory and vocabulary development. Further evidence on the nature of the relationship. *Applied Cognitive Psychology* **13**: 65–77.

Gelb, I.J. (1965). *A Study of Writing*, 2nd edn. Chicago: University of Chicago Press.

Goldin-Meadow, S. and McNeill, D. (1999). The role of gesture and mimetic representation in making language the province of speech. In: Corballis, M.C. and Lea, S.E.G. (eds), *The Descent of Mind. Psychological perspectives on hominid evolution*. Oxford: Oxford University Press, pp. 155–172.

Goldin-Meadow, S., McNeill, D. and Singleton, J. (1996). Silence is liberating: removing the handcuffs on grammatical expression in the manual modality. *Psychological Review* **103**: 34–55.

Goody, J. (1986). *The Logic of Writing and the Organization of Society*. Cambridge: Cambridge University Press.

Goody, J. and Watt, I.P. (1963). The consequences of literacy. *Comparative Studies in Society and History* **5**: 304–345.

Gregory, R. (1981). *Mind in Science*. Harmondsworth: Penguin Books.

Hjelmquist, E. and Dahlgren Sandberg, A. (1996). Sounds and silence: Interaction in aided language use. In: von Tetzchner, S. and Jensen, M.H. (eds), *Augmentative and Alternative Communication: European perspectives*. London: Whurr, pp. 137–152.

Kluender, K., Diehl, R. and Killeen, P. (1987). Japanese quail can learn phonetic categories. *Science* **237**: 1195–1197.

Knecht, H., Pike-Tay, A. and White, R. (1993). Introduction. In: Knecht, H., Pike-Tay, A. and White, R. (eds), *Before Lascaux. The complex record of the early upper Paleolithic*. Boca Raton: CRC Press.

Lawick-Goodall, J. van (1968). The behavior of free-living chimpanzees in the Gombe Stream Reserve. *Animal Behavior Monograph* **1**: 165–311.

Lawick-Goodall, J. van and Lawick H. van (1966). Use of tools by the Egyptian vulture, *Neophron percnopterus*. *Nature* **212**: 1468–1469.

Lieberman, P. (1991). *Uniquely Human: The evolution of speech, thought, and selfless behavior*. Cambridge, MA: Harvard University Press.

Lieberman, P. (1998). *Eve Spoke: Human language and human evolution*. New York: WW Norton.

Lock, A. (1999). On the recent origin of symbolically-mediated language and its implications for psychological science. In: Corballis, M.C. and Lea, S.E.G. (eds), *The Descent of Mind. Psychological perspectives on hominid evolution*. Oxford: Oxford University Press, pp. 324–355.

Lundberg, I. (1991). Phonemic awareness can be developed without reading instruction. In Brady, S.A. and Schankweiler, D.P. (eds), *Phonological Processes in Literacy: A tribute to Isabelle Y. Liberman*. Hillsdale, NJ: Lawrence Erlbaum, pp. 47–53.

McManus, C. (1999). Handedness, cerebral lateralization, and the evolution of language. In: Corballis, M.C. and Lea, S.E.G. (eds), *The Descent of Mind. Psychological perspectives on hominid evolution*. Oxford: Oxford University Press, pp. 194 –217.

Olson, D. (1994). *The World on Paper*. Cambridge: Cambridge University Press.

Ong, W. (1982). *Orality and Literacy*. London: Methuen.

Ramus, F., Hauser, M.D., Miller, C., Morris, D. and Mehler, J. (2000). Language discrimination by human newborns and by Cotton-Top Tamarin Monkeys. *Science* **288**: 349–351.

Schmandt-Besserat, D. (1986). Tokens: Facts and interpretations. *Visible Language* **20**: 250–272.

Street, B.V. (1984). *Literacy in theory and practice*. Cambridge: Cambridge University Press.

Turing, A. (1950). Computing machinery and intelligence. *Mind* **59**: 433–460.

Vandermeersch, B. (1995). The first modern men. In: Changeaux, J.-P. and Chavaillon, J. (eds), *Origins of the Human Brain*. Oxford: Clarendon Press, pp. 3–10.

Waal, F. de (1998). *Chimpanzee Politics*. Baltimore, MD: Johns Hopkins University Press.

White, R. (1989). Visual thinking in the ice age. *Scientific American* 74–81.

Whiten, A. (1999). The evolution of deep social mind in humans. In: Corballis, M.C. and Lea, S.E.G. (eds), *The Descent of Mind. Psychological perspectives on hominid evolution*. Oxford: Oxford University Press, pp. 173–193.

CHAPTER 2

Dyslexia: how it started and some of the steps towards the present

CURT VON EULER

The terms 'word blindness', 'alexia' and 'dyslexia' were coined by neurologists such as Professors Adolfl Kussmaul (1877) and Rudolf Berlin (1877, 1887) to denote the loss of the ability to read as a consequence of, presumably minor, brain damage. Berlin (1887) seems to be the first to have coined the term 'dyslexia' to denote a condition of a somewhat less complete loss of the reading ability compared with alexia.

Professor Joseph Dejerine, a well-renowned neurologist and pioneer in the emerging field of what, today, is known as neuropsychology, understood that an insightful and detailed examination of patients suffering from pure alexia not only might be of benefit to the patients, but would also provide new knowledge about the cognitive processes of reading. Dejerine (1892) has given an extensive account of such a case followed by a postmortem examination of the brain. This case report of one of Dejerine's patients, called Monsieur C., provides one of the first and most detailed descriptions of the fine-grained organisation of brain functions.

Monsieur C. was a well-to-do French businessman in his late 60s who had experienced attacks of numbness in his right arm and leg, and a slight blurring in his speech. These symptoms soon disappeared, although he then found that he could not read. He therefore consulted his ophthalmologist who found nothing wrong with C.'s eyes and referred him to Joseph Dejerine. Dejerine examined C. very carefully and followed his course closely, noting all the fine details of his condition and cognitive capacities. He found that Monsieur C. had lost the vision of the right half of the visual field, leaving the left half completely intact. Dejerine further found that, although C. was 'blinded' to letters and written and printed words and thus, medically speaking, was alexic, he had a completely unimpaired ability to express himself orally, to understand spoken information, to recognise and without any hesitation name objects and persons, and to recall and give detailed descriptions of past events. Monsieur C. had retained his ability to write both spontaneously, expressing his own thoughts, and what was dictated to him, but he was unable to read what he had written. (A similar condition had previously been described by Kussmaul, 1877.) With his tactile sense, however, Monsieur C. could immediately understand messages written on the skin of his arm. He had no difficulty in reading numbers, performing elaborate calculations and following what happened to his investments on the stock market.

About four and a half years after his first stroke Monsieur C. suffered a second one, which deprived him selectively of the ability to write, leaving all his other cognitive functions intact. Thus, in addition to his alexia, he had now also become agraphic.

Ten days after his second stroke, Monsieur C. died. Dejerine was permitted to perform a postmortem examination of the brain. He could clearly recognise the destruction caused by the first and the second stroke. The first one had destroyed the connections between the preserved part of the visual system in the right hemisphere and the language-processing areas in the left hemisphere were damaged.

The two syndromes exhibited by Monsieur C. – first pure alexia and later alexia with agraphia – are examples of relatively rare, selective, 'isolated' disorders after small circumscribed brain injuries, leaving the intellectual, linguistic and perceptual capacities intact. The knowledge about these acquired selective losses of the ability to read and write are also of great interest because they shed light on the important problems of congenital difficulties in learning to read and write, i.e. congenital or developmental dyslexia.

Congenital word blindness, or congenital dyslexia, was recognised and well described more than 100 years ago. In 1896, Dr W. Pringel Morgan published a detailed report about a bright boy aged 14 who suffered from great specific difficulties to learn to read and write, but had no other learning difficulties. Two weeks after Morgan's report, Dr James Hinshelwood published a similar report (Hinshelwood, 1896), and the next year Dr James Kerr published an account of his examinations of children who suffered from great specific reading and writing difficulties despite normal intelligence (Kerr, 1897). In 1900, Hinshelwood wrote about his analysis of two cases of congenital word blindness. Later he wrote an extensive account of several cases of both congenital and acquired word blindness, describing the great similarities between these two forms of word blindness, the causal origins of which are very different (Hinshelwood, 1917).

To the pioneers in this field, the British physicians Morgan, Hinshelwood, Kerr and others, it seemed most likely, in the light of the studies of Déjerine, that this specific learning disability was caused by a developmental disturbance restricted to language-related areas of the brain. A similar conclusion was reached by the German child neurologist Dr V. Lasser in a report on cases of congenital dyslexia (*Braylexie*) (Lasser, 1919). Hinshelwood had already, in his first account, suggested that this congenital defect was localised to gyrus angularis on the left side.

In the USA, Dr Samuel T. Orton, in the 1920s and 1930s, became engaged in the problems of specific reading and writing difficulties (Orton, 1928, 1937). He carefully examined children with congenital word blindness. Orton found nothing wrong with their perceptual or linguistic capacities but made the important observation that they had specific difficulties in associating written symbols with speech sounds.

One of Orton's crucial contributions was that he developed new, more effective methods for remediation of dyslexic children. Orton also made the important observation that many dyslexic children exhibit a particular difficulty with those letters for which orientation is crucial for identification, e.g. *b*, *d* and *p*, *q*, and that they often 'mirror wrote'. Orton found that quite a few of these children have a tendency to read words from right to left, confusing, for example, *was* and *saw* (Orton, 1937).

These ground-breaking recognitions of congenital word blindness, or congenital dyslexia, as well as Dejerine's fundamental reports, came into disrepute and were neglected for a long time by many of the leading psychologists. It was argued, to some extent based on the holistic views of brain function advanced by Karl Lashly, that learning of all modalities was believed to be controlled by a common, unitary brain function. According to this opinion, a deficit in the ability to learn to read and write could not coexist with ease of learning in other fields and with normal or above-normal intellectual capacities. This belief long held sway. It was not until ethologists such as Konrad Lorenz, Nikolaus Tinbergen, Karl von Frisch and their co-workers had shown convincingly that specific learning abilities – and disabilities – occur commonly in animals and humans that this became fully accepted by researchers in the field of psychology of learning and memory.

During the last three or four decades the problems of developmental dyslexia have been the subject of intense research activities, primarily in the USA, the UK, Canada and the Scandinavian countries. In Norway, Professor Hans-Jörgen Gjessing started and led the Bergen Project, with Ingvar Lundberg as the Swedish research partner. This project became an important ground for dyslexia research in Scandinavia. In Sweden the first international conference on dyslexia was held in Stockholm in 1980 (Zotterman, 1982). Ingvar Lundberg played an important role in preparing the programme for this symposium.

At this conference it was felt that it would be of great value for the furthering of dyslexia research if interdisciplinary approaches were promoted. An international multidisciplinary academy for dyslexia research was planned by Dr Per Uddén. This should be a forum for leading scientists in the fields of relevance to dyslexia research to exchange facts and ideas. With a broad international support, including among others Professors Norman Geschwind of Harvard University (USA) and Oliver Zangvill of Cambridge University (UK), the Academia Rodinensis Pro Remediatione or the Rodin Remediation Academy was formed. It was formally founded in October 1984 at a big international symposium held at St Andrews, Scotland.

Through its name the Academy wished to honour Auguste Rodin's father, Jean Baptiste Rodin, for his more than adequate treatment of his gravely dyslexic, albeit superbly gifted son. The name further implies that anyone with a functional deficit ought to receive help to overcome his or her problems and developmental capacities to their full extent.

The aims of the Academy are to promote interdisciplinary research on dyslexia, to develop better, more efficient and fine-tuned methods for identification of the problems and their remediation, and to spread information about the advances in the field. The activities of the Academy have been focused mainly on arranging multidisciplinary symposia and conferences on different aspects of dyslexia and its underlying problems. To the present time, the Academy has arranged 25 international symposia in 16 years. Currently the Academy has 100 active scientific members (among them seven Nobel laureates) and about 190 corresponding scientific members; all are well-known scientists in their fields, ranging over neurobiology, cognitive science, psychology, neuropsychology, linguistics, genetics, education and rehabilitation sciences. Professor Ragnar Granit, Nobel laureate in 1967, was elected the first President of the Academy, and Princess Marianne Bernadotte was appointed Honorary President. As a member of the Council of the Academy and chairman of the prize committee for the Norman Geschwind–Rodin prize, Ingvar Lundberg has made very important contributions to the Academy.

One of the cornerstones in this research is the studies by Albert Galaburda and his co-workers on postmortem material from the brains of people who had had dyslexia (Geschwind and Galaburda, 1985). These studies showed that the brains of dyslexic individuals did not exhibit normal asymmetry. Instead, the right planum temporale was larger than normal and of the same size as the left planum. These brains further exhibited a large number of ectopies on the cortical surface, predominantly on the left hemisphere. The prevalence of symmetry in the planum temporale regions on the two sides was later confirmed using magnetic resonance imaging (MRI) in live dyslexic individuals. In an MRI study, Ingvar Lundberg together with his Norwegian colleagues (Larsen et al., 1989) found a complete correspondence between brain symmetry and phonological problems. This demonstrated, for the time, a direct connection between the dyslexic anomalies in the structure of the brain and the cognitive deficit characteristic of this disorder.

The dyslexia research seems to have found its way into the fields of neuroscience, linguistics, psychology and neuropsychology. In all these areas great advances have been made. It has been well established that developmental dyslexia is a congenital neurocognitive disorder that most often causes phonological deficits. The specific cognitive capacities that are prerequisites for the ability to learn to read and write have been identified. The main obstacles standing in the way of acquiring literacy have been recognised. There is much new knowledge about the neural structures and cognitive functions behind the relative slowness in the rate of information processing that is characteristic of dyslexic people.

Results of great importance both for the understanding of the role of phonological problems in reading acquisition and for successful remediation of dyslexic children have been obtained by Ingvar Lundberg and his co-workers. They have shown that phonological deficits can already be identified at the pre-school level and that these problems can be eliminated by early pre-school training that is aimed at creating a well-functioning phonological awareness in children with deficits in this respect, and providing children with a disposition towards dyslexia with a normal or near-normal ability to learn to read and write. These results (see, for example, Lundberg, 1991) have been amply verified by several research groups. Great effort has been devoted to find different ways to take advantage of the great plasticity of the brain for remedial purposes.

The role of genetic factors in the case of a disposition for dyslexia has received much attention. The author would like to draw attention to the extensive work of Bertil Hallgren from the Karolinska Institut (Hallgren, 1950). More recently, the genetic research has followed other strategies. Great attempts have been made to identify the genes that are responsible for induction of a dyslexic disposition. Such genes have been localised to chromosomes 6 and 15 and, according to results from one family, also to chromosome 2. The Colorado project, within which frame much of the gene localisation has been carried out, also contains the extensive twin study. The fine-grained modular organisation of the language functions would seem to enable the occurrence of a fairly specific vulnerability of the phonological processing mechanisms. The precise interaction of the genes in brain tissues is not yet known.

As pointed out by Frith and Frith (1998), it is ironic that the genetically based developmental dyslexia should be recognised by its impairment of the ability to acquire the artificial art of reading and writing, an art that can hardly be considered to be coded in our genes. The biological mechanism that is crucial to acquisition of literacy seems to be an intact phonological processing module. Although a lack of phonological awareness is often associated with some delay in speech development, this deficit is most often rapidly compensated for. Remaining signs of this defect are usually fairly subtle and not readily detectable in ordinary speech. In confrontation with the artificial art of reading and writing, however, the phonological problems will cause very serious difficulties in acquiring literacy.

Advances in the biological sciences have very often followed suit on ground-breaking developments in the fields of technology. This is certainly true in the case of dyslexia research. The techniques of positron emission tomography (PET), MRI, functional MRI (fMRI) and magnetoencephalography have lent themselves to important new results in this field. Examples of this are presented in several of the chapters in this volume, as are the presentations of the 'state of the art' in dyslexia research and the predictions on where we go from here.

References

Berlin, R. (1877). Wortblindheit. *Archiv für Psychiatrie und Nervenkrankheiten* **XV**: 276-278.

Berlin, R. (1887). *Eine besondere Art der Wortblindheit (Dyslexie)*. Wiesbaden: J.E. Bergmann.

Dejerine, J. (1892). Contribution à l'étude anatomo-pathologique et clinique des différentes variétés de cécité verbale. *Mémoires de la Société de Biologie* 4: 61-90.

Frith, U. and Frith, C. (1998). Modularity of mind and phonological deficit. In: Euler, C. von, Lundberg, I. and Llinas, R. (eds), *Basic Mechanisms in Cognition and Language*, Vol. 70. Amsterdam: Wenner-Gren International Series, pp. 3-17.

Geschwind, N. and Galaburda, A.M. (1985). Cerebral lateralization: Biological mechanisms, associations, and pathology: I. A hypothesis and a program for research. *Archives of Neurology* **45**: 428-459.

Hallgren, B. (1950). Specific dyslexia (congenital word-blindness): A clinical and genetic study. *Acta Psychiatrica et Neurologica Scandinavica Supplementum* **65**.

Hinshelwood, J. (1896). The visual memory for words and figures. *British Medical Journal* **ii**: 1543-1544.

Hinshelwood, J. (1917). *Congenital Word-blindness*. London: Lewis.

Kerr, J. (1897). School hygiene in mental, moral, and physical aspects. *Journal of the Statistical Society* **60**: 613-680.

Kussmaul, A. (1877). Die Störungen der Sprache. *Handbuch der speziellen Pathologie und Therapie*, 12. Leipzig: H. Ziermssen.

Larsen, J.P., Höjen, T., Lundberg, I. and Ödegaard, H. (1989). MRI-evaluation of size and symmetry of the planum temporale in adolescents with developmental dyslexia. *Brain and Language* **39**: 289-301.

Lasser, V. (1919). Angeborene Wortblindheit (Bradylexie), beim nicht schwachsinnigen Kind. *Zeitschrift für Kinderheilkunde* **22**: 124-130.

Lundberg, I. (1991). Reading difficulties can be predicted and prevented: A Scandinavian perspective on phonological awareness and reading. In: Hulme, C. and Snowling, M. (eds), *Reading Development and Dyslexia*. London: Whurr, pp. 180-199.

Morgan, W.P. (1896). A case of congenital word blindness. *British Medical Journal* **ii**: 1378–1379.

Orton, S.T. (1928). Specific reading disability – Strephosymbolia. *Journal of the American Medical Association* **90**: 1095–1099.

Orton, S.T. (1937). *Reading, Writing, and Speech Problems in Children*. London: Chapman & Hall.

Zotterman, Y., ed. (1982). *Dyslexia – Neuronal, Cognitive and Linguistic Aspects*. Wenner-Gren Center International Symposium Series. Oxford: Pergamon Press.

CHAPTER 3

Literacy in the past millennium

DAVID R. OLSON

The millennium just ended was marked not by such dramatic inventions as that of writing systems or even of the alphabet, because those were ancient inventions passed on as traditional crafts, but rather by changes in readership and in the increasingly diverse uses of literacy in public and private life. Expanding uses of literacy were a consequence of social and political changes, which in turn brought with them changing goals for schooling and changed pedagogies. The technologies of literacy, including a more readable script, the printing press, and cheap and durable writing surfaces were important factors both in the ways that writing was used and in school teaching methods, but they were secondary to the functions that writing has to serve.

The uses of literacy

At the beginning of the millennium, writing played an important role in the exercise of power in every major civilisation whether in Europe, China, India or pre-conquest America. But, in contrast with the modern world, writing was used almost exclusively for administrative purposes such as accounting or keeping records of who paid or owed taxes, for example, for religious purposes, for the writing and reading of Sacred Texts, or for historical or monumental purposes, assuring respect by recording the great and heroic deeds of ancestors. All of these had an organising effect on social life. Aristotle was correct when he said that writing is the keystone of civilisation, the society of cities. In modern times writing is the key to large-scale social organisation, what we now call bureaucracy.

By the end of the millennium, although not abandoning those traditional functions, literacy had come to play a central role in almost every aspect of social and personal life. No event of significance, ranging from declarations of war to simple birthday greetings, passes without appropriate written documentation. Contracts are sealed by means of a written signature. Goods in a market or street names, all bear written inscriptions. Activities from cooking to knitting to word processing are scripted, set out in manuals. Inventions are patented, ideas copyrighted. Births are marked by a certificate, deaths by a mark on a gravestone.

Knowledge has been identified with writing at least since the fourteenth century when Richard de Bury claimed that 'The treasure of wisdom is chiefly contained in books' (de Bury 1345/1945). Certainly writing has served as the archive of knowledge. Writing helps to mark off the knower from the known (Havelock, 1963), the known being treated not just as common knowledge, but as the knowledge stored in the archive. No enquiry then or now could begin before asking the question 'What is known about x?' and making the appropriate search of the archive.

It may be argued that writing and reading thereby imposed a particular form on knowledge, establishing such formal genres as narrative fiction, encyclopaedias and scientific prose. Early modern scientists such as Robert Boyle and Robert Hooke honoured Francis Bacon's injunction to distinguish clearly the 'patterns in the world' from 'the dreams of the imagination', or as we would now say observations from inferences. Boyle, for example, left what he called a 'conspicuous internal' between the report of his experimental findings – which anyone could have seen had they been with him in the laboratory – and his occasional discourses on their interpretation. Robert Hooke, too, reported his observations with a microscope by distinguishing observations from mere guesses. He wrote:

> Whenever [the reader] finds that I have ventur'd at any small Conjectures, at the causes of the things I have observed, I beseech him to look upon them only as doubtful Problems, and uncertain ghesses, and not as unquestionable Conclusions.
>
> (Olson, 1994, pp. 173–174)

This strategy for reading the 'Book of Nature' was essentially the strategy that had earlier been worked out for reading the 'Book of Scripture' at the time of the Reformation. Luther preached that one must distinguish the true authority of the Scripture, its plain meaning available for all to see, from what he called the 'Doctrines of the Church'. The meaning of Scripture was to be found not in the dogmas of the Church, but upon deeper reading of the text. Consequently, it may be argued that there was a close relationship between the Protestant method of reading Scripture and the method of reading the 'Book of Nature', i.e. of doing their science, by the early modern scientists, many of whom were Protestants. Common to both was this essentially new way of writing and reading texts. The method was set out by the Royal

Society of London, which, according to its historian Thomas Sprat, required 'a mathematical plainness of style' that shunned digressions, amplifications and swellings of style to create what we still honour as scientific prose, prose that, so far as possible, means neither more nor less than what it says.

This way of using writing is also a way of speaking and a way of thinking – thinking in a literal, explicitly logical way. This claim has attracted much controversy in the face of the fact that both talk and action presuppose a certain logic if they are to be coherent and successful. However, the claim is rather that literate practices give an emphasis to justification and the provision of reasons, i.e. the construction of explicit warrants for beliefs. It was no longer appropriate to justify action on the basis of thinking and wanting, but rather on the basis of validity of claims and their deductibility from general laws. Although everyone, it seems, can think in terms of hypothetical if–then terms, it requires schooling and literacy to learn to treat the 'if clause' as a premise from which valid deductions may be drawn. Thus, Luria's (1976) famous report of the Siberian peasant who failed to draw a valid inference is less a failure of logic than an unfamiliarity with the literate habit of treating assertions as premises from which valid inferences may be drawn, rather than treating them as expressions of dubious personal belief. The difference is captured in the contrast between a belief and an assumption. This is a distinction that children are taught during their school years as part of their literacy training in science – their scientific literacy.

For these and similar reasons, literacy has come to be a part of the functioning of bureaucracies in the modern world. A bureaucracy is a 'machine' that is designed to operate according to explicit roles and rules, with the goal of producing a certain effect whether in government, economics, justice, science or education. Even science is best viewed as an institutional or bureaucratic process based in part on the creation, criticism and circulation of documents. A scientific finding becomes part of the disciplinary knowledge only when published in a legitimate, peer-reviewed text. Scientists earn their place in this institution by learning to create and use these documents according to the norms and rules of accepted practice.

The spread of literacy into every walk of life was important, not only because it democratised literacy but because it gave the very idea of 'text' a prominent place in society. The autonomy given to the text was to be repeated in many contexts in which written documents came to be seen as authoritative. The written law, the written contract, the written scripture, the written scientific article, came to be seen as having the authority previously accorded to personal authority, whether Pope, King or scribe. Although many writers from Pope Urban VIII to Stanley Fish deny the authority of 'text', written documents came to be seen as having a use and an authority throughout the modern world (Geisler, 1990; Baron, 2000). The authority of the textual tradition provides the motivation towards inscription found everywhere in the modern world whether in contracts, law or science – or even in the publication of a *Festschrift*.

Schooling and literacy

The changing use of literacy in society was reflected in the purposes and patterns of schooling. The religious schools of the Middle Ages served to train leaders and administrators in the Church and, to the extent that they were open to a more general public, to teach people how to participate in religious life. A major change occurred when the institution of the school shifted from being the servant of the Church to the preparation of experts for secular culture. Murray (1978) discussed the growing role of specialised non-religious knowledge in the West. One twelfth-century writer claimed 'The glory of any kingdom has always grown vigorously so long as schools of the liberal sciences flourished in it' (Murray, 1978, p. 117). It was an expression of the growing awareness of the importance of the 'powers of the 'trained' mind for government and the military' (Murray, 1978, p. 130), a training in which mathematics came to play a prominent role. Grendler (1989) traced a similar pattern in thirteenth-century Italy: '. . . in 1333 the Commune of Chioggia decreed that judges and other civic officials must read and write to hold their jobs' (Grendler, 1989, p. 12). Secular social roles such as judge or administrator required the special training that was to be provided by the newly established universities. With the universities came schools that trained people so that they would be eligible for admission to and benefit from those universities. Thus, the fifteenth century saw the growth of the preparatory schools, such as the one that was attached to Magdalen College, Oxford.

The close tie between literacy and function is shown in the work of Egil Johansson (1981). In Sweden, mass literacy education was achieved without an elaborate school system because parents were expected to take care of children's learning. The Church Law of 1686 required the Lutheran churchmen to check the reading proficiency of both adults and children in a solemn annual examination of their ability to read certain sacred texts. Failure could bar one from marriage or other sacraments of civil and religious life. The result was one of the highest levels of literacy in Europe, although it was a form of literacy tied explicitly to a particular religious function. Such specific functions have always been the motivation for learning to read; literacy had to be seen as having a use.

An extensive study of literacy in eighteenth-century north-west Germany (Hofmeister, Prass and Winnige, 1998) has shown the importance of three primary factors in the growth of literacy rates, as indicated by the ability to

sign one's name and to read and write – namely, adequate schools, administrative functions mediated by writing and the ties of economic activities to
more distant markets. Protestantism was also found to be an important factor.

Indeed, a profound change in the history of literacy and schooling
occurred with the development of the idea that everyone should be a reader
– the 'massification' of literacy. The idea grew up with the Reformation with
the view that even laypeople should have the opportunity to encounter the
word of God for him- or herself. The Lutheran Reformation in Germany was
quickly followed by the development of schools to teach children to read and
memorise the Scriptures (Strauss, 1981; Hofmeister, Prass and Winnige,
1998). Such schools were financed by the State but organised by the Church,
which taught what it chose as long as appropriate deference was paid to the
Monarch. Through schooling, literacy was distributed across the masses.

Although we tend to think of literacy as a general skill in reading and
writing, literacy in this early period continued to be closely tied to specific
functions. The invention of the printing press made an abundance of written
materials available both for educational purposes and to meet the needs and
interests of the increasingly literate population. But, again, the driving force
was the interest and use of the learners rather than the intention of the
authorities. If the ability to read and write was not found to be useful for
religious life, business or enjoyment, it tended to wither.

Universal public schooling, employing a secular curriculum and compulsory attendance laws, was largely the product of the growth of nationalism
and the rise of the nation state. Here, literacy was turned not only to the
ancient purposes of training of expertise for the religious or secular institutions of society, but also for creating national identity, a willingness to pay
taxes and, if necessary, to fight. Nations, Anderson (1983) points out, were
born when the Enlightenment and political revolutions were 'destroying the
legitimacy of the divinely ordained, hierarchical dynastic realm' (Anderson,
1983, p. 6). Nation states picked up for themselves rights and obligations that
were previously held by Prince, Church or family. Literacy and education
were two of these. Literacy was seen as a way of identifying and extending a
vernacular language as a national language, thereby heightening the identity
of the people as well as a means of filling the new roles in the administration
of the nation state. To meet these goals, the state provided funds for the
establishment of public schools, which grew as the society as a whole
became more literate. Schooled literacy has, it appears, always been an
important instrument of national identity. France having adopted, after the
French Revolution, a republican form of government was determined to
create an informed citizenry. Such a citizenry with a national identity could
be guaranteed only through universal schooling in the vernacular, i.e. in the
French language.

The role of language and literacy in national identity is documented by Coulmas (2000), who pointed out that the collapse of the Soviet Union has been accompanied by renewed interest not only in local languages, but also in the development of a distinctive national script, e.g. in Moldova, the Soviet regime had promoted Cyrillic script to foster ties with the Soviet Union and to mark off the Moldavians from their Romanian neighbours who used a Roman script. When the Soviet Union collapsed, the Moldavians rejected the Cyrillic script and their revival of the Roman script allowed them to recognise the identity of Moldavian and Romanian. Thus, literacy is not just about human competence, but also about national identity. The issue resurfaces in the Americas in the form of French–English debates in Canada and the idea of a 'national' language in the USA.

With the growth of nationalism, the function of the school changed from serving professional, personal or family needs to fulfilling national needs, to which those earlier needs were seen as subservient. To survive, a nation needs to defend itself against external threat and from internal strife, it needs to foster the welfare of its people, especially the welfare of its economic class (who may otherwise move away!), and it needs to train the professionals needed for public administration and the professions. Further, it needs to educate its citizens so that they see or at least believe that the state serves their interests and needs, thereby fostering compliance with the rule of law and avoiding civic strife. The creation of education as the instrument of the nation state was responsible for the 'big' categories of educational reform – elementary versus advanced education, education versus basic skills, credentials, passing and failing, dropouts, standards and the national curriculum, which specifies what everyone (in a particular society) must know.

By the end of the twentieth century, schools came to see the functions of literacy less as those of defending the nation or serving the bureaucracies of the society, and more as an instrument of human competence and human fulfilment. Although literacy as a virtue is much exaggerated, it continues to be much more a form of competence that allows for participation in the great bureaucratic structures of society be they law, science or literature. Literacy is a criterion for admission to new opportunities; consequently, literacy is no less central to schooling now than it was 500 years ago. Literacy in this sense is, however, much more inclusive than the simple ability to read and write; it is the knowledge of how to create and make use of the documentary resources of a literate society.

Education of literacy

Educational methods for the teaching of reading remained more or less the same over the first nine centuries of the millennium, although what was taught changed in important ways. Mediaeval Roman education taught literacy using methods that were 'slow, thorough, and relentlessly pedantic', involving, from an early age, 'the practice of writing and reading out the letters of the alphabet in all sorts of combinations before proceeding to syllables and complete words' (Green, 1994, p. 26). This pedagogy which continued through the eighteenth century was based on the then current assumptions about knowledge:

> The subject matter, whether beginning reading, Latin grammar, advanced rhetoric, or abbaco [reckoning with an abacus], had to be divided into very small individual bits of knowledge. Teachers and textbooks taught by breaking a skill into its smallest components, drilling them intensively, and then assembling the bits to make the whole.
>
> Grendler (1989, p. 409)

This education was driven by at least two factors. First, reading was taught independently of writing, writing remaining in some countries as a monopoly held by a guild, so one could not use writing as a means of teaching reading. More importantly, learning to read was not learning to read one's mother tongue, a vernacular language, but rather learning to read Latin, a dead language in which most of the important texts had been and continued to be written. Thus, one had no knowledge of an oral language that could be appealed to in learning to read. One was learning not to recognise the known, but to 'sound out' a foreign language, Latin. Here, one learned to talk by learning to read! This method is far from obsolete; it remains part of 'folk pedagogy', the belief that leads parents in much of the West to buy alphabet books for their children and in their habit of teaching them to recite the ABC. We now know, partly through the efforts of Ingvar Lundberg and his colleagues, that one of the most important roots of learning to read is to reflect upon the properties of one's own speech; this move was impossible in learning to read Latin, yet in many parts of the world the ancient education of 'sounding out' remains.

Shortly after the translation of the Bible into German, Valentin Ickelsamer (1501-1542), a friend of Luther, developed what would now be called the phonological method, i.e. teaching reading by moving from the sounds of actual speech to the letters representing those sounds. In his *The Shortest Way to Reading* (1527), he wrote:

> Take the name Hans: you have four sound changes in this word, which are represented by four letters. First, you hear a strong exhaling noise, as when someone heaves a deep sigh. This is the H, which you breathe into the vowel A. Following this, there is a sound through the nose and finally you hear a sibilant like the hissing of a snake.
>
> Strauss (1981, p. 102)

This idea became central to what one may think of as the 'new phonics' for the teaching of reading: learning to read by finding a mapping between the known structures of speech and the visible features of the script. We may credit the Libermans (Shankweiler and Liberman, 1972) with the idea that, in learning to read, one must make a completely new analysis of the sound patterns of speech. This analysis is quite different from that required for ordinary oral production and perception. In learning to read, one must learn to hear, i.e. analyse, speech in a new way, namely into categories that map on to the specific properties of the written code. It is for this reason that the metalinguistic training studies pioneered by Lundberg, Olofsson and Wall (1980) were so important; they showed how a new awareness of the properties of speech-facilitated literacy development.

The author would add two caveats. It is not reflective awareness in general that is at play, so much as the reflective analysis of speech into the categories mandated by the script. Thus the Piagetian studies of language and metalanguage are somewhat misleading. Knowledge of the metalanguage is not a natural development as much as learning how to hear the language in order to map it to a particular script, whether character, syllable or alphabet.

Second, it is a mapping not just to sound patterns, but to morphemic and syntactic structure. Children have to learn to recognise words not just phonemes and syllables, and syntactic structure as well as meanings. Both these semantic and syntactic structures have to be brought into awareness in order to find the required mappings. Children know many words but are not aware that they are words; that is why they call caterpillar a short word and why, when reading 'Three little pigs' with one word covered up, they think it now reads 'Two little pigs' (Homer and Olson, 1999). Similarly, that is why they have difficulty in judging where to put a full stop or a comma in their writing; they have to learn to analyse their less formally organised speech into these restricted categories.

I recently encountered a children's reader prepared for German schools in the early part of the twentieth century which presented its text as follows:

Hei ni und Le ne. Hei ni und Le ne hel fen schon der Ma ma wi schon und wa schen.

Clearly, the text has the intention of aiding the recognition of the syllables of the language, just as some teachers of reading encourage attention to the individual letters to help the recognition of the individual phonemes. What is lost is the lexical identities that are equally or more important in reading. Even the author can read this small German text syllabically, but may not grasp the meaning. This text encourages the former with perhaps loss of the latter.

Reading is sometimes represented by cognitive psychologists as a matter of knowing and following rules or procedures in a way that is analogous to a computer program. Wittgenstein (1958), to whom we owe the most careful analysis of what is involved in learning or following a rule, argued:

> Knowing how to play a game or being master of a technique does not involve simply knowing rules (if it involves rules at all)

but knowing what the rules are for, what the game is, what he called the 'Witz of the game'. Strategy in chess, for example, is not just following rules – a mistake in chess is not just moving a rook as if it were a pawn but of, say, leaving the queen unguarded (Staten, 1985, p. 106). It is that deeper understanding that lies behind, and gives point to, the rules. When children fail to acquire a 'rule' or procedure in learning to read, it is as likely that they have not grasped the point of the rule – the action achieved by the rule – as being unable to learn the rule itself. As whole language writers have pointed out, it is easy to get distracted by many rules if one does not know the point of the game, namely grasping meaning.

The new understanding of the importance of linguistic awareness in learning to read brings to light the critical role of implicit knowledge in any educational context. Children have implicit knowledge of the structure of speech, including implicit knowledge of grammar. A grammatical rule such as the use of the objective form of a pronoun after a preposition (e.g. 'for you and me' versus for 'you and I') is easy to learn if one can discover the regular form in one's own implicit knowledge or intuition, but difficult to learn otherwise. Teaching reading traditionally ignored the role of the learner's prior implicit knowledge or intuition. As noted, it was thought that learning to read could be built up from elementary constitutive elements, the letters of the alphabet and their 'sounds', which could then be organised into 'syllables', and finally into meaningful units, 'words'. The new understanding of learning to read begins at the other end by recruiting the linguistic intuitions that children already possess, albeit implicitly, in their ability to speak. Thus the letter 't' comes to represent the sound that the child can hear, with practice and some instruction, at the end of the word 'cat'. It is the implicit knowledge of speech, when analysed and reorganised into constituents and patterns, such as words and, ultimately, phonemes, that the child brings to understanding the written symbols. Thus, children are not merely taught to read; they are learning to perceive their own speech in a new way, i.e. they are learning how the structures of their speech may be analysed and re-represented by a visual code. Although this view was pretty well in place by the end of the millennium, it has yet to make a profound impact on educational practice.

Reading difficulty

The millennium created many new types of people, not just citizens as defined by a constitution, criminals as defined by courts of law, and managers as defined by the charter of a business firm, but also educationally relevant types of people such as learning disabled, gifted, hyperactive and dyslexic people. People with dyslexia exist only because of the norms established in a society to measure reading skill. There have always been non-readers and poor readers, reluctant readers and cynical readers, but our putative science has institutionalised some of these by designing texts that serve to define such categories as 'people with functional illiteracy' and 'people with dyslexia', for whom special procedures are thought to be appropriate. Only at the end of the century did writers begin to show how such categories are socially constructed and to raise questions about their meaning (Hacking, 1990). I raise two concerns: the nature of the phenomenon and its educational usefulness in understanding learners.

The 'there' there problem

The cognitive revolution is generally understood as an attempt to replace explanations based on traits, dispositions, skills and habits by explanations based on knowledge. Success is attributed to the fact that the subject knows something whereas failure is traced to not knowing or not understanding. Thus, a reader is one who knows and understands something that a non-reader does not. Although poor reading may be analysed in terms of knowledge or lack of knowledge which, ideally, could be addressed through education, dyslexia harks back to non-cognitive analysis of dispositions and skills, and in that sense is a pre-cognitive scientific notion.

The attempt to study dyslexia as a process or disposition has not been without some promise. Population studies have succeeded in isolating a trait or disposition that shows the standard patterns of heritability. Dyslexia, as we say, runs in families. Or is it that reading ability runs in families? Just how do the traits that are biologically distributed in the population as a whole relate to the knowledge or lack of knowledge to be found in particular individuals? I want to consider the reasons for thinking that a trait that shows patterns of genetic heritability has little or nothing to tell us about either knowledge or individuals.

Dyslexia, unlike blindness or cancer, is not simply present or absent, but rather is defined in terms of a statistical, institutional norm. Thus the 'dyslexic' child is the worst reader in the class, the 'attention deficit' child is the most disruptive in the class, the 'gifted' child is the one with a highest tested IQ in the class, etc. The class average and the normal distribution provide the norm relative to which these children are considered anomalous.

The dyslexic child is one who falls two standard deviations below the mean.

Tails of distributions are always invitations for enquiry. Porter (1995) has pointed out the uses and limitations of appeals to numbers in the formation of arguments. He writes:

> The tables for marriage revealed that each year a small number of men in their twenties married septuagenarian women. Here was a phenomenon that could be investigated. The curious statistician could compare the rates in different countries, or according to religious faith and inheritance laws, in order to understand this aspect of social life.
>
> Porter (1995, p. 37)

Such an analysis may advance one's career but not one's science.

Psychologists for the past century have attempted to isolate the special properties of those individuals falling at the tails of various distributions, while ignoring the institutions that create these categories and, in a sense, these pathologies. Indeed, it has been argued that reading difficulties are social problems rooted in linguistic practices of the home and in the mass teaching practices of the school. Thus, if appropriate non-classroom instruction is provided, in many cases such dyslexia disappears (Clay, 1998).

The term 'dyslexia' creates a nominal class implying a discontinuity from the population as a whole, whereas in fact it is defined in terms of a statistical distribution. Designating the tail of the distribution as a class implies that it is a thing, a disease say, that one either does or does not have. Cancer is not normally distributed in the population; it is a discrete class, a thing that one either does or does not have; dyslexia, unlike a genuine disease, is defined only by reference to statistical norms and, in my view, is inappropriately labelled as a class. The correct designation would be low reading ability relative to the statistical norm. As for any trait, reading skill is distributed 'normally' in the population. Co-varying IQ and the number of years in school do not alter the fact that children with dyslexia fall into the tail of a normal distribution. If dyslexia were a disease independent of the normal distribution of reading skill, one would expect to have two distributions – one for dyslexia and one for reading ability. But, in fact, dyslexia is just poor reading given a normal IQ and the opportunity for learning.

What is distributed in the population, then, is not dyslexia but reading ability, the variability captured by the normal curve. Where there is variability in a population, selective pressures can apply; however, the selection is not for or against dyslexia, but for a trait common to all readers although differentially distributed in the population. Selection applies not only to the tails of a distribution, but also to the trait distributed in the population as a whole.

This may be seen more clearly by contrasting a genuine disease, e.g. cancer, with an institutional category such as dyslexia. For a disease, the symptoms may be distinguished from the disease. On the basis of the symptoms, e.g. a spot on a mammogram, one infers the presence of the disease – uncontrolled cell division. The actual presence of the disease is determinable independently of those predicting symptoms. The disease is the 'thing' of which the symptoms are an indication. One can assess the reliability of the symptom as a predictor of the presence of the disease. For dyslexia, on the other hand, there are only symptoms that are correlated with each other. There is no disease, no 'thing' that can be ascertained independently of the symptoms predicting it. There is no 'there' there, as Gertrude Stein famously said when asked about her impressions after a visit to Oakland. So, predictive tests do not predict a criterion, but rather predict each other; the tests are intercorrelated but there is no 'thing', no criterion, of which they are predictive.

The 'who has it' problem

In an interesting series of studies, Hoffrage and Gigerenzer (1998) showed that the predictive value of such diagnostic tests as the mammogram for the diagnosis of breast cancer is quite limited. That predictive value is grossly overestimated by most people because of the tendency to ignore the prevalence of the symptoms in the population as a whole is a factor taken into account in Baysian statistics. Thus, to cite their example, for a woman aged 40 who participates in a routine screening, the chance of having cancer is 1%. If she actually has cancer, the probability that she will have a positive mammogram is about 80%. They found that most physicians report to a woman with a positive mammogram that the probability that she has cancer is about 0.8, 80% – highly likely indeed. In fact, if the appropriate Baysian probabilities are calculated, the probability is only about 0.08, or 8% – highly unlikely. The flaw in reasoning comes from ignoring the base rates, the prevalence of the symptoms in the population as a whole. This may be presented as follows:

1000 women are tested

10 have cancer		990 do not	
8 test positive	2 test negative	95 test positive	895 test negative

The Baysian calculation may be approximated by computing with the actual frequencies: of the 103 people who test positive, only 8 have the disease. Hence, if one tested positive, the probability that she has the disease is approximately $p = 8/(8 + 95) = 0.08$ – an order of magnitude lower than frequently reported by physicians.

Setting aside the fact that there is no such 'thing' as dyslexia, we may apply Baysian logic to the use of diagnostic tests for dyslexia in an individual poor reader. Here invented numbers are used. Real scores are by nature impossible because no one knows who really has this putative affliction, all we know is who has the symptoms (i.e. there is no cancer):

1000 children

| 100 (10%) have 'it' | | 900 do not | |
| 80 score badly | 20 score well | 200 score badly | 700 score well |

The Baysian calculation, again approximated by computing with actual frequencies, is as follows:

$$p = 80/(80 + 200) = 0.3$$

i.e. a one in three chance that the person who scored badly was actually dyslexic.

Under such circumstances, is a teacher wise to infer dyslexia on the basis of poor performances on a reading test? No, because the teacher would be right in only one-third of the cases. The odds of being right in the individual case are too small to be useful. The teacher is better off just noting that performance is poor and directing his or her attention to what it is that the poor reader is having trouble with – it could be any one of many gaps in knowledge or any one of many misunderstandings, which a competent teacher, if time was available, could address.

The problem is more general than just deciding who has dyslexia. Whenever a psychological test is used to predict performance on some criterion test, predictions are extremely low in individual cases. With the help of German colleagues Renata Valtin and Oliver Thiel at the Humboldt University, we have calculated the likelihood of a student who is classified at the extreme of a distribution (about the top 10% of ability on a standard IQ test) actually being among the top scorers of an achievement test with which it correlates 0.5. The finding is that only half of the top performers in a class come from the high ability group. Combining six classes and cross-classifying the gifted/non-gifted with being in the top one-third of the class on an achievement test yields the following:

Achievement		Gifted	Not gifted
	Good (A)	15	28
	Poor (B or C)	6	71

Notice that most of the high achievers are from the not gifted group. Even if we equate the number of participants designated as gifted and the number of individuals in the category of highest achievers, the high achievers are as likely to be from the not gifted group as from the gifted group. A typical class reported by Thiel is as follows:

		Gifted	Not gifted
Achievement	Excellent	1	2
	Other	2	16

Again, notice that more of the high scorers come from the not gifted group, illustrating the limited value of the diagnostic test in individual cases. This is a simple consequence of the fact that diagnostic measures correlate with criterion performances by only about 0.5 even in the best cases. Again, correlations are of limited usefulness in individual cases, e.g. in predicting who will do well in a particular class or on a particular test even if in the class as a whole the correlation is highly significant.

Note, however, that, for the epidemiologists, the population geneticist or the functioning of an institution, a small difference may be important. A university admissions committee may not need to know who 'really' has ability or disability as long as the selection device is better than nothing for the population as a whole; evolution does not need to discriminate in the individual case as long as the distribution as a whole is altered by natural selection. So, let those who study populations continue with their work, but do not expect that they will have anything of interest to say to education. Education is oriented to the intentional states, the knowledge and under-standing of individual learners, and those states should be the focus of atten-tion of researchers and the object of educational interventions.

Conclusion

If we are to understand reading and learning to read, we may well begin by considering the factors that explain why some people do not read. The biggest factor is that there is no script, no writing systems available for much of the world's population (Figure 3.1).

If there is a script, it may not be learned because there is no important role for writing and reading to play in the economic, religious or public life of the people; literacy can thrive only in a literate society, e.g. if resources are distributed by largesse, on the personal whim of an authority rather than on the basis of rules and contracts, literacy will wither. If literacy is in fact impor-tant, i.e. if literacy is a route to opportunity, people may still fail to learn to read and write because of an absence of well-functioning schools. Even if there are schools, the teachers may be employing inappropriate educational methods or education that fails to meet the needs of the individual learner. Even if the educational structure is in place, the learner may still misinterpret or ignore important aspects of knowledge that are needed to understand what reading is all about, e.g. that it is a visible representation of what could be said. Even if they understand all that, they may fail to invest the required effort. Note that all of these steps so far are under intentional control, they

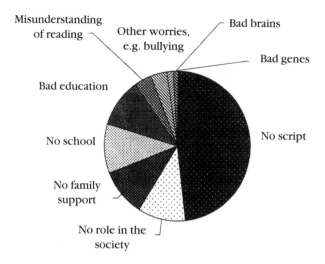

Figure 3.1. Why people around the world cannot read.

rely on things that one may do and for which one may accept responsibility. The final step – namely, that one lacks or at least has fewer of the mental structures required to compute a certain function – may be a cause of a failure to learn to read well, but even here we can never be sure in the diagnosis of a particular individual. What is worse is that such non-intentional characterisation removes the responsibility for learning from the child, which is, surely, the teachers' most important educational resource.

The major problems about literacy that remain unsolved at the end of the millennium involve the difficulties in extending literacy into the non-literate world, i.e. the spread of literacy and the development of literate institutions into contexts and nations in which they may be useful. This should not be seen as a new evangelism, but rather as providing resources that people in less developed countries find useful for furthering their own ends. Second, we still do not understand just what our literacy is doing to us, other than causing eye strain. Third, we don't understand the problems of poor readers, partly because we do not understand well the general problem of human diversity.

References

Anderson, B. (1983). *Imagined Communities: Reflections on the origin and spread of nationalism*. New York: Verso.

Baron, N. (2000). *From Alphabet to E-mail: How written English evolved and where it is heading*. London: Routledge.

Clay, M. (1998). *By Different Paths to Common Outcomes*. York, ME: Stenhouse.

Coulmas, F. (1999). *The Nationalization of Writing*. (Mimeo.) Duisburg, Germany: Sprache und Geschichte, Gerhard-Mercator-University.

de Bury, R. (1345/1945). *The Philobiblon of Richard de Bury*. New York: Duschnes.

Geisler, C. (1990). *Academic Literacy and the Nature of Expertise: Reading, writing and knowing in academic philosophy*. Hillsdale, NJ: Erlbaum.

Green, D.H. (1994). *Medieval Listening and Reading: The primary reception of German literature 800–1300*. Cambridge: Cambridge University Press.

Grendler, P.F. (1989). *Schooling in Renaissance Italy: Literacy and learning 1300–1600*. Baltimore, MD: Johns Hopkins University Press.

Hacking, I. (1990). *The Taming of Chance*. Cambridge: Cambridge University Press.

Havelock, E.A. (1963). *Preface to Plato*. Cambridge: Cambridge University Press.

Hoffrage, U. and Gigerenzer, G. (1998). Using natural frequencies to improve diagnostic inferences. *Academic Medicine* **73**: 538–540.

Hofmeister, A., Prass, R. and Winnige, N. (1998). Elementary Education, Schools, Literacy, and the Demands of Everyday Life: Northwest Germany ca. 1800. *Central European History* **31**: 329–384.

Homer, B. and Olson, D.R. (1999). Literacy and children's conception of language. *Written Language and Literacy* **2**: 113–137.

Johansson, E. (1981). The history of literacy in Sweden. In: Graff, H. (ed.), *Literacy and Social Development in the West: A reader*. Cambridge: Cambridge University Press, pp. 151–182.

Lundberg, I., Olofsson, Å. and Wall, S. (1980). Reading and spelling skills in the first school years predicted from phonemic awareness skills in kindergarten. *Scandinavian Journal of Psychology* **21**: 159–173.

Luria, A.R. (1976). *Cognitive Development: Its cultural and social foundations*. Cambridge: Cambridge University Press.

Murray, A. (1978). *Reason and Society in the Middle Ages*. Oxford: Oxford University Press.

Olson, D.R. (1994). *The World on Paper*. Cambridge: Cambridge University Press.

Porter, T.M. (1995). *Trust in Numbers: The pursuit of objectivity in science and public life*. Princeton, NJ: Princeton University Press.

Shankweiler, D. and Liberman, I.Y. (1972). Misreading: A search for causes. In: Kavanagh, J.F. and Mattingly, I.G. (eds), *Language by Ear and by Eye*. Cambridge, MA: MIT Press, pp. 293–317.

Staten, H. (1985). *Wittgenstein and Derrida*. Oxford: Blackwell.

Strauss, G. (1981). Techniques of indoctrination: The German Reformation. In: Graff, H. (ed.), *Literacy and Social Development in the West: A reader*. Cambridge: Cambridge University Press, pp. 96–104.

Wittgenstein, L. (1958). *Philosophical Investigations*, 3rd edn. Trans. by G.E.M. Anscombe. New York: Macmillan.

Chapter 4

Reading disabilities among very-low-birthweight children: implications for using different exclusion criteria in defining dyslexia

STEFAN SAMUELSSON

The generally accepted definition of dyslexia or specific reading disability is poor reading that occurs without general intelligence problems (this is normally operationalised as a discrepancy between reading achievement and intellectual potential as measured by standardised intelligence tests). As a consequence of this definition of reading disability, dyslexia has traditionally been regarded as a discrete disorder and, thus, distinguished from 'garden-variety' (ordinary) poor readers (generally learning-disabled readers) characterised by low intelligence and low reading achievement. This emphasis on the IQ–achievement discrepancy as a defining characteristic of dyslexia is also outlined as the single most critical exclusion criterion in the currently most influential definition given in the *Diagnostic and Statistical Manual of Mental Disorders* (DSM-IV – American Psychiatric Association, 1994). In actual practice, only poor readers with average or better intelligence, i.e. individuals who satisfy IQ discrepancy as a standard exclusionary criterion, are likely to be defined as having dyslexia. More importantly, it is also widely accepted that poor readers with an IQ–reading discrepancy are qualitatively different from 'garden-variety' poor readers with low IQ scores, and that this difference constitutes one critical source of information guiding the need for and the amount of remediation.

However, several recent studies have seriously challenged the discrepancy-based definition of dyslexia and in particular the assumption that people with dyslexia are qualitatively different from 'garden-variety' poor readers (Siegel, 1992; Fletcher et al., 1994; Stanovich and Siegel, 1994; Foorman et al., 1996; Ellis, McDougall and Monk, 1996; Siegel and Himel, 1998; Vellutino, Scanlon and Lyon, 2000). In fact, comparisons between readers with dyslexia and poor readers, on cognitive tests measuring reading skills, vocabulary, visual processing, phonological and orthographic decoding skills and short-term memory, have rather consistently revealed non-significant differences. It has also been demonstrated that readers with dyslexia and poor readers do not respond differently to educational intervention (Vellutino, Scanlon and Lyon, 2000), and there are no substantial differences obtained in the rate of growth in reading as a function of intelligence (Siegel, 1988; Share, McGee and Silva, 1989). In fact, the similarities between readers with dyslexia and poor readers are remarkable as long as the tests measure reading subskills or reading-related cognitive skills (Toth and Siegel, 1994). Together, these results indicate that the deficits in reading or cognitive subskills obtained in readers with dyslexia and poor readers are closely matched, and that reading difficulty represents the lower end of a normal continuum of reading skills (Shaywitz et al., 1992).

Thus, the research addressing the validity of the term 'dyslexia', defined by a strong emphasis on discrepancy from IQ or expected reading level, has demonstrated that there is little evidence for the assumption that the reading problems exhibited by dyslexic poor readers have different causes compared with 'garden-variety' poor readers. However, intellectual impairment is only one exclusionary criterion employed in classic definitions of dyslexia (compare World Health Organization, 1993; American Psychiatric Association, 1994). In addition to low intelligence, poor reading among people with dyslexia should not be attributed to factors such as sensory deficits, neurological dysfunction, emotional and behavioural problems, absence of appropriate instruction and deprived cultural background. Along with the assumption underlying reading disability and low intelligence, these factors are also assumed to be associated with poor reading acquisition. However, in the case when poor reading is assumed to be caused by one or several of these exclusionary criteria, it can also be assumed that this deficit should affect achievement in other domains outside the reading area, e.g. arithmetical skills and memory functioning (Stanovich and Siegel, 1994). Thus, based on recent research, dyslexic poor readers and 'garden-variety' poor readers do not differ much on reading-related cognitive skills, but they do seem to differ in some other non-reading areas such as cognitive tasks highly related to intellectual capacity (Fletcher et al., 1994; Stanovich and Siegel, 1994).

Most research focusing on potential differences between readers with dyslexia and 'garden-variety' poor readers have used intellectual abilities as the only critical distinguishing variable between the groups and, thus, most of the excluding variables have been very much ignored. The major issue addressed in the present chapter is further examination of whether it is appropriate to distinguish between the two groups when using neurological dysfunction and behavioural problems as additional exclusionary criteria.

For this purpose, the author has combined two samples of children: one group of 70 very-low-birthweight (VLBW) children and one group of 72 normal birthweight (NBW) children, all of whom had been participants in previous studies (e.g. Samuelsson et al., 1999, 2000). For the present purpose, unlike most investigations of reading disabilities, it was important to make sure that a broad range of individual differences with regard to intellectual abilities, as well as the prevalence of both hyperactive behaviour and neurological problems, were present in the sample. In general, VLBW children represent a group at higher risk for delays in various domains compared with NBW children, including school-related abilities such as reading, spelling and mathematics, in addition to other abilities such as intelligence, language, speech, memory and visual motor performance (Aram et al., 1991; Saigal et al., 1991; Hack et al., 1992; Breslau et al., 1994; Dammann et al., 1996; Horwood, Mogridge and Darlow, 1998; Samuelsson et al., 1999). This general pattern of impaired developmental outcome covering school-related functions is also found among neurologically intact VLBW children; therefore differences between VLBW and NBW children are not simply attributable to those relatively few VLBW children with neurological deficits (Aram et al., 1991; Saigal et al., 1991; Hack et al., 1992; Middle et al., 1996; Samuelsson et al., 1999; Bylund et al., 2000).

By combining a sample of VLBW children and a sample of NBW children, it is therefore reasonable to assume that all levels of intellectual, behavioural and neurological functioning should be represented in the total sample of 142 children. Poor readers in the sample will be divided into dyslexic and 'garden-variety' poor readers, following three different subdivisions, with the purpose of gradually defining a group of readers with dyslexia who have a substantial IQ–achievement discrepancy with intact neurological functioning, as well as no signs of hyperactive behaviour.

Participants

VLBW children

The study population was taken from five hospitals that had both obstetric and paediatric departments; one is a university hospital with a regional neonatal intensive care unit in south-east Sweden. The VLBW group included all live-born infants with a birthweight of 1500 g or less, born between 1 February 1987 and 30 April 1988. The VLBW group consisted of 107 infants born to 97 mothers; 23 of the mothers (25 infants) were referred to the university hospital before birth and 8 after birth, where a total of 72 (67%) were treated. A total of 86 (80%) survived the neonatal period; 82 of these were examined at 4 years of age (see Bylund et al., 1998) and 70 (81% of survivors) were re-examined at 9 years of age. Eight families declined to participate: four had moved out of the region and four children were excluded because their mental or motor disability was too severe for psychological testing. Neonatal data for the 70 VLBW children were as follows: mean birthweight 1210 g (standard deviation or SD = 195), mean gestational age 30.9 weeks (SD = 2.56); 8 children had intracranial haemorrhage neonatally and 11 had been mechanically ventilated (5 days on average, SD = 2.7). All VLBW children had normal hearing and vision (or corrected-to-normal vision) and attended mainstream school. However, the prevalence of special education was significantly higher among VLBW children compared with the NBW children (43% vs 9%).

The NBW children in this sample were selected as follows: for each VLBW child who survived the first 48 h, one full-term child who was next in the order to the VLBW child with the same sex and maternal parity was chosen. A few mothers refused to participate, in which case the next NBW child in the order was chosen. A total of 86 NBW children was initially recruited, 83 of whom were examined at 4 years of age and 72 (84%) re-examined at 9 years. Nine families declined to participate and five families had moved out of the region. Neonatal data for the NBW children were as follows: mean birthweight 3530 g (SD = 502), mean gestational age 40.0 weeks (SD = 1.33); all passed an uneventful neonatal period.

The groups of VLBW and NBW children did not differ significantly with regard to maternal age and parity, sex, number of siblings, number of parental separations, parent's educational level or maternal smoking during pregnancy.

Measures

General academic achievement tasks

Non-verbal intellectual ability

The Raven Standard Progressive Matrices (Raven, Court and Raven, 1983) were employed to divide the children into different levels of non-verbal intellectual abilities.

Reading ability

The reading test was made up of 12 short passages followed by one to three multiple-choice questions primarily measuring reading comprehension. The test consisted of 36 questions and the testing time was restricted to 8 minutes.

Vocabulary

Word knowledge was measured by a test comprising 24 target words. In the test, the children were instructed to choose one of four alternatives that constituted a synonym to the target word. All words were read aloud by the teacher.

Mathematics

A total of 61 items (covering addition, subtraction, multiplication and division) was presented to the children and they worked alone for a maximum of 1 hour. The test was adopted from the Swedish National Agency for Education, and has been used to screen arithmetic skills among grade 2 children. The test did not include any arithmetic story problems.

Word-decoding tasks

Phonological choice task

The phonological decoding test was designed to force children to read using phonological decoding. The children viewed pairs of non-words (there were 25 pairs on each page in the test booklet) and were instructed to indicate, as quickly as possible, which non-word sounded exactly like a real word when pronounced. The number of correct non-words chosen within 2 minutes was taken as a measure of phonological decoding skill.

Non-word-reading task

Phonological decoding skill was also measured by a 48-item list of pronounce-able non-words. All non-words were orthographically legal and were constructed following the rules of Swedish phonology. The items appeared one at a time on a computer screen, with no time limit, and were printed in lower-case letters (Geneva font, 24 point). The number of correctly pronounced non-words was taken as a measure of phonological decoding skill.

Orthographic choice task

In this task, the children viewed pairs of words (there were 25 pairs of words on each page in the booklet) and were instructed to indicate, as quickly as possible, which word was spelled correctly. One word in each pair was misspelt, but was phonologically identical to the correctly spelt word when pronounced. Again, the number of words correctly identified within 2 minutes was taken as a measure of orthographic decoding skill.

Orthographic reading

In this test, 60 words (Geneva font, 24 point) were presented on a computer screen, one at a time, for very brief exposure periods (100 ms). The number of correctly read words (both regular and irregular) was taken as a measure of orthographic decoding skill, with the underlying assumption being that brief exposure imposes constraints on the information processes such that the use of phonological word decoding is made more difficult, whereas the use of orthographic word decoding is encouraged (Høien and Lundberg, 1989).

Lexical decision

In the test, children were presented with a series of words and non-words, and their instruction was to decide as quickly as possible whether or not each stimulus was a real word. There were 48 real words and 54 non-words in the test. The stimuli were presented on a computer screen and the children made their decisions by pressing the right or left button on a response console. Both accuracy and latency scores were recorded.

Neurological examination

Neurological functions in both VLBW and NBW children participating in this study had been graded on several occasions before this study using a standardised classification system. These examinations were conducted by the paediatrician who had followed the child from birth. On the basis of this classification system, each child was diagnosed into one of four groups: neurologically normal (i.e. having no noticeable neurological deviations at all), minor neurological deviations (problems with coordination, perception and behaviour, but with no need for any treatment), moderate neurological deviations (i.e. mild cerebral palsy, speech deviations and/or epileptic seizures for which there is a need for treatment) and severe neurological deviations (i.e. children with severe cerebral palsy, impaired vision, deafness, epilepsy and clear intellectual handicaps).

Behavioural ratings

To measure individual differences in hyperactive behaviour, a questionnaire comprising 13 items was used. Although the questions measuring hyperactive behaviour were closely related to the diagnostic criteria for attention deficit hyperactivity disorder (ADHD) established in DSM-IV, they were adjusted to a classroom setting and, thus, the questionnaire has not been used to identify ADHD as a discrete diagnostic category. The questionnaire was completed by each child's teacher. Each item in the questionnaire was followed by four response alternatives and an average score for each child was used as a measure of hyperactive behaviour.

Procedure

Both VLBW and NBW children visited one of the five hospitals in the region at 9 years of age (± 1 month) for a neurological examination. After this examination, a trained psychologist administered all word-decoding and general academic achievement tests, except for the test measuring mathematical skills and vocabulary. All data for reading skill and intellectual ability for both VLBW and NBW children were collected by the same experimenter. After this test session, the experimenter requested permission from the parents to contact their child's classroom teacher for the additional tests (i.e. vocabulary, arithmetic ability and behavioural ratings).

Results and discussion

To evaluate potential differences between readers with dyslexia and 'garden-variety' poor readers, one-third of the children (n = 52) with the lowest scores (< 12 points) on the reading ability task were defined as poor readers. The remaining 90 children with reading scores above 12 points were regarded as normal readers. It should be noted that this reading task mainly emphasises word-decoding skills (correlations between reading ability and lexical decision were 0.86 for accuracy and 0.87 for response time). It might also be added that the cut-off score of 12 points represents almost a 2-year lag compared with normal readers. The relatively large proportion of poor readers in the sample is explained mainly by the fact that VLBW children in general are at higher risk for delays in reading acquisition. It should also be made clear that this cut-off score represents only the lower portion of a continuum of reading skills, and not a real cut-off in the distribution of reading skills (see Shaywitz et al., 1992).

Mean performance for the total sample of children for the Raven's matrices was 30 points (this is close to the 50th percentile obtained in the norms for the test). In the first subdivision, all poor readers with an IQ score less than 30 points were defined as 'garden-variety' poor readers, whereas the poor readers with IQ scores at or above 30 points were defined as dyslexic readers. Although there is no *a priori* IQ cut-off score to be used when dividing poor readers with average and low non-verbal intellectual abilities, this subdivision clearly includes several intermediate cases where some dyslexic readers have IQ scores that are only slightly better compared with those poor readers with relatively high IQ scores.

As can be seen in Table 4.1, there is a striking similarity on all reading-related tasks between the dyslexic group and the 'garden-variety' poor reader group. The only difference between the groups, except for the scores on Raven's matrices, was the mathematical skills. These findings clearly replicate previous studies that suggest that differences between readers with dyslexia and 'garden-variety' poor readers are most likely to appear outside the reading domain in general and more specifically outside the phonological faculty (Stanovich, 1988; Fletcher et al., 1994; Stanovich and Siegel, 1994).

The distribution of normal readers, readers with dyslexia and 'garden-variety' poor readers among VLBW and NBW children is displayed in Table 4.2. More than one-third (34%) of all VLBW children were identified as 'garden-variety' poor readers compared with only 15% among the NBW children. The opposite pattern occurs with regard to the dyslexia classifica-

Table 4.1. Performance of the three groups on general academic achievement tasks and word-decoding skills following the first subdivision

Measure	Dyslexic readers (n = 17)	'Garden-variety' poor readers (n = 35)	Normal readers (n = 90)
	General academic achievement tasks		
Raven's matrices			
Accuracy (/60)	**35.8** (3.8)	**20.4** (5.4)	32.4 (9.1)
Mathematics			
Accuracy (/61)	**34.1** (12.6)	**28.0** (14.1)	44.0 (10.2)
Vocabulary			
Accuracy (/24)	8.3 (3.0)	8.9 (3.4)	11.9 (3.8)
Reading ability			
Accuracy (/33)	7.6 (4.5)	6.5 (4.2)	21.0 (5.7)
	Word decoding tasks		
Lexical decision			
Accuracy (/102)	45.2 (24.9)	37.4 (22.2)	84.6 (13.2)
RT in seconds	2.49 (0.34)	2.55 (0.27)	1.65 (0.42)
Non-word reading			
Accuracy (/48)	25.3 (9.8)	23.4 (8.8)	32.7 (5.3)
Phonological choice			
Completed items	10.4 (7.1)	8.6 (4.4)	17.1 (6.3)
Orthographic reading			
Accuracy (/60)	22.9 (12.8)	15.4 (10.8)	40.9 (10.9)
Orthographic choice			
Completed items	5.7 (4.0)	6.1 (5.3)	21.3 (8.7)

Significant differences between readers with dyslexia and 'garden-variety' poor readers using the Tukey–Kramer procedure are marked in bold and standard deviations are given in parentheses.

tion and, thus, VLBW children are significantly less likely to be classified as dyslexic compared with NBW children.

In the second subdivision, IQ discrepancy was increased between the two groups by excluding those 'garden-variety' poor readers who had IQ scores between 20 and 29 points (i.e. percentile scores between 25 and 50, respectively, according to the norms). In this second subdivision, the number of 'garden-variety' poor readers was reduced from 35 to 19 and, therefore, 16 intermediate cases with IQ scores close to those of the dyslexic group were removed. The mean difference in non-verbal IQ between readers with dyslexia and 'garden-variety' poor readers was increased from 15 to almost 20 points on the Raven task.

Table 4.2. The distribution of dyslexic readers, 'garden-variety' poor readers and normal readers among VLBW and NBW children following three different subgroup divisions

Subgroup	VLBW children	NBW children
	The first subdivision (n = 142)[a]	
Normal readers	39 (56)	51 (71)
Dyslexic readers	7 (10)	10 (14)
'Garden-variety' poor readers	24 (34)	11 (15)
	The second subdivision (n = 126)[b]	
Normal readers	39 (64)	51 (78)
Dyslexic readers	7 (11)	10 (16)
'Garden-variety' poor readers	15 (25)	4 (6)
	The third subdivision (n = 117)[c]	
Normal readers	39 (69)	51 (84)
Dyslexic readers	2 (4)	6 (10)
'Garden-variety' poor readers	15 (27)	4 (6)

[a]$\chi^2 = 6.93$, $p < 0.05$; [b]$\chi^2 = 8.38$, $p < 0.05$; [c]$\chi^2 = 9.77$, $p < 0.01$.
Numbers in parentheses are percentages.

As can be seen in Table 4.3, this new set of comparisons revealed that dyslexic readers performed significantly better than 'garden-variety' poor readers on two of three orthographic processing tasks. However, there were still no significant differences between the groups on the two tasks measuring phonological decoding skills. Again, these results agree with the phonological-core variable-difference model proposed by Stanovich (1988), indicating that both readers with dyslexia and 'garden-variety' poor readers seem to share the same underlying phonological processing deficits. Although the obtained differences in orthographic processing have not been systematically observed in previous work focusing on the distinction between readers with dyslexia and 'garden-variety' poor readers (e.g. Fletcher et al., 1994; Stanovich and Siegel, 1994), there have been several other studies demonstrating an increased tendency for dyslexic readers to compensate with visual–orthographic skills (Snowling and Frith, 1981; Pennington et al., 1986; Olson et al., 1989). Siegel, Share and Geva (1995) further suggest that, in some cases, dyslexic readers might have superior orthographic processing skills than same-age normal readers. These findings might indicate that poor readers with significant IQ–achievement discrepancies are more likely to use visual–orthographic decoding as an alternative strategy in developing reading skills (Figure 4.1).

Table 4.3. Performance of the three groups on general academic achievement tasks and word-decoding skills following the second subdivision

Measure	Dyslexic readers (n = 17)	'Garden-variety' poor readers (n = 19)	Normal readers (n = 90)
	General academic achievement tasks		
Raven's matrices			
Accuracy (/60)	**35.8** (3.8)	**16.1** (3.0)	32.4 (9.1)
Mathematics			
Accuracy (/61)	**34.1** (12.6)	**22.3** (14.6)	44.0 (10.2)
Vocabulary			
Accuracy (/24)	8.3 (3.0)	8.2 (3.7)	11.9 (3.8)
Reading ability			
Accuracy (/33)	7.6 (4.5)	4.9 (4.2)	21.0 (5.7)
	Word-decoding tasks		
Lexical decision			
Accuracy (/102)	**45.2** (24.9)	**28.8** (20.6)	84.6 (13.2)s
RT in seconds	2.49 (0.34)	2.61 (0.28)	1.65 (0.42)
Non-word reading			
Accuracy (/48)	25.3 (9.8)	22.2 (10.6)	32.7 (5.3)
Phonological choice			
Completed items	10.4 (7.1)	8.4 (4.5)	17.1 (6.3)
Orthographic reading			
Accuracy (/60)	**22.9** (12.8)	**12.4** (10.5)	40.9 (10.9)
Orthographic choice			
Completed items	5.7 (4.0)	4.8 (5.0)	21.3 (8.7)

Significant differences between readers with dyslexia and 'garden-variety' poor readers using the Tukey–Kramer procedure are marked in bold and standard deviations are given in parentheses.

In fact, when dividing all children in the present sample into four different IQ bands ranging from 1 or more SD below the mean to 1 or more SD above the mean, and then measuring levels of orthographic and phonological decoding within each IQ band, a consistent increase in orthographic decoding skill was found as a function of IQ. It was also found that levels of phonological decoding skill remain relatively stable across IQ bands. A similar pattern of a larger increase in orthographic compared to phonological decoding skills as a function of IQ was also found for two additional tests measuring orthographic (i.e. orthographic choice task) and phonological skills (i.e. phonological choice task). This relationship between IQ ranges

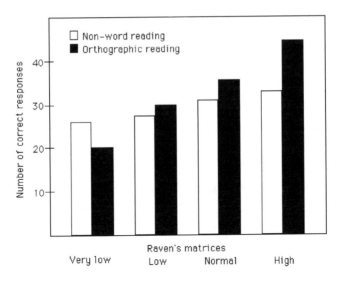

Figure 4.1. Phonological and orthographic decoding skills as a function of four different IQ bands.

and levels of orthographic and phonological decoding skills is consistent with results obtained by Fletcher et al. (1994), Siegel (1988, 1989), and Stanovich and Siegel (1994), especially regarding the findings that poor phonological decoding skills are relatively independent of intellectual capacity, and that a deficit in phonological processing is the main cause underlying reading difficulties.

Once again, the distribution of readers with dyslexia and 'garden-variety' poor readers across VLBW and NBW children clearly indicates that VLBW children are more likely to be classified as 'garden-variety' poor readers, whereas NBW children will be defined more often as dyslexic readers (see Table 4.2).

In the third subdivision, all dyslexic children with moderate and minor neurological deviations, and those deviating more than 1 SD compared with normal readers on the questions measuring hyperactive behaviour, were excluded from the subgroup of dyslexic readers. Adding these exclusion variables, the number of dyslexic readers was reduced from 17 to only 8 children (Table 4.4) and, at this stage, it is reasonable to argue that the group of dyslexic readers does in fact satisfy standard exclusionary criteria.

In more detail, 11 children (53%) among 'garden-variety' poor readers had minor-to-moderate neurological deviations and their mean score on hyperactive behaviour was 1.51 (SD = 0.69), whereas a mean score of 0.50 (SD = 0.20) for hyperactive behaviour was achieved among the dyslexic readers.

Table 4.4. Performance of the three groups on general academic achievement tasks and word-decoding skills

Measure	Dyslexic readers (n = 8)	'Garden-variety' poor readers (n = 19)	Normal readers (n = 90)
	General academic achievement tasks		
Raven's matrices			
Accuracy (/60)	**37.1** (3.9)	**16.1** (3.0)	32.4 (9.1)
Mathematics			
Accuracy (/61)	**35.0** (13.6)	**22.3** (14.6)	44.0 (10.2)
Vocabulary			
Accuracy (/24)	9.3 (3.5)	8.2 (3.7)	11.9 (3.8)
Reading ability			
Accuracy (/33)	7.5 (4.0)	4.9 (4.2)	21.0 (5.7)
	Word-decoding tasks		
Lexical decision			
Accuracy (/102)	**49.5** (23.8)	**28.8** (20.6)	84.6 (13.2)
RT in seconds	2.40 (0.39)	2.61 (0.28)	1.65 (0.42)
Non-word reading			
Accuracy (/48)	27.2 (3.2)	22.2 (10.6)	32.7 (5.3)
Phonological choice			
Completed items	11.0 (3.8)	8.4 (4.5)	17.1 (6.3)
Orthographic reading			
Accuracy (/60)	**28.4** (11.7)	**12.4** (10.5)	40.9 (10.9)
Orthographic choice			
Completed items	6.4 (4.0)	4.8 (5.0)	21.3 (8.7)

Significant differences between readers with dyslexia and 'garden-variety' poor readers using the Tukey–Kramer procedure are marked in bold and standard deviations are given in parentheses.

There were no differences in hyperactive behaviour between dyslexic and normal readers (0.50 vs 0.54). However, 10 normal readers (11%) had minor-to-severe neurological deviations.

Comparisons between readers with dyslexia and 'garden-variety' poor readers revealed that the dyslexic readers outperformed 'garden-variety' poor readers on task-measuring mathematical skills and orthographic processing skill. However, mean differences on phonological tasks remained non-significant. There was also a significant difference in the distribution of reading subgroups between VLBW and NBW children. In fact, closer inspection of Table 4.2 illustrates that the proportion of VLBW children defined as dyslexic readers gradually decreases as the number of excluding variables increases.

Summary and conclusion

The results from this study add to the growing body of evidence that documents that IQ–achievement discrepancy definitions of reading disability do not distinguish between readers with dyslexia and 'garden-variety' poor readers on tasks measuring phonological processing skills. Differences between readers with dyslexia and 'garden-variety' poor readers were obtained only for arithmetic skills and orthographic word-decoding skills (both related to general ability measured by non-verbal IQ). However, the findings presented in this chapter also challenge several other exclusionary variables that have a bearing on traditional definitions of dyslexia. It was found that even if 'garden-variety' poor readers were compared with dyslexic readers who not only manifested a significant IQ–achievement discrepancy, but also exhibited normal neurological functioning together with few signs of behavioural problems, there were still no differences in word-decoding tasks emphasising phonological skills. In other words, even if the difference between readers with dyslexia and 'garden-variety' poor readers were gradually increased on factors used as standard exclusionary criteria, such as neurological, behavioural and intellectual problems, the differences between the groups would be obtained only outside the phonological processing module.

On the basis of these data, it is also evident that VLBW children represent a group of children at higher risk of being under-identified as dyslexic readers, in spite of the fact that the number of VLBW children classified as poor readers is almost three times larger than for NBW children. This finding indicates larger differences between VLBW and NBW children on tests measuring non-verbal intelligence compared with tests measuring reading-related skills (see Saigal et al., 1991; Hack et al., 1992). Thus, the obtained differences between VLBW and NBW children in the distribution of readers with dyslexia and 'garden-variety' poor readers are mainly the result of more severe impairments in general cognitive abilities compared with their deficits in reading abilities. This finding relates to previous work indicating that the use of IQ–achievement discrepancy in defining dyslexia might under-identify some groups of children as dyslexic readers (Fletcher et al., 1994; Stanovich and Siegel, 1994; Siegel and Himel, 1998) and, thus, the necessity of making sure that children at higher risk for being excluded from the diagnosis of dyslexia are not excluded from the remediation that they need. At present, there is no evidence suggesting that poor readers with low IQs have more difficulty remediating, or that they are in need of a different strategy for remediation.

References

American Psychiatric Association (1994). *Diagnostic and Statistical Manual of Mental Disorders*, 4th edn revised. Washington, DC: American Psychiatric Press.

Aram, D.M., Hack, M., Hawkins, S., Weissman, B.M. and Borawski-Clark, E. (1991). Very-low-birthweight children and speech and language development. *Journal of Speech and Hearing Research* **34**: 1169-1179.

Breslau, N., DelDotto, J.E., Brown, G.G., Kumar, S., Ezhuthachan, S., Hufnagle, K.G. and Petersen, E.L. (1994). A gradient relationship between low birth weight and IQ at age 6 years. *Archives of Pediatric and Adolescent Medicine* **148**: 377-383.

Bylund, B., Cervin, T., Finnström, O. et al. (1998). Morbidity and neurological function of very low birthweight infants from the newborn period to 4 y of age. A prospective study from the Southeast region of Sweden. *Acta Pædiatrica Scandinavica* **87**: 758-763.

Bylund, B., Cervin, T., Finnström, O. et al. (2000). Very low-birth-weight children at 9 years: School performance and behavior in relation to risk factors. *Prenatal and Neonatal Medicine* **5**: 124-133.

Dammann, O., Walther, H., Allers, B. et al. (1996). Development of a regional cohort of very-low-birthweight children at six years: Cognitive abilities are associated with neurological disability and social background. *Developmental Medicine and Child Neurology* **38**: 97-108.

Ellis, A.W., McDougall, S.J.P. and Monk, A.F. (1996). Are dyslexics different I. A comparison between dyslexics, reading age controls, poor readers and precocious readers. *Dyslexia* **2**: 31-58.

Fletcher, J.M., Shaywitz, S.E., Shankweiler, D.P. et al. (1994). Cognitive profiles of reading disability: Comparisons of discrepancy and low achievement definitions. *Journal of Educational Psychology* **86**: 6-23.

Foorman, B.R., Francis, D.J., Fletcher, J.M. and Lynn, A. (1996). Relation of phonological and orthographic processing to early reading: Comparing two approaches to regression-based, reading-level-match designs. *Journal of Educational Psychology* **88**: 639-652.

Hack, M., Breslau, N., Aram, D., Weissman, B., Klein, N. and Borawski-Clark, E. (1992). The effect of very low birth weight and social risk on neurocognitive abilities at school age. *Journal of Developmental and Behavioral Pediatrics* **13**: 412-420.

Horwood, L. J., Mogridge, N. and Darlow, B.A. (1998). Cognitive, educational, and behavioural outcomes at 7 to 8 years in a national very low birthweight cohort. *Archives of Disease in Childhood* **79**: 12-20.

Høien, T. and Lundberg, I. (1989). A strategy for assessing problems in word recognition among dyslexics. *Scandinavian Journal of Educational Research* **33**: 185-201.

Middle, C., Johnson, A., Alderdice, F., Petty, T. and Macfarlane, A. (1996). Birthweight and health and development at the age of 7 years. *Child Care Health and Development* **22**: 55-71.

Olson, R.K., Wise, B., Conners, F., Rack, J. and Fulker, D. (1989). Specific deficits in component reading and language skills: Genetic and environmental influences. *Journal of Learning Disabilities* **22**: 339-348.

Pennington, B.F., McCabe, L.L., Smith, S.D., Lefly, D.L., Bockman, M.O., Kimberling, W.J. and Lubs, H.A. (1986). Spelling errors in adults with a form of familial dyslexia. *Child Development* **57**: 1001-1013.

Raven, J.C., Court, J.H. and Raven, J. (1983). *Manual for Raven's Progressive Matrices and Vocabulary Scales,* Part three, Section 7, *Research.* London: H.K. Lewis.

Saigal, S., Szatmari, P., Rosenbaum, P., Campbell, D. and King, S. (1991). Cognitive abilities and school performance of extremely low birth weight children and matched term control children at age 8 years: A regional study. *Journal of Pediatrics* **118**: 751–760.

Samuelsson, S., Bylund, B., Cervin, T. et al. (1999). The prevalence of reading disabilities among very-low-birth-weight children at 9 years of age – Dyslexics or poor readers. *Dyslexia* **5**: 94–112.

Samuelsson, S., Finnström, O., Leijon, I. and Mård, S. (2000). Phonological and surface profiles of reading difficulties among very low birth weight children: Converging evidence for the developmental lag hypothesis. *Scientific Studies of Reading* **4**: 197–217.

Share, D.L., McGee, R. and Silva, P.A. (1988). IQ and reading progress: A test of the capacity notion of IQ. *Journal of the American Academy of Child and Adolescent Psychiatry* **28**: 97–100.

Shaywitz, S.E., Escobar, M.D., Shaywitz, B.A., Fletcher, J.M. and Makuch, R. (1992). Distribution and temporal stability of dyslexia in an epidemiological sample of 414 children followed longitudinally. *New England Journal of Medicine* **326**: 145–150.

Siegel, L.S. (1988). Evidence that IQ scores are irrelevant to the definition and analysis of reading disability. *Canadian Journal of Psychology* **42**: 201–215.

Siegel, L.S. (1989). IQ is irrelevant to the definition of learning disabilities. *Journal of Learning Disabilities* **22**: 469–479.

Siegel, L.S. (1992). An evaluation of the discrepancy definition of dyslexia. *Journal of Learning Disabilities* **25**: 618–629.

Siegel, L.S. and Himel, N. (1998). Socioeconomic status, age and the classification of dyslexics and poor readers: The dangers of using IQ scores in the definition of reading disability. *Dyslexia* **4**: 90–104.

Siegel, L.S., Share, D. and Geva, E. (1995). Evidence for superior orthographic skills in dyslexics. *Psychological Science* **6**: 250–254.

Snowling, M.J. and Frith, U. (1981). The role of sound, shape, and orthographic cues in early reading. *British Journal of Psychology* **72**: 83–87.

Stanovich, K.E. (1988). Explaining the differences between the dyslexic and the garden-variety poor reader: The phonological-core variable-difference model. *Journal of Learning Disability* **21**, 590–604.

Stanovich, K.E. and Siegel, L.S. (1994). Phenotypic performance profile of children with reading disabilities: A regression-based test of the phonological-core variable-difference model. *Journal of Educational Psychology* **86**: 24–53.

Toth, G. and Siegel, L.S. (1994). A critical evaluation of the IQ–achievement discrepancy based definition of dyslexia. In: van den Bos, K.P., Siegel, L.S., Bakker, D.J. and Share, D.L. (eds), *Current Direction in Dyslexia Research.* Lisse: Swets & Zeitlinger, pp. 45–70.

Vellutino, F.R., Scanlon, D.M. and Lyon, G.R. (2000). Differentiating between difficult-to-remediate and readily remediated poor readers: More evidence against the IQ–achievement discrepancy definition of reading disability. *Journal of Learning Disability* **33**: 223–238.

World Health Organization (1993). *International Classification of Mental and Behavioural Disorders: Diagnostic criteria for research.* Geneva: WHO.

CHAPTER 5

Word recognition: the impact of phonological and orthographic components

TORLEIV HØIEN

Research on word recognition in reading has been a particularly active field since the birth of experimental psychology more than 100 years ago (Høien and Lundberg, 2000).

Word recognition refers to the process of recognising and pronouncing written words, and thereby accessing their meanings. This skill takes time to build, and it is acquired by repeated encounters with words, primarily through text reading. Being able to recognise immediately most of the words in a given text gives the reader a high degree of 'automaticity' in reading. Lexical access processes need to be executed efficiently and automatically, so as not to overtax processing resources.

This automaticity is the hallmark of skilful reading (LaBerge and Samuels, 1974; Perfetti, 1985, 1992; Stanovich, 1991; Wolf and Segal, 1992; Bowers and Wolf, 1993; Bowers et al., 1994). Freed from the task of having to figure out which words are on the page, the skilled reader can devote his or her mental resources to comprehension processes, and comprehension of course is the ultimate aim of all skilful reading.

Comprehension refers to the more demanding cognitive processes that make it possible for the reader to extract the meaning from the text, think about it, draw conclusions and make inferences. However, unlike word recognition, reading comprehension cannot be automated; it requires attention and higher-level cognitive abilities in order to function adequately.

Although word recognition and comprehension are different types of reading skills, good comprehension clearly depends on efficient word recognition. An abundance of research evidence has shown that accurate and automatic word decoding is a necessary prerequisite for skilful reading, and that the main stumbling block for less-skilled readers is the process of word recognition (Adams, 1990; Gough, Ehri and Treiman, 1992; Ehri, 1998).

According to the classic dual-route theory of word recognition, a written word can either be identified directly by recognition of the orthographic pattern (the orthographic strategy) or indirectly by a grapheme–phoneme translation (the phonological strategy). Current modifications of this theory acknowledge both processes as being involved more or less simultaneously (Seidenberg and McClelland, 1989; Hulme, Snowling and Quinland, 1991; Coltheart et al., 1993; Brown and Loosemore, 1995; Bjaalid, Høien and Lundberg, 1997).

The orthographic strategy allows the reader to decode the word immediately, i.e. to go directly from the word's orthographic representation (the letter sequence on the page) to the word's sound and meaning. An orthographic representation is the memory of the visual structure and spelling patterns that identify the individual word on the page, and the orthographic representation provides a direct link between a word's spelling and its pronunciation and meaning. These representations allow rapid identification of individual words as whole units, or as units composed of familiar-looking 'subunits,' such as word stems, prefixes and suffixes, and common sequences of letters (Gough, Juel and Griffith, 1992; Torgesen, Wagner and Rashotte, 1997; Ehri, 1998; Goswami, 1998).

Skilled readers primarily use the orthographic strategy when decoding words. They have seen the words in print hundreds or thousands of times before, so they recognise them immediately. But, when confronted with an unfamiliar word, or an experimentally devised non-word, the reader needs to use the phonological strategy (Share and Stanovich, 1995). When reading phonologically, the word is broken down into letters or short segments of letters. These letter segments are phonologically recoded ('sounded out') and the sounds are blended together to create a smooth string of sounds. This string of sounds – the word's phonological identity – is the raw material used for recognising the word.

It is clear from Share and Stanovich (1995) that phonological reading skills provide a necessary, but not a sufficient, support for the development of good reading ability. Acquisition of fluent reading skills depends on the establishment of a multitude of orthographic representations for word recognition in long-term memory (Ehri, 1992; Share and Stanovich, 1995), and skilful reading is also characterised by the ability to employ strategies flexibly, depending on the task at hand. However, the relative impact of the phonological and the orthographic skills at different levels of word-reading development is far from clear, and it might well be the case that skilled and less-skilled decoders use different strategies when encountering words. Therefore, in the present study the main focus will be on a comparison of how skilled and less-skilled readers decode words. More particularly, we look at the relative impact of phonological and orthographic strategies on word recognition among skilled and less-skilled children at different grade levels.

As already noted, word recognition is a skill that takes time to develop (Cunningham and Stanovich, 1998). Full automaticity is often not reached until the end of compulsory school (Jacobson and Lundberg, 2001). A critical question concerning less-skilled readers is whether their poor performance is the result of a delayed development, where the lag eventually will be overcome, or whether the problem has the character of a basic deficit. By studying children of different ages, it is possible to compare less-skilled readers in the older age group with normal younger readers at the same skill level. Different patterns in the relationship between subprocesses in word recognition would then suggest basic differences in performing the word-recognition task, and this would give tentative support to the deficit hypothesis rather than the lag hypothesis.

Studies

Participants

A total of 469 children, divided into three age groups (11, 13 and 15 year olds), participated in the study. They were selected from 21 classes from different areas in Sweden. All children in the selected classes participated, including those who had Swedish as second language – 7%. Table 5.1 gives an overview of the number of children participating in the study.

Table 5.1. Participants at each grade level

	Grade 4 *Number*	*Grade 6* *Number*	*Grade 8* *Number*
Boys	77	90	74
Girls	69	82	77
Total	146	172	151

Test battery

A computer-based test battery called KOAS (Assessment of Strategies for Word Identification) was used in assessing word and non-word decoding (Høien and Lundberg, 2000). The test battery included one subtest to assess word recognition ability in general, and two subtests to assess each of the main decoding strategies: orthographic and phonological reading. For all subtests, the number of correct answers and response time were recorded. The response time refers to the time interval between the presentation of the word on the computer screen and the pupil's answer, and only correct responses were used when calculating mean reaction time. By using a computer with a voice key, a very exact measurement of the reaction time was possible. The items were presented in lower case letters (size 32 × 16 pixels, Herculus) with dark letters on a light-blue background. Before presenting a subtest, three practice items with feedback correction were provided. The test battery also comprised two subtests assessing general oral and manual reaction time.

Assessing word-recognition ability

This test included 48 words which varied in length (three, five and seven letters), frequency (high, low), content/function words and orthographic complexity (regular spellings versus irregular). Immediately before each word presentation, a fixation point appeared on the screen to help the child focus on where the word would appear. When the pupil started pronouncing the word, the microphone was activated and the word disappeared from the screen, and a dark masking field appeared on the screen where the word had been exposed. The experimenter recorded whether the response was correct or not by pressing a button on the keyboard.

Assessment of the phonological strategy

The phonological decoding ability was assessed by two subtests: reading non-words and phonological choice.

Reading non-words

In the present test, 36 non-words were presented, which varied in length (three, five and seven letters) and complexity (consonant clusters or not). All of the items were pronounceable and formed no obvious analogies to real words. As in the word-decoding tests, the stimuli were exposed on the computer screen and the experimenter recorded correct or incorrect responses on the keyboard; the response times for correctly decoded words were recorded automatically.

The test situation is arranged such that other strategies can be used only to a minimal extent. This test situation is obtained if the task is to read a completely unknown, regular word. It is, however, difficult to make quite certain that the stimulus word is 100% unknown to the reader, and thus it is not completely possible to exclude use of the orthographic strategy. On the other hand, if one uses non-words that are very unlike real words, we can assume that the decoding result will depend largely on the functional level of the phonological strategy.

Phonological choice task

The pupil was presented with 34 pairs of non-words on the screen. One of the non-words was homophonic to a real word, the other was not. The task was to select the non-word that would be pronounced like a well-known real word. To solve this task, a phonological strategy is necessary because orthographic support is not available.

Assessing the orthographic strategy

Brief exposure of word

In this first task, 48 words were presented on the screen one at a time during very brief exposures (200 ms). The words varied in length (three, five and seven letters), frequency (high, low) and orthographic complexity (regular, irregular). To obliterate the iconic 'after-image' of the word, a dark masking field appeared immediately after the word was presented, and the masking field remained on the screen for 5 seconds. The assumption behind this subtest is that the brief exposure imposes constraints on the information processing, thereby thwarting the use of the more laborious phonological strategy and encouraging the use of the orthographic route. Therefore, a marked decrease in performance on this task would indicate difficulty in using the orthographic strategy.

Orthographic choice

In this task participants listened to a sentence, and then two homophone words were presented on the screen side by side. The participants had to choose as quickly as possible the word that fitted the context. Both words were real words and are pronounced exactly the same, but spelled differently. Answering correctly here depends on orthographic skill, because the orthographic pattern is the only basis for the choice. The participants pushed a 'yes' or 'no' button (a right or left arrow) to indicate which was the correct word for the sentence. A total of 30 trials was used.

Reaction time

Manual response

An arrow appeared pointing randomly either to the right or to the left side of the computer screen. The test participant was asked to press as quickly as possible the corresponding left or right arrow button on the keyboard. The time difference between stimulus presentation and response was used as an indicator of manual reaction time. A total of 30 trials was used.

Oral response

This subtest assessed the oral response time. Two digits (1 and 3) were presented randomly on the screen, and the task was to name the digits as quickly as possible. The time interval between stimulus presentation and oral response was used as an indicator of oral reaction time. A total of 30 trials was used.

Procedure

The test administration and results scoring were carried out by teachers who previously had participated in a training programme to learn how to use the computer test appropriately and how to interpret the results.

Results and comments

Descriptive data and some preliminary analyses

At all grade levels speed accounted for substantially more variance in word recognition than accuracy. The word-recognition speed, when partialling out the impact of age and manual and oral reaction time, accounted for about 70% of unique variance in word recognition, whereas accuracy contributed to explain an additional 19.5% of unique variance after controlling for variance in age, accuracy, and manual and oral reaction time. The lower impact from accuracy may result partly from the ceiling effect, but it may also reflect the more important role played by the speed factor in acquiring efficient word-reading ability. In the further analyses, accuracy (as percentage correct) and speed (in seconds) were combined in a composite score obtained by dividing accuracy score with word reaction time.

Differences in word recognition among children in grades 4, 6 and 8

An analysis of co-variance was run with word recognition (composite scores) as dependent variable, grade level and sex as group factors, and manual and oral reaction times as co-variates. Before running the analyses of co-variance, the homogeneity of the slope was tested. No interaction was found between grade level and the co-variates. In Figure 5.1 the mean index values for each grade level are displayed.

As expected, the analysis showed significant differences in word-recognition ability between children at various grade levels ($F = 9.340$ and degrees of freedom or d.f. = 2, $p < 0.001$), and post-hoc testing (Bonferroni) revealed that the increase in mean score was statistically significant both between grades 4 and 6 and between grades 6 and 9. Follow-up analyses showed that word-reading time had a higher impact than accuracy in explaining differences in word recognition across all grade levels.

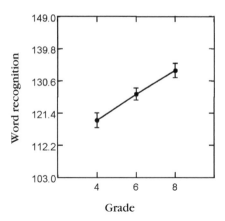

Figure 5.1. Increase in word-recognition ability across grade level.

Both manual and oral reaction time had a significant impact on the word-recognition ability across all grade levels. The impact of oral reaction time on word recognition was substantial ($F = 182.727$, d.f. $= 1$, $p < 0.001$). The task used in this test was a very simple naming task (naming a digit, either 1 or 3). However, no significant change in oral reaction time across grade level was found.

No overall sex differences were found ($F = 0.154$, $p = 0.694$), but the sex-by-grade interaction was significant at the 0.09 level. In Figure 5.2 the mean results for boys and girls are shown.

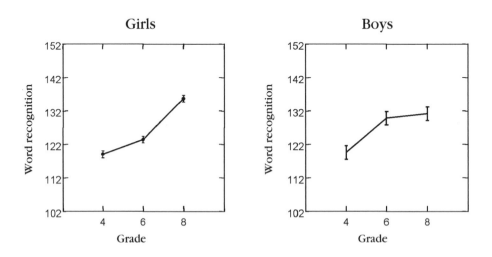

Figure 5.2. Increase in word-recognition across grade level for girls and boys.

When assessing larger samples of children, no significant sex differences are found in mean scores (Naidoo, 1972; Shaywitz et al., 1990). Our study gives additional evidence to previous research findings. However, at all grade levels the standard deviation (SD) was higher among boys than among girls, demonstrating that more boys than girls are found among both less-skilled and skilled word readers. As far as poor reading is concerned, our results are in accordance with earlier studies reporting a higher frequency of boys than girls among poor readers (Critchley, 1970; Finucci and Childs 1981). However, a post-hoc testing (Bonferroni) showed a significant sex difference in favour of girls (p <0.01) from grade 6 to 8. Further studies are needed to clarify which factors are causing these sex-by-grade differences. It may turn out that the observed sex differences among poor readers across grade levels are to some extent the result of variation in motivational factors (Tracey and Morrow, 1998; Guthrie and Wigfield, 1999; Guthrie et al., 1999).

Separate analyses of co-variance were performed with orthographic and phonological skills as dependent variables, grade level and sex as group factors, and manual and oral reaction time as co-variates. The results obtained were similar to those already reported for word recognition, showing a significant impact on the dependent variables as a function of grade level (p < 0.001). Furthermore, the special sex-by-grade interaction pattern found when assessing word recognition also appeared when assessing orthographic and phonological skills.

The impact of phonological and orthographic skills on word recognition

To study the impact of phonological and orthographic skills on word recognition, both correlation analyses and hierarchical regression analyses were used.

Table 5.2 shows the correlation matrix based on the composite values for all test variables used in the present study. As a result of age differences among the children, Table 5.2 presents the residual correlation coefficients after partialling out differences caused by grade level variation.

The correlation between tests of word recognition (Wordrec) and reading briefly presented words (Orth1) was substantial (0.785), whereas the correlation between the two orthographic tests (Orth1 and Orth2) was only 0.383. The high correlation between Wordrec and Orth1 makes one wonder whether this orthographic test is only representing another version of a word-recognition test rather than being an assessment of genuine orthographic skills. The task similarity between these two subtests should not be neglected but, as mentioned, the Orth1 test was constructed for maximal constraint of the benefit of using a phonological reading strategy by presenting the words very briefly (200 ms), and each word presentation was

Table 5.2. Correlations between different test scores

	Wordrec	Orth1	Orth2	Phon1	Phon2	Oral	Manual
Wordrec	1.000						
Orth1	0.785	1.000					
Orth2	0.359	0.383	1.000				
Phon1	0.547	0.550	0.399	1.000			
Phon2	0.361	0.351	0.508	0.539	1.000		
Oral	-0.535	-0.492	-0.114	-0.228	-0.151	1.0000	
Manual	-0.243	-0.246	-0.140	-0.215	-0.219	0.271	1.000

Wordrec = word recognition; Orth1 = reading briefly presented words; Orth2 = homophone word decision; Phon1 = non-word-reading; Phon2 = homophone choice; oral = oral reaction time; manual = manual reaction time. All values were significant ($p < 0.01$).

followed by a masking field to obliterate iconic 'after-image.' Therefore, we assume that reading briefly presented words yields specific information about orthographic processing skills.

The low correlation between the two orthographic tests was somewhat surprising, and may indicate that each of them to a certain extent is assessing different aspects of orthographic skill. However, we should also keep in mind that the Orth2 test provides only two response alternatives and therefore 50% accuracy may be obtained by guessing. This may highly decrease the reliability of a test (Olson et al., 1994; Vellutino, Scanlon and Tanzman, 1994).

Table 5.2 shows that the correlation between word recognition and non-word reading was higher than between word recognition and phonological choice (0.547 and 0.361, respectively). The correlation between the two phonological tasks – non-word reading (Phon1) and phonological choice (Phon2) – was 0.539, showing that both of them to a certain extent are measuring the same underlying construct. However, the phonological choice test also allows the participant to score 50% accuracy by guessing.

Both oral and manual reaction times correlated significantly with word recognition. The oral reaction time accounted for 28.6% of the variance in word recognition, whereas manual reaction time accounted for only 5.9% of the variance. Previous studies on the speed of naming various stimuli such as digits, colours and letters indicate that speed is a good predictor of fluent word reading (Denckla and Rudel, 1976; Ehri and Wilce, 1983; Perfetti, 1985; Stanovich 1986; Ehri, 1994), and our results give further evidence to these findings.

The results in Table 5.2 do not provide the unique contribution of each factor as a result of the interrelationship of the various tests used in the analysis. Therefore, the unique contribution of each independent factor was estimated by using a general model for regression analysis to estimate the residual correlation coefficient (also called the partial correlation coefficient). The results are displayed in Table 5.3.

The results showed that both tests Orth1 and Phon1 had a significant impact on word recognition. Whereas the correlation between word recognition and orthographic skill increased from grade 4 ($r = 0.576, p < 0.001$) to grade 8 ($r = 0.672, p < 0.001$), the most remarkable finding was the decrease of impact of phonological reading from grade 6 ($r = 0.238, p < 0.01$) to grade 8 ($r = 0.007, p = NS$). Clearly, among children in general, the impact of the orthographic skill on word recognition seems to increase by age, whereas the influence from phonological skill decreases.

Oral reaction time, measured by digit naming, contributed to explain uniquely 8.9–14.4% of the variance in word recognition across the age span. Wolf (1991) claims that naming tasks, e.g. object naming or digit naming, tap cognitive–linguistic factors that are more highly correlated with orthographic reading than phonological decoding, and a number of studies have shown that there is an unexplained variability in orthographic reading skill in children even after partialling out effects of general ability, phonological abilities and print exposure (Stanovich and West, 1989; Cunningham and Stanovich, 1991; Bowers and Wolf, 1993; Bowers et al., 1994; Manis, Seidenberg and Doi, 1994; Wimmer, Mayringer and Landerl, 1998). Our results lend support to the hypothesis that rapid naming has a unique impact on variation in word-reading ability. In the present study, a confrontation naming task was used, whereas in other studies serial naming (RAN) has often been employed.

The results of the correlation analyses were confirmed by analyses of co-variance. Separate analyses were performed for each grade level, using word

Table 5.3. Unique contribution of phonological and orthographic skills and reaction times on word recognition

	Grade 4	Grade 6	Grade 8
Number		Word recognition	
Orth1	0.576**	0.527**	0.672**
Phon1	0.206*	0.238*	0.086 NS
Orth2	0.189 NS	0.021 NS	0.012 NS
Phon2	0.031 NS	0.011 NS	0.009 NS
Manual	– 0.017 NS	–0.016 NS	–0.015 NS
Oral	–0.380*	–0.298*	–0.316*

$**p < 0.001, *p < 0.01$; NS, not significant. The numbers refer to partial correlation coefficients.

recognition as dependent variable and phonological and orthographic skill as independent factors.

Among the six independent factors included in the regression analysis, only three subtests contributed significantly to explain variance in word recognition: Orth1 (reading briefly exposed words), Phon1 (non-word reading) and Oral (oral reaction time) (Table 5.4).

Table 5.4. Impact of phonological and orthographic factors on word-recognition ability at different grade levels

Word recognition	Grade 4	Grade 6	Grade 8
Orth1	63.0**	68.5**	74.5**
Phon1	4.1**	3.3**	2.2**
Oral reaction	2.3**	2.0**	2.8**

**$p < 0.001$. The numbers refer to R^2 increase.

Differences between skilled and less-skilled decoders

Separate partial correlation analyses were performed with the less-skilled decoders. At each grade level, the children who scored below −1 SD for their grade level in word recognition were selected. Our main interest was to ascertain whether the relative importance of the various subskills among the less-skilled decoders was different from those in children in general. The results are displayed in Table 5.5.

Table 5.5. Impact of phonological and orthographic skills and oral reaction times on word recognition ability among less-skilled decoders

Word recognition	Grade 4 (n = 17)	Grade 6 (n = 25)	Grade 8 (n = 24)
Orth1	0.263*	0.500**	0.672*
Phon1	0.090 NS	−0.230*	−0.238*
Oral	−0.080 NS	−0.006 NS	0.075 NS

**$p < 0.001$; *$p < 0.01$; NS, not significant. The numbers refer to partial correlation coefficients.

The results on Phon2, Orth2 and Manual reaction showed no significant impact and are not shown in Table 5.5.

The impact of orthographic skill on word recognition among less-skilled decoders increased substantially from grade 4 to grade 8. At grade 4, orthographic skill accounted for only 6.9% of the variance in word recognition, whereas, among grade 8 children, the orthographic factor accounted for 33.2% of the variance.

It is quite remarkable to observe that phonological skill (non-word reading) did not have any significant impact on word recognition among less-skilled readers. Our results may indicate that less-skilled decoders are employing compensatory strategies, e.g. visual cue analysis, when reading words (Høien and Lundberg, 1988; Ehri, 1998).

The design of the study allowed a comparison of reading-disabled older students with younger students at the same word-recognition level of skill. A comparison was done between 21 poor decoders in grade 8 and 21 reading-level-matched normal decoders in grade 4. The poor decoders where those scoring below −1 SD on the combined accuracy/latency index score on word recognition. Separate Student t-test analyses were performed with briefly presented words and non-word reading as dependent variables.

Regarding orthographic reading, no differences between the groups could be found ($t = -0.517, p = 0.608$), whereas, in phonological reading, the older, poor decoders performed significantly lower than younger reading-level-matched control group ($t = 2.526, p = 0.01$).

These results give support to previous research claiming that the word-decoding problems among poor decoders are caused by phonological difficulties, which seem to endure at least into adolescence (Scarborough, 1984; Bruck, 1992; Ehri and Saltmarsh, 1995; Elbro, Nielsen and Petersen, 1994; Torgesen and Burgess, 1998). Although some researchers have reported that the poorly decoding older children performed significantly higher on orthographic tests than younger skill-level-matched children (Olson et al., 1990, 1994), our results did not give evidence for these findings. It might be the case that the type of test we used (reading briefly presented words) is not sensitive enough to pick up minor variance in orthographic skills. Therefore a follow-up analysis was performed using the other orthographic subtest, the orthographic choice test (Orth2), as dependent variable. However, this orthographic test did not yield any significant differences between the two groups either ($t = 0.0431, p = 0.723$).

Concluding remarks

When assessing word recognition ability, both accuracy and speed should be assessed. In particular, the speed factor seems to be very important when explaining variance in word reading. No overall significant sex differences were found in word recognition, non-word decoding and orthographic skills. Significant differences were found between children at various grades, and the older children scored the highest. Our study provides additional evidence to previous findings showing that both phonological and orthographic decoding strategies are important for achieving skilful word-recognition ability. For most readers, the road to efficient orthographic knowledge depends on phonological competence. The less-skilled readers in grade 8 scored significantly lower than the younger skill-level-matched students on non-word reading, showing that the phonological deficit underlying word-decoding difficulties seems to be very resistant to treatment. The older less-skilled readers seem to be more dependent on orthographic strategies in word recognition, compared with normal skilful decoders. For less-skilled decoders struggling with phonological difficulties, the orthographic strategy might be serving as a compensatory strategy.

References

Adams, M. (1990). *Beginning to Read: Thinking and learning about print*. Cambridge, MA: MIT Press.

Bjaalid, I.-K., Høien, T. and Lundberg, I. (1997). Dual-route and connectionist models: A step towards a combined model. *Scandinavian Journal of Psychology* **38**: 73–82.

Bowers, P. and Wolf, M. (1993). Theoretical links between naming speed, precise timing mechanisms and orthographic skill in dyslexia. *Reading and Writing: An Interdisciplinary Journal* **5**: 69–85.

Bowers, P., Golden, J., Kennedy, A. and Young, A. (1994). Limits upon orthographic knowledge due to processes indexed by naming speed. In: Berninger, V. (ed.), *The Varieties of Orthographic Knowledge I: Theoretical and developmental issues*. Dordrecht: Kluwer, pp. 173–218.

Brown, G. and Loosemore, R. (1995). A computational approach to dyslexic reading and spelling. In: Leong, C. and Joshi, R. (eds), *Developmental and Acquired Dyslexia: Neuropsychological and neurolinguistic perspectives*. Dordrecht: Kluwer, pp. 195–220.

Bruck, M. (1992). Persistence of dyslexics' phonological awareness deficits. *Developmental Psychology* **26**: 439–454.

Coltheart, M., Curtis, P., Atkins, P. and Haller, M. (1993). Models of reading aloud: Dual route and parallel distributed processing accounts. *Psychological Review* **100**: 589–608.

Critchley, M. (1970). *The Dyslexic Child*. London: Heinemann.

Cunningham, A. and Stanovich, K. (1991). Tracking the unique effects of print exposure in children: Associations with vocabulary, general knowledge, and spelling. *Journal of Educational Psychology* **83**: 264–274.

Cunningham, A. and Stanovich, K. (1998). The impact of print exposure on word recognition. In: Metsala, J. and Ehri, L. (eds), *Word Recognition in Beginning Literacy*. Mahwah, NJ: Erlbaum, pp. 195–220.

Denckla, M. and Rudel, R. (1976). Naming of object drawing by dyslexic and other learning disabled children. *Brain and Language* **3**: 1–16.

Ehri, L. (1992). Reconceptualizing the development of sight word reading and its relationship to recoding. In: Gough, P., Ehri, L. and Treiman, R. (eds), *Reading Acquisition*. Hillsdale, NJ: Erlbaum, pp. 107–143.

Ehri, L. (1994). Phases of development in learning to read words by sight. *Journal of Research in Reading* **18**: 116-125.

Ehri, L. (1998). Grapheme-phoneme knowledge is essential for learning to read words in English. In: Metsala, J. and Ehri, L. (eds), *Word Recognition in Beginning Literacy.* Mahwah, NJ: Erlbaum, pp. 3-40.

Ehri, L. and Saltmarsh, J. (1995). Beginning readers outperform older disabled readers in learning to read words by sight. *Reading and Writing: An Interdisciplinary Journal* **7**: 295-326.

Ehri, L. and Wilce, L. (1983). Development of word identification speed in skilled and less skilled beginning readers. *Journal of Educational Psychology* **75**: 3-18.

Elbro, C., Nielsen, I. and Petersen, D. (1994). Dyslexia in adults: Evidence for deficits in non-word reading and in the phonological representation of lexical items. *Annals of Dyslexia* **44**: 295-326.

Finucci, J. and Childs, B. (1981). Are there really more dyslexic boys than girls? In: Ansara, A., Geschwind, N., Galaburda, A., Albert, M. and Gartrell, M. (eds), *Sex Differences in Dyslexia.* Towson: Orton Dyslexia Society, pp. 1-9.

Goswami, U. (1998). The role of analogies in the development of word recognition. In: Metsala, J. and Ehri, L. (eds), *Word Recognition in Beginning Literacy.* Mahwah, NJ: Erlbaum, pp. 21-47.

Gough, P., Ehri, L. and Treiman, R. (eds) (1992). *Reading Acquisition.* Hillsdale, NJ: Erlbaum.

Gough, P., Juel, C. and Griffith, P. (1992). Reading, spelling and the orthographic cipher. In: Gough, P., Ehri, L. and Treiman, R. (eds), *Reading Acquisition.* Hillsdale, NJ: Erlbaum, pp. 35-49.

Guthrie, J. and Wigfield, A. (1999). How motivation fits into a science of reading. *Scientific Studies of Reading* **3**: 199-200.

Guthrie, J., Wigfield, A., Metsala, J. and Cox, K. (1999). Motivational and cognitive predictors of text comprehension and reading amount. *Scientific Studies of Reading* **3**: 231-256.

Hulme, C., Snowling, M. and Quinland, P. (1991). Connectionism and learning to read: Steps towards a psychologically plausible model. *Reading and Writing: An Interdisciplinary Journal* **3**: 159-168.

Høien, T. and Lundberg, I. (1988). Stages of word recognition in early reading acquisition. *Scandinavian Journal of Educational Research* **3**: 163-182.

Høien, T. and Lundberg, I. (2000). *Dyslexia: From theory to intervention.* Dordrecht: Kluwer.

Jacobson, C. and Lundberg, I. (2001). Early prediction of individual growth in reading. *Reading and Writing: An Interdisciplinary Journal* **13**: 273-296.

LaBerge, D. and Samuels, J. (1974). Toward a theory of automatic information processing in reading. *Cognitive Psychology* **6**: 293-323.

Manis, F., Seidenberg, M. and Doi, L. (1994). See Dick RAN: Rapid naming and the longitudinal prediction of reading subskills in first and second graders. *Scientific Studies of Reading* **3**: 129-158.

Naidoo, S. (1972). *Specific Dyslexia.* London: Pitman.

Olson, R., Wise, B., Conners, F. and Rack, J. (1990). Organization, heritability, and remediation of component word recognition and language skills in disabled readers. In: Carr, T. and Levy, B. (eds), *Reading and Its Development: Component skills approaches.* New York: Academic Press.

Olson, R., Forsberg, H., Wise, B. and Rack, J. (1994). Measurement of word recognition, orthographic, and phonological skills. In: Lyon G. (ed.), *Frames of Reference for the Assessment of Learning Disabilities*. Baltimore, MD: Brookes, pp. 242-277.

Perfetti, C. (1985). *Reading Ability*. New York: Oxford University Press.

Perfetti, C. (1992). The representation problem in reading acquisition. In: Gough, P., Ehri, L. and Treiman, R. (eds), *Reading Acquisition*. Hillsdale, NJ: Erlbaum, pp. 15-174.

Scarborough, H. (1984). Continuity between childhood dyslexia and adult reading. *British Journal of Psychology* **75**: 329-348.

Seidenberg, M. and McClelland, J. (1989). A distributed, developmental model of word recognition and naming. *Psychological Review* **96**: 523-568.

Share, D. and Stanovich, K. (1995). Has the phonological recoding model of reading acquisition and reading disability led us astray? *Issues in Education* **1**: 1-57.

Shaywitz, S., Shaywitz, B., Fletcher, J. and Escobar, M. (1990). Prevalence of reading disability in boys and girls. *Journal of the American Medical Association* **264**: 998-1002.

Stanovich, K. (1986). Matthew effects in reading: Some consequences of individual differences in the acquisition of literacy. *Reading Research Quarterly* **21**: 360-407.

Stanovich, K. (1991). Word recognition. Changing perspectives. In: Barr, R., Kamil, M., Mosenthal, P. and Pearson, P. (eds), *Handbook of Reading Research*, Vol 2. New York: Longman, pp. 418-452.

Stanovich, K. and West, R. (1989). Exposure to print and orthographic processing. *Reading Research Quarterly* **24**: 402-433.

Torgesen, J. and Burgess, S. (1998). Consistency of reading-related phonological processes throughout early childhood: Evidence from longitudinal-correlational and instructional studies. In: Metsala, J. and Ehri, L. (eds), *Word Recognition in Beginning Literacy*. Mahwah, NJ: Erlbaum, pp. 161-188.

Torgesen, J., Wagner, R. and Rashotte, C. (1997). Approaches to the prevention and remediation of phonologically based reading disabilities. In: Blachman, B. (ed.), *Foundations of Reading and Dyslexia. Implications for early intervention*. London: Erlbaum, pp. 287-304.

Tracey, D. and Morrow, L. (1998). Motivating contexts for young children's literacy development: Implications for word recognition. In: Metsala, J. and Ehri, L. (eds), *Word Recognition in Beginning Literacy*. Mahwah, NJ: Erlbaum, pp. 341-356.

Vellutino, F., Scanlon, D. and Tanzman, M. (1994). Components of reading ability: Issues and problems in operationalizing word recognition coding. In: Lyon, G. (ed.), *Frames of Reference for the Assessment of Learning Disabilities*. Baltimore, MD: Brookes, pp. 279-329.

Wimmer, H., Mayringer, H. and Landerl, K. (1998). Poor reading: A deficit in skilled automatization or a phonological deficit? *Scientific Studies of Reading* **2**: 321-340.

Wolf, M. (1991). Naming speed and reading: The contribution of the cognitive neuro-sciences. *Reading Research Quarterly* **26**: 123-141.

Wolf, M. and Segal, D. (1992). Word finding and reading in the developmental dyslexias. *Topics in Language Disorders* **13**: 51-65.

CHAPTER 6

Components of reading comprehension as predictors of educational achievement

CARSTEN ELBRO AND ELISABETH ARNBAK

External validity of literacy classifications

It is easy to classify adults into groups of good and poor readers. A reading test and a cut-off point are the only two requirements. As reading is such a specialised ability, most tests of reading are highly homogeneous and reliable. The problem is the arbitrariness of the cut-off point. In other words, the problem is the validity of the classification. Studies of adult literacy levels rarely include empirical support for their choice of cut-off points.

One solution is the prescriptive (axiomatic) definition. The recent Organisation for Economic Co-operation and Development (OECD) study of adult reading literacy (Second International Adult Literacy Survey or SIALS) may serve as an illustration of this type of solution (OECD, 1997; Jensen and Holm, 2000). In this study functional literacy is defined as a scaled score above 275 on the OECD literacy scale. It is simply assumed that literacy skills at this level are generally necessary for adults to be able to work and participate in everyday life in modern societies. At this level of literacy, readers are supposed to be able to extract information from texts based on simple criteria or inferences. By this definition, 46% of the adult Danish population have recently been found to have less than sufficient functional reading skills (Jensen and Holm, 2000). This figure may be compared to 27.8% in Sweden, 33.2% in Norway, 36.7% in Finland, and 52.1% in the UK.

Ten years earlier, only 12% of Danish adults were categorised as poor readers (Elbro, Møller and Nielsen, 1991, 1995). The difference between the two studies of Danish adults is striking, given the fact that they employed similar sampling techniques and similar everyday sorts of texts. The only explanation for the vastly divergent results resides with the selection of different cut-off points. Apparently, the more recent study has set the minimum requirement for functional literacy at a much higher level than the

69

previous study. The recent study has had an immediate and dramatic impact on Danish educational policies. A law about new preparatory courses for adults has been issued, and many new courses have been set up at a great pace. Yet it is unknown whether there is any real cause for concern as long as it has not been demonstrated that adults with a score lower than 275 (or any other) are really handicapped by poor reading.

Another solution to the cut-off problem is to give it up. Different education and jobs require different reading skills. Different everyday lives require different reading skills, and different adults set different goals and value their own skills differently. No two adults have exactly the same requirements for literacy. So one should set as many criteria as there are adults and different reading purposes. This view, of course, is not particularly productive in the literature on functional literacy, although it has probably warned many researchers against becoming entangled in the field.

A third solution, and our preferred one, is to make the selection of cut-off point(s) an issue for empirical investigation. This is a view we share with many of the contributors to the literature (e.g. Verhoeven, 1994; Smith, 1998). The question is which (low) literacy levels are associated with which educational, occupational or social constraints. To answer this question, the educational or social constraints are treated as external correlates that may serve to validate a particular definition of low functional literacy.

To our knowledge, every single published study of the relationship between literacy levels and educational levels has found substantial correlations. There is a strong link between literacy levels and various indicators of educational and social levels. However, correlation does not imply causation. There is a scarcity of longitudinal prediction studies, and perhaps not even a single major experimental study.

A recent Danish study may serve to illustrate how low literacy levels may constrain educational achievement. This study may also illustrate the external, predictive validity of a measure of functional literacy. So, the first part of this chapter focuses on the general relationship between literacy levels and educational achievement. The second part goes into detail with specific relationships between components of reading comprehension and educational achievement. The question is which subcomponent processes of reading best predict how well students will cope with their studies.

Reading comprehension predicts educational achievement: a study of Danish adults and young adults

The main purpose of this section is to show that it is indeed possible to define literacy levels below which educational (and vocational) opportunities are significantly constrained. A recent Danish study of adults and young adults in education may illustrate this possibility.

The original study comprised a total of 773 participants from five groups of adults and young adults (Arnbak and Elbro, 1999). They were dyslexic adults attending special education, adults in reading courses for adults with milder literacy problems, adults in O-level classes (secondary school level), young adults in vocational training and young adults in upper secondary school (A-level). Two of these groups of participants are brought into focus here, namely young adults in vocational training and adults in O-level classes. These groups were of particular interest for two reasons: the participants covered a wide range of literacy levels, and they all aimed to take formal examinations at the end of the school year, against which their literacy levels could be compared. Full datasets were available from about 130 participants from each of the two groups.

Literacy levels of the participants were assessed by means of a reading comprehension test and a test of word decoding. The reading comprehension test has a selection of everyday texts similar in type and complexity to those used in recent Danish and international studies of adult literacy (e.g. OECD, 1997; Jensen and Holm, 2000). There were 16 texts and a total of 60 multiple-choice questions. The texts were organised in three blocks with 20 questions in each: schematised texts, documents and narratives (newspaper stories). Participants were given an equal amount of time to try to answer as many questions as possible for each text block (three × 15 minutes). The texts and comprehension questions are described in further detail in Arnbak and Elbro (1999), and they have recently been published (Arnbak, 2001).

A word-decoding test was also administered to the participants. The reason was that we wished to be able to separate variance associated with decoding from variance in text comprehension. The decoding test is a pseudo-homophone test that taps into phonological recoding in word decoding (see also Olson et al., 1985). The task of the subject is to select the non-word out of four non-words that may sound like a real word if read aloud (e.g. *tro*, *sil*, *tys*, *sof*, where *sil* is the expected answer because it may sound like the real word *sill*). The test is a group-administered silent reading test with 38 items. The correlation with oral reading of non-words has previously been reported at $r = 0.82$ (Elbro, Nielsen and Petersen, 1994).

Educational achievement (the dependent variable) was registered about 6 months after the measurement of the reading abilities. This was done by means of student and teacher questionnaire. The questionnaires covered aspects of reading directly (e.g. 'How well do you think that each of your students reads?') and they also covered aspects of the students' educational achievement, typically in the form of examination marks.

Reading comprehension turned out to have moderate-to-strong correlation with practically all measures of educational achievement (see Arnbak and Elbro, 1999), e.g. differences in reading comprehension in young adults predicted variance in examination marks in spoken and written Danish ($r = 0.47$, $n = 128$, $p < 0.001$), in oral English (first foreign language, $r = 0.54$, $n = 96$, $p < 0.001$) and in written maths ($r = 0.57$, $n = 52$, $p < 0.001$, a varying number of participants took examinations in various subjects). Reading comprehension even predicted how often the young adults were absent from school. Poor comprehenders tended to be away from school more than average or good comprehenders. In the adult group, reading comprehension predicted examination marks in Danish (oral and written combined) quite well ($r = 0.60$, $n = 132$, $p < 0.001$).

For the sake of simplicity, the remaining analyses focus on examination marks in spoken and written Danish as the only dependent variable (external variable). Figures 6.1 and 6.2 illustrate in detail the relationship between reading comprehension and (later) examination marks in oral Danish.

In Denmark the average examination performance is awarded an 8 on a scale from 0 to 13. High or low marks are used very rarely and the present distribution from 5 to 11 is fairly typical. Figure 6.1 shows that no students

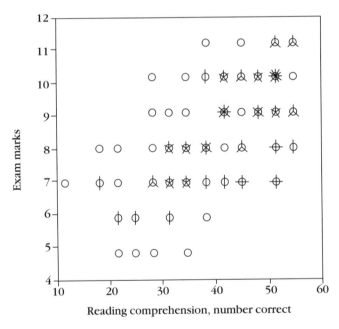

Figure 6.1. Examination results for oral and written Danish plotted against reading comprehension with everyday texts. Adults taking school leaving exams (O-levels) ($r = 0.60$, $n = 132$, $p < 0.001$). The symbols: o represents one participant; the number of lines emanating from other points indicate the number of participants represented by the points.

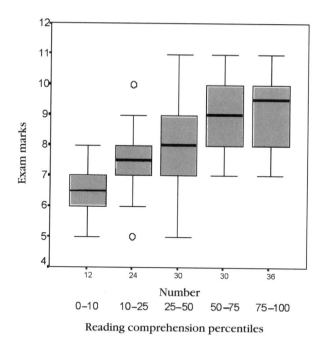

Figure 6.2. Box plot of examination results as a function of reading comprehension scores. Based on the same data as Figure 6.1. Fifty per cent of the scores fall within the boxes. Outliers are marked by small circles.

with poor reading abilities achieved high marks. This indicates that good reading comprehension is necessary in order to achieve a high mark in this particular course. The same thing is shown in Figure 6.2 with just five score groups on reading comprehension. Based on the present findings, it would seem fair to tell adult students with scores in the 10th percentile that they should be prepared for examination marks below average in oral and written Danish – unless they make an extraordinary effort.

In summary, reading comprehension certainly predicts educational outcome. It is thus possible to define cut-off points below which poor reading comprehension predicts limited educational achievement. Such a predictive relationship may even be strong enough to permit specific guidance for students with low reading comprehension.

Components of reading comprehension that predict educational achievement

The second part of this chapter focuses on specific relationships between components of reading comprehension and educational achievement. It may be that some components of reading comprehension are better predictors of educational achievement than others – and perhaps even better than reading comprehension in general.

This section focuses on some of the well-known components of reading comprehension: decoding (pseudo-homophone detection), speed and accuracy of text reading, and reading of different types of texts – schematised texts, documents and narrative prose. Correlations between components of reading comprehension and examination marks in Danish are shown in Table 6.1.

In the young adults, decoding by itself predicted examination grades almost as well as the measures of text comprehension ($r = 0.44$ vs 0.47 for the overall reading comprehension score). However, text comprehension predicted significant variance in examination grades even when decoding was taken into account (partial $r = 0.29$, $p < 0.01$). Comprehension accuracy (percentage correct of items attempted) by itself accounted for significant variance in examination grades after controlling for decoding. Conversely, text reading speed (number of items attempted) did not. Comprehension efficiency (number of correct items within the time limit) was the strongest predictor in both groups of participants.

In the adults, decoding also predicted a fair amount of variance in later examination grades. However, text comprehension appeared to predict relatively more of the variance in examination grades than among the young

Table 6.1. Correlations between components of reading comprehension and examination marks in Danish in young adults in vocational training and in adults in O-level classes. Bivariate correlations – with partial correlations controlling for decoding added in parentheses

Components of reading comprehension	Young adults (n = 128)	Adults (n = 132)
	Decoding	
Efficiency	0.44***	0.39***
	Text comprehension	
Speed	0.33***(0.12)	0.53*** (0.43***)
Accuracy	0.46*** (0.33***)	0.50*** (0.42***)
Efficiency	0.47*** (0.29**)	0.60*** (0.51***)
	Comprehension of different types of text	
Schematised texts	0.37*** (0.19*)	0.49*** (0.39***)
Documents	0.41*** (0.21*)	0.54*** (0.44***)
Narratives	0.46*** (0.30**)	0.58*** (0.49***)

* $p < 0.05$; ** $p < 0.01$; *** $p < 0.001$.

adults. We can only speculate about possible reasons for this. One difference between the groups of possible importance is the level of education: as a group, the young adults were better educated than the adults – at least, formally. The young adults had all recently completed secondary school, in most cases with O-level examinations. The adults were only aiming to take a school-leaving examination in order to be able to continue into some form of further education. Hence, we would expect greater variance in vocabulary and knowledge among the adults than among the young adults. This variance is likely to be associated more specifically with text comprehension than with word decoding, and might explain the differences between the groups.

The reading comprehension test comprised three blocks of texts with 20 questions in each block. This design allowed for a comparison of the predictive value of reading of various types of texts: schematised texts, documents and narratives. In both groups of participants, narratives were slightly better predictors of examination grades than other types of texts. This may reflect the traditional strong focus on literary texts in the teaching of Danish in secondary schools in Denmark. However, the same pattern of results was found with other indicators of educational achievement. We believe that the questions for the narrative texts may have required more advanced comprehension strategies. The psychological and social relationships related by the narrative texts were rather simple, but definitely more complex than those in the other two types of text.

To sum up, some component processes in reading comprehension appear to be better indicators of educational achievement than others – and hence, perhaps, of greater interest to future studies of adult literacy. It is interesting that word decoding still plays a significant role in the educational attainment of adults.

Prior knowledge: highlighting or concealing the message of the text?

Prior knowledge is one of the most important prerequisites for understanding a text (e.g. Pearson and Fielding, 1991). One reason is that texts are explicit only to the extent that the author assumes necessary. Texts would be tediously lengthy otherwise. In some cases, the reader may even draw upon prior knowledge and guess at least some of what the text says. It is a commonly held view that readers have to use prior knowledge actively in order to comprehend texts (e.g. Pressley, 2000). There is some evidence that specific text comprehension problems may be caused by passive reading – in the sense that the passive comprehender makes too little use of his or her background knowledge when attempting to recreate the contents of a text (e.g. Oakhill, 1994). Passive comprehenders are not just lacking knowledge;

the problem seems to be that they fail to activate whatever relevant knowledge they have got (Cain and Oakhill, 1999).

The constructive use of prior knowledge and inference-making abilities is often emphasised in definitions of reading comprehension, e.g. 'We define reading comprehension as the process of constructing meaning through interaction and involvement with written language' (Snow, 2001).

However, one may ask if any meaningful interaction with written language deserves the term 'comprehension'. Specifically, it would seem reasonable to expect the reader to construct (or reconstruct) a mental representation of the contents of the text that bear a certain resemblance to the original ideas of the author of the text. Readers are not generally assumed to read texts as freely as 'the Devil reads the Bible'. One important consequence of this more well-defined requirement for comprehension is that reading texts allows for learning to take place. Readers may indeed add to their pre-existing knowledge and even revise what they already knew.

From the perspective of learning from text, prior knowledge may have more than one role to play. Prior knowledge not only may be necessary for building inferences and relating the text to the world outside it, it may also stand in the way of learning from text. Sometimes learning implies incongruity and revision of prior knowledge (e.g. Kintsch, 1980). In such cases, the ability to disregard, or overrule, prior knowledge may be seen as a central component of learning from text. If the reader is more inclined to trust his or her knowledge than what the text says, then little may be learned from the text. From the author's perspective, some readers may appear relatively unteachable.

Studies of the obstructive functions of prior knowledge are few. In a study of 80 fifth grade disabled readers, McCormick (1992) found that the single most frequent source of error in responses to inferential questions was over-reliance on background knowledge. Instead of relating text to background knowledge, the disabled readers produced many answers that just reflected their pre-existing beliefs. It is reasonable to assume that the participants' problems with word decoding may have made them more dependent than normal readers on prior knowledge. For this reason, the results should be generalised to normal readers only with caution. Perhaps normal readers do sometimes over-rely on prior knowledge, but they are likely to do so less often than disabled readers.

Alvermann, Smith and Readence (1985) studied average sixth graders' reading of science texts. The students were asked to write what they knew about particular topics before they were given texts to read about these topics. The texts were selected because they contained some pieces of information that conflicted with commonly held views. It turned out that those sixth graders who activated conflicting beliefs before they read the texts also answered fewer of the corresponding questions correctly. The interference effect appeared to be limited to the potentially conflicting questions. No differences were found between 'activators' and 'non-activators' on the other, neutral questions about the texts. The conclusion is that prior knowledge may interfere with comprehension. However, the study shows that this may happen only under certain conditions, namely when conflicting beliefs are consciously activated before reading. The study does not indicate how detrimental conflicting beliefs are under normal reading conditions, nor does it address the question of the practical implications of such conflicts for learning from text.

To our knowledge, the complex role of prior knowledge in text comprehension has not been studied with respect to its consequences for educational achievement. A post-hoc analysis of the data from the text comprehension test was performed in order to shed light on this issue.

The complex role of prior knowledge as predictor of educational achievement

The multiple choice format could be well suited for studying the complex role of prior knowledge. An example from the present reading comprehension test may illustrate how this could be done (see Alvermann, Smith and Readence, 1985).

Four questions about a text on fire alarms

1. Where would you place the fire alarm in a two-bedroom flat if you have only one fire alarm?:
   (a) near where you spend most of the time (the lounge)
   (b) near the main entrance (the escape route)
   (c) near where you sleep (the bedroom)
   (d) near inflammable things (the kitchen).
2. Is it OK to put a fire alarm up on a wall?:
   (a) yes, but not above a radiator
   (b) yes, about half-way between floor and ceiling
   (c) yes, about a foot from the ceiling
   (d) no, smoke rises towards the ceiling.
3. How often should a fire alarm be tested?:
   (a) once a year
   (b) once a week
   (c) when you change the battery
   (d) twice a year.
4. How many Danes' lives could be saved if all homes had fire alarms? _____

The four questions about fire alarms (smoke detectors) are not equally easy to answer without the text. Prior knowledge and reasoning based on prior knowledge do help more towards the correct reply to some of the questions than to others. Try to answer the questions before you read on.

For example, it is reasonable to expect that a fire alarm should be put up in the bedroom (answer 1c). Placed there it may wake you up before you are choked by the smoke or caught in flames. This reply is also in line with the instructions in the text. In this case prior knowledge is certainly helpful. A question like this would not normally appear in a reading comprehension test because a correct reply does not necessarily depend on having understood the text. Let us refer to this type of question as *predictable*.

The second question is much more typical for reading comprehension tests. It is difficult to know or to infer where it would be advisable to put a fire alarm on a wall. The response in accordance with the text is 2c, about a foot from the ceiling. Chances are about 25% that you chose the correct response. For convenience, let us refer to such questions as *neutral*.

The third question is a tricky one. We suppose that most people who install fire alarms forget about them as long as the alarms do not set off or indicate that a new battery is needed. But the advice in the text is to check a fire alarm once a week (3b)! In comparison with prior knowledge, this is probably surprising, and we refer to such counterintuitive items as *surprising*.

The fourth question is another kind of comprehension question in the sense that it is very hard to predict the correct reply. It is even harder than with question number 2. Certainly, some replies will be more qualified guesses than others but, as with telephone numbers, it is very hard to guess the exact number. For simplicity, we will assume that prior knowledge is not *applicable* with this type of question.

Each of the 60 questions of the reading comprehension test was categorised as either predictable, neutral, surprising or not applicable. The categorisation was based on results from a separate study in which 26 undergraduate students were asked to select the best answers without having read the texts. A question was categorised as predictable if the right response was selected by a significantly larger proportion of the students than would be expected by chance (binomial distribution, with $p = 0.25$ and $n = 26$). Conversely, questions with a significantly low score were categorised as surprising (except for open-ended questions). And questions in between, i.e. questions with about 25% correct responses, were neutral.

Responses to the predictable questions and the surprising questions were of particular interest to the post-hoc analysis. Correct responses to the predictable questions were supposed to reflect positive, constructive use of prior knowledge. Conversely, the surprising questions were supposed to tap

Table 6.2. Correlations between different types of comprehension questions and examination marks in Danish in young adults in vocational training and in adults in O-level
classes. Bivariate correlations (with partial correlations controlling for decoding added in
parentheses)

Reading comprehension questions	Young adults ($n = 128$)	Adults ($n = 132$)
Predictable ($n = 19$)	0.46*** (0.27**)	0.62*** (0.53***)
Neutral ($n = 20$)	0.40*** (0.22*)	0.52*** (0.43***)
Surprising ($n = 11$)	0.47*** (0.30**)	0.56*** (0.46***)
Not applicable ($n = 10$)	0.25** (0.11)	0.29** (0.19*)

* $p < 0.05$; ** $p < 0.01$; *** $p < 0.001$.

into the reader's ability to override prior knowledge and learn from text. It
was hypothesised that the two types of questions would provide independent contributions to the prediction of educational achievement. It may be
added as a methodological point that both types of questions are usually
avoided in the construction of multiple choice tests.

Interestingly, both the predictable questions and the surprising questions
correlated with educational achievement at about the same level as the
unabridged reading comprehension test. The typical ('neutral') questions
appeared to correlate slightly less strongly with examination marks. The
open-ended questions ('not applicable') were somewhat easier than the
other questions (mean score 94% correct). The restricted variation may
explain why the scores on these questions (NA) correlated less strongly with
examination marks. However, the three types of multiple-choice questions
had about equal means (62–76% correct) and variances, so possible differences between the prediction power of these questions were unlikely to be
caused by simple psychometric effects.

In order to see whether predictable and surprising questions contributed
independently to the prediction of examination marks, multiple regression
analyses were performed in each of the participating groups separately
(Tables 6.3 and 6.4).

Regression analyses showed that responses to both surprising questions
and predictable questions accounted for variance in examination marks,
even after differences in decoding and neutral questions had been
accounted for. This suggests that standard comprehension questions do not
necessarily capture all educationally relevant information about reading
comprehension.

More interestingly, surprising questions contributed to the prediction of
examination marks even after further control for scores on predictable

Table 6.3. Summaries of linear regressions: examination marks predicted by word decoding and components of reading comprehension (adults in O-level courses, $n = 132$)

Model Step	R^2	R^2 change	F change	p change
1 Decoding and neutral questions	0.31	0.31	28.2	0.000
2 Surprising questions	0.36	0.05	10.2	0.002
3 Predictable questions	0.42	0.06	13.5	0.000
2 Predictable questions	0.39	0.09	18.1	0.000
3 Surprising questions	0.42	0.03	5.9	0.02

Table 6.4. Summaries of linear regressions: examination marks predicted by word decoding and components of reading comprehension (young adults in vocational training, $n = 128$)

Model Step	R^2	R^2 change	F change	p change
1 Decoding and neutral questions	0.23	0.23	18.6	0.000
2 Surprising questions	0.27	0.03	5.7	0.02
3 Predictable questions	0.28	0.01	1.6	0.21
2 Predictable questions	0.25	0.02	3.0	0.08
3 Surprising questions	0.28	0.03	4.3	0.04

questions. This suggests that ability to override prior knowledge and expectations and learn something unexpected from a text contributed positively towards educational achievement in both populations.

Finally, responses to both surprising and predictable questions contributed independent variance to examination marks in the adult population. This independence is important because it may reflect a basic dissociation between the two functions of prior knowledge mentioned earlier: the constructive function and the obstructive function.

At the moment we have no strong explanation why we did not find quite as distinct contributions from the two types of questions in the young adults. It is important, however, to keep in mind that the surprising questions did predict educational achievement over and above decoding and standard comprehension questions. So gaining unsuspected new knowledge from text may be an important ability in this group, too. We suspect that the aforementioned smaller variance in the knowledge and vocabulary among the young adults than in the adults may explain the smaller impact of prior knowledge in the young adults.

Conclusion

We believe the primary contribution of this chapter to be methodological. The chapter had two main points. First, it demonstrates that it is possible to define low levels of functional literacy with reference to educational achievement. One way to do so is to look for reading comprehension scores below which educational achievement (e.g. examination marks) is clearly constrained. Many other indicators of educational or social functioning could have been used. The basic idea is that any cut-off point between acceptable and unacceptably low functional literacy needs external validation. If no validation is provided, reading research may ultimately lose its credits, because very different proportions of the population may be claimed to be reading handicapped by different studies.

The second point is concerned with which components of reading comprehension best predict educational achievement. A post-hoc analysis of a recent study of literacy showed that it may be possible to separate two important components in text comprehension. The components are (1) use of prior knowledge to support comprehension of text and (2) the ability to disregard prior knowledge while learning something new and counterintuitive from text. We suggest that these two components may be studied by means of different types of questions in a multiple choice format: questions with predictable answers and questions with counterintuitive answers, respectively.

The post-hoc analysis indicated that both components may contribute independent variance to educational achievement, at least in adults, even when decoding and simple reading comprehension are controlled. Also, in the young adults, ability to overrule prior beliefs and learn something new from text seemed to contribute independent variation to educational achievement. However, differences in use of prior knowledge did not contribute independent variance when other aspects of reading comprehension were controlled for.

To sum up, we suggest that use of prior knowledge may form the basis of two, partly independent dimensions in reader's comprehension and learning from text. One dimension has to do with the constructive use of background knowledge to form a coherent mental representation of the content of the text. Readers who fail in this respect have been termed 'passive readers'. Another dimension has to do with the ability to override and revise prior knowledge and beliefs. Readers who fail in this may be termed 'unteachable'. Hence, we suggest that readers may be more or less active comprehenders and, independently, more or less teachable.

Of course, one should be careful about interpreting results from a post-hoc analysis too rigorously. The regression analyses in the present study were based on a post-hoc categorisation of the items. This means that categories were not balanced across texts or text groups. So, the independence of the variables may to some extent stem from differences between texts, and not solely from differences between some underlying constructs. Future research is needed to sort out this and other possible confounders. We are currently running a study with this aim.

Acknowledgement

The study received economic support from the Danish Ministry of Education (contract 1996-12018-28). We are most grateful to the participating teachers and their students.

References

Alvermann, D.E., Smith, L.C. and Readence, J.E. (1985). Prior knowledge activation and the comprehension of compatible and incompatible text. *Reading Research Quarterly* **20**: 420-436.

Arnbak, E. (2001). *Læsetekster for unge og voksne*. Copenhagen: Dansk Psykologisk Forlag.

Arnbak, E. and Elbro, C. (1999). Læsning, læsekurser og uddannelse. *Om unge og voksnes funktionelle læsefærdighed i uddannelse og på læsekurser vurderet med et nyt materiale*. Copenhagen: Centre for Reading Research, University of Copenhagen, Copenhagen.

Cain, K. and Oakhill, J.V. (1999). Inference making ability and its relation to comprehension failure in young children. *Reading and Writing: An Interdisciplinary Journal* **11**: 489-503.

Elbro, C., Møller, S. and Nielsen, E.M. (1991). Danskernes læsefærdigheder. *En undersøgelse af 18-67-åriges læsning af dagligdags tekster*. Copenhagen: Projekt Læsning og Undervisningsministeriet.

Elbro, C., Møller, S. and Nielsen, E.M. (1995). Functional reading difficulties in Denmark. A study of adult reading of common texts. *Reading and Writing: An Interdisciplinary Journal* **7**: 257-276.

Elbro, C. Nielsen, I. and Petersen (1994). Dyslexia in adults: Evidence for deficits in nonword reading and in the phonological representation of lexical items. *Annals of Dyslexia* **44**: 205-226.

Jensen, T.P. and Holm, A. (2000). *Danskernes læse-regne-færdigheder - i et international lys*. Copenhagen: AKF Forlaget.

Kintsch, W. (1980). Learning from text, levels of comprehension or: Why anyone would read a story anyway. *Poetics* **9**: 87-98.

McCormick, S. (1992). Disabled readers' erroneous responses to inferential comprehension questions: Description and analysis. *Reading Research Quarterly* **27**: 55-77.

Oakhill, J. (1994). Individual differences in children's text comprehension. In: Gernsbacher, M. (ed.), *Handbook of Psycholinguistics*. New York: Academic Press, pp. 821-848.

OECD (1997). *Literacy Skills for the Knowledge Society*. Paris: OECD.

Olson, R.K., Kliegel, R., Davidson, B.J. and Foltz G. (1985). Individual and developmental differences in reading disability. In: MacKinnon, G.E. and Waller, T.G. (eds), *Reading Research: Advances in theory and practice*, Vol 4. New York: Academic Press, pp. 1-64.

Pearson, P.D. and Fielding, L. (1991). Comprehension instruction. In: Barr, R. et al. (eds), *Handbook of Reading Research*, Vol. 2. Mahwah, NJ: Erlbaum, pp. 815-860.

Pressley, M. (2000). What should comprehension instruction be the instruction of? In: Kamil, M.L. et al. (eds), *Handbook of Reading Research*, Vol. III. Mahwah, NJ: Lawrence Erlbaum, pp. 545-562.

Smith, M.C. (ed.) (1998). *Literacy for the Twenty-first Century: Research, policy, practices, and the National Adult Literacy Survey*. Westport, CT: Praeger Publishers.

Snow, C. (ed.) (2001). Reading for Understanding: Towards an RandD Program in Reading Comprehension. RAND Reading Study Group. Prepared for the Office of Educational Research and Improvement (OERI),US Department of Education. (http://www.rand.org/multi/achievementforall).

Verhoeven, L. (ed.) (1994). *Functional Literacy. Theoretical issues and educational implications*. Amsterdam: John Benjamins.

CHAPTER 7

Shadows over phonological awareness training: resistant learners and dissipating gains

PEKKA NIEMI AND ELISA POSKIPARTA

The purpose of this chapter is to shed light on issues that have been overshadowed by the impressive success attributed to phonological awareness and its role in learning to read. More specifically, we argue that neither prognostic nor training studies have paid enough attention to three relevant problems. First, very few training studies include a follow-up extending over several years, thus leaving the question of the child's final reading status more or less open. Second, there obviously are children at risk whose reading improves hardly at all with training in phonological awareness. Third, about half of the variance in beginning readers' decoding ability remains unexplained even after most informed measures of pre-reading phonological awareness. If observations such as these are supported by more than casual evidence, especially in view of the usual bias towards reporting positive results, the celebrated status of phonological awareness faces the fate of many other great ideas, i.e. its power is less than currently assumed.

Generally speaking, it is not difficult to agree that the discovery of phonological awareness has exerted a major effect on the study of starting to read and the treatment of its problems. A child on the verge of mastering the trick is able to observe correctly the length of a word and the number of syllables in it, as well as their relative position. A little later, she or he performs the same feat with individual phonemes and, finally, develops an astonishing skill of manipulating word parts intentionally. The ultimate feats are intelligent spoonerisms and secret languages that are eagerly practised, often with the explicit aim to fool adults who are around. It is no surprise that linguistic skills such as these comprise a growth platform for decoding and spelling skills. One might even argue that phonological awareness basically means reading and writing in the absence of letters. In fact, since the 1970s, evidence supporting the significance of phonological awareness for reading acquisition has accumulated beyond doubt, e.g. children as young as

2;10–3;9-years show a variation in their ability to detect rhyme and alliteration that reliably predicts their reading skill 2–3 years later (Bryant, MacLean and Bradley, 1990). Phonological awareness training given before formal reading instruction results in clear-cut gains in learning to read that extend over several years (Lundberg, Frost and Petersen, 1988; Lundberg, 1994). What is more, both the spontaneous development and the training results appear to be quite specific. The early ability to detect rhyme and alliteration in the study of Bryant, MacLean and Bradley (1990) made a contribution to reading skill variation even after controlling for more general linguistic abilities and intelligence. The training-induced gains in word-recognition ability in the study of Lundberg, Frost and Petersen (1988) did not generalise to arithmetic.

The following discussion draws heavily on our longitudinal study of 252 pre-schoolers in Turku, Finland (e.g. Kinnunen, Vauras and Niemi, 1998; Poskiparta, Niemi and Vauras, 1999). This study featured extensive cognitive, linguistic and motivational testing, totalling 10–12 hours, and was carried out in the spring of the year the children were to enter grade 1 at the age of 7 years. Equally extensive follow-up tests were performed during the late spring term of grade 3, and less extensively up to grade 6. Measures relevant to reading skill extended up to grade 3. Readers at risk were identified in each year, starting from pre-school. They were subjected to interventions designed according to current knowledge of decoding and reading comprehension.

In the course of this research we learned that more often than not results ran against our well-informed expectations (see Niemi et al., 1998). Surprises included pupils resistant to treatment, reading failures in the presence of at least average cognitive prerequisites, and almost non-existent productive writing in spite of average reading and spelling ability and intelligence. When faced with these undesired results, we sought contact with groups that were running similar longitudinal projects. As usual, fortune favoured a prepared mind and we realised to our satisfaction that others had also experienced the same kinds of problems.

Training in phonological awareness in grade 1: help reaches those who need it

Altogether 240 children remained in the sample at the school start; 16% of them could already read and were therefore excluded from the study of reading acquisition. Two schools were designated as intervention schools (97 pupils) and the other two as control schools (105 pupils). In the intervention schools 45 children with the lowest scores in phonological awareness were re-tested in the beginning of grade 1; 26 of them scored zero or just above and were identified as children at risk. These children comprised the target group for the intervention. Each of them had a pair-wise-matched control pupil in the control group. Matching was based on phonological awareness in the first place, and supported by a test of listening comprehension and the *Wechsler Intelligence Scale for Children* – Revised (WISC-R).

A training programme similar to that of Lundberg, Frost and Petersen (1988) was carried out during the autumn term. There were two research questions:

- Is training equally effective for all children irrespective of cognitive level?
- What component of phonological awareness is most sensitive to training given that the initial level is virtually zero?

In Finland, special education is regularly provided for children who are judged to need it. It turned out that 11 of the 26 control children belonged to this group. It was characteristic of these children that they scored significantly lower than remaining children at risk on many variables: letter naming, WISC-R Verbal score, working memory and counting skills. As a result of the initial matching, there were no differences in phonological awareness and listening comprehension. Consequently, four groups were formed: cognitively inferior control children who received traditional special education (n = 11), their matched pairs among the intervention children (n = 11), cognitively near-average control children not receiving additional support (n = 15) and their matched pairs among the intervention children (n = 15).

The results were reported in detail by Poskiparta, Niemi and Vauras (1999). In general, they were a replication of those showing the effectiveness of training. The whole intervention group scored significantly above the entire control group in terms of the total score on phonological awareness. What is more, the effect was mostly the result of the drastic improvement among the intervention children with inferior cognitive level, relative to the control children receiving traditional special education. Interestingly, the cognitively near-average control children seemed to benefit as much from the regular classroom instruction as their matched pairs in the intervention group benefited from training. This finding suggests that our original diagnosis of phonological awareness was based on too stringent a test and resulted in an over-sampling of children at risk. The component of phonological awareness most amenable to training was sound blending. The post-test showed a large difference among the cognitively inferior children in favour of the training group – 7.0/10 and 1.8/10, respectively.

Transfer of training to word recognition, lexical decision and spelling was tested 4–5 months after training at the end of grade 1. Both intervention groups and the cognitively near-average control group performed at approximately the same level, comparable to that of other pre-school non-readers who did not participate in the intervention. The poorest results were achieved by the cognitively inferior control group receiving traditional special education. A comparison with the matched pairs who received training in phonological awareness showed robust effect sizes: 0.98 for picture–word comparison, 1.01 for lexical decision for words, 0.77 for lexical decision for non-words, 1.88 for word spelling and 0.77 for sentence spelling.

All in all, these results suggested that training was still beneficial in grade 1 and helped the pupils with a poor prognosis to rise to the reading and spelling level of other pre-school non-readers. The road to success was through learning how to blend the phonemes that are heard one at a time. At this stage, we had every reason to be confident with regard to the reading careers of our intervention children. However, three unforeseen surprises were about to emerge, one 2 years later and the other two almost at once.

Disappointment: gains that result from training dissipate in 2 years?

It would be natural to ask whether positive training results lead to permanent good reading. The only way to find out about this is to carry out a longitudinal study extending over a number of years. With this aim in mind, we searched an extensive European database recently compiled by Schneider and Stengård (1999). To our surprise, this important question had received meagre attention. There were 144 studies featuring a longitudinal design and 44 of them included some sort of intervention. However, very few studies had addressed the long-term maintenance of the effects of phonological awareness training, a finding similar to that observed by Bus and Ijzendoorn (1999) who reported the longest follow-up period to be 2 years and 5 months.

A handful of studies have reported sustained effects until the end of grade 2 (Olofsson, 1993; Lundberg, 1994; Borstroem and Elbro, 1997; Schneider et al., 1997, 1999; Petersen, 2001). Similar training effects have been found even at the end of grade 3 (Olofsson, 1993; Lundberg, 1994; Petersen, 2001; W. Schneider, personal communication). An outstanding exception is the study of Byrne, Fielding-Barnsley and Ashley (2001), in which weak positive training effects on list reading as late as grade 5 were observed. Encouragingly, permanent word-reading gains have been found for children showing very little or no phonological awareness in pre-school before training (Olofsson, 1993; Lundberg, 1994; Schneider et al., 1999). However, a feature worth mentioning is that none of the above studies included measures of reading fluency. Word-reading ability was tested by means of picture-to-word comparison, with the exception of the sentence-to-word comparison used in the study of Lundberg (1994) and the list reading of

Byrne, Fielding-Barnsley and Ashley (2001). Their merits notwithstanding, these measures do not tap fast and accurate reading of continuous text in an optimal way.

Our longitudinal data allowed us to explore the long-term development of the positive training effects found in grade 1. The relevant tests included the same picture-to-word comparison as used by Lundberg (1994) and Olofsson (1993). In addition to that, we also used the reading aloud of narrative and lexical decision tasks to explore the speed and accuracy aspects of word recognition and continuous reading. The participants were the 11 low-performing pupils who showed strong training-induced gains in grade 1, and their respective controls. The data were collected at the end of grades 2 and 3 (for details, see Niemi, Poskiparta and Vauras, 2001).

Figure 7.1 depicts the word-recognition performance of grade 2 intervention children with low cognitive ability, their matched controls who received traditional special education and other pre-school non-readers who received regular classroom teaching. A planned contrast between the intervention and control group proved significant, the effect size being 0.78.

Lexical decision for words with 7–12 letters also showed superiority of the intervention children over their matched controls, with the effect size being 0.65. The respective group data are given in Figure 7.2.

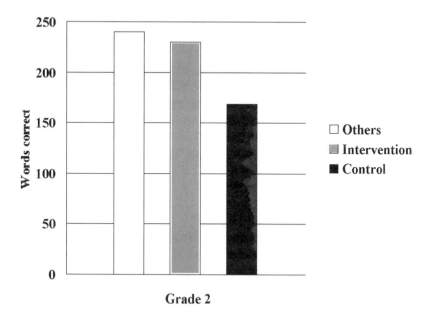

Figure 7.1. Word recognition performance in a picture-to-word comparison test (OS-400). Maximum = 400 correct during 15 min.

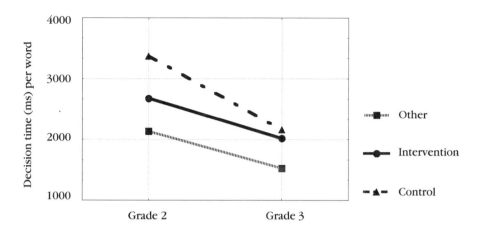

Figure 7.2. Mean lexical decision times for words.

Story reading was based on a text of 135 words. The difference between intervention and control groups was symptomatic only with the effect size being 0.55. The performance of the intervention group was clearly below that of other pre-school non-readers who represent the mainstream reading skill. Reading errors showed a pattern favouring even more other pre-school non-readers (4.8%), with intervention children (10.9%) making almost as many errors as their matched controls (12.3%).

In grade 3, both lexical decision and story-reading data suggested that the gains resulting from training in phonological awareness in grade 1 had disap-

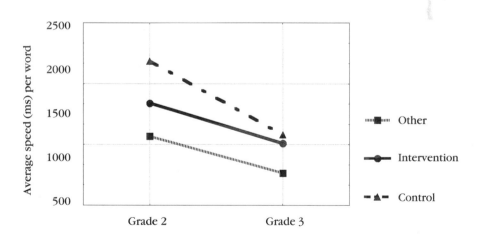

Figure 7.3. Average speed of reading aloud of continuous text.

peared. The intervention children were now farther apart from mainstream readers than from their original matched control children. This resulted in significant interactions involving grade level and group. Post-hoc HSD (honestly significant difference) tests showed that the source was lack of difference between intervention and control groups ($p = 0.981$ for lexical decision and $p = 0.716$ for spelling).

Is there any explanation for such a negative development? Clearly, the intervention had a long-term effect. It should also be noted that every pupil in the intervention group moved up from grade 2 to grade 3, whereas three control children repeated either grade 1 or grade 2. Nevertheless, the question still arises as to whether there are any processes that gradually steer children at risk in a different direction from mainstream readers. Our data did not allow for a penetrating analysis. However, some potentially important observations were made. When asked about their reading habits in grade 1, the children at risk preferred to read cartoons rather than texts. In grade 3, only one of 18 read factual books and encyclopaedias, whereas 19% of mainstream readers did so. This tendency coincides with a pronounced preference for watching TV rather than reading. The proportions were 89% and 57%, respectively. On the whole, intervention children and their matched controls did not differ from each other in terms of their reading habits. This turned our attention towards the motivational side of reading.

'Resistant learners' and beginning reading

Behind the success of phonological training, a seldom discussed problem lurks. After all, the group means hide within them the individual children who do not benefit from training. More specifically, these children seem unable to transfer their newly acquired phonological awareness to reading and spelling (Torgesen, Wagner and Rashotte, 1994, 1997; Olson et al., 1997).

In addition to the aforementioned intervention in phonological awareness in grade 1 (Poskiparta, Niemi and Vauras, 1999), our study also included computer-assisted training in word recognition (Poskiparta, Vauras and Niemi, 1998), featuring feedback given by a speech synthesiser. This training was given in grade 2. Altogether 30 pupils participated in one or both of these interventions. Niemi et al. (1999) divided them into three equally large groups depicting their permanent position as a reader and speller during grades 1 and 2. The children in the three groups were good decoders with average spelling ability, good spellers with average decoding ability and resistant learners. The reference was the average performance of other former pre-school non-readers at a corresponding time. The resistant learners scored consistently below this level both in decoding ($z = -0.6$) and in spelling ($z = -1.1$).

Our original idea was to try to delineate sources of unsuccessful learning in the comprehensive database collected at the pre-school age. However, this attempt turned out to be a disappointment. No pre-school measure distinguished the groups. We tested for phonological awareness, working memory, metacognitive knowledge, WISC-R, naming and writing letters, invented spelling, counting skills and motivational orientation. An intriguing finding was also that differences in decoding and spelling notwithstanding, the groups performed equally on tests of listening and reading comprehension in grades 1 and 2.

In the end, we managed to find only one factor bearing a relationship to the inferior performance of resistant learners – their motivational disposition towards performance situations. Motivational disposition refers to one of three relatively permanent modes of orientation (Olkinuora and Salonen, 1992; Salonen, Lepola and Niemi, 1998). Task orientation is manifested as a child's intrinsically motivated tendency to approach, explore and master the challenging aspects of a learning task. Ego-defensive orientation means a child's tendency to alleviate negative feelings and reduce motivational-emotional tension by, for example, avoidance behaviour, substitute activities, and negative verbal and non-verbal expressions. Social dependence orientation shows as a tendency to please the teacher, and to seek his or her help and approval. When a certain motivational disposition interacts with situational cues, a specific coping pattern is launched. Task orientation favours problem-solving, whereas ego-defensive and social-dependency coping patterns counteract it. The latter tendencies are assumed to be associated with poor quality problem-solving and surface-level processing because the pupil's resources are engaged in achieving goals alien to productive learning.

A trained observer assessed the behaviour of the children on three occasions. In grade 1, resistant learners showed less task orientation and more socially dependent behaviour than good readers. A similar difference in social dependency was observed in grade 2. In grade 3, resistant learners showed a significant increase of ego-defensive behaviour relative to other groups. In other words, they displayed avoidance, inhibition of action, and belittling utterances about themselves and their performance more often than other pupils. However, these tendencies were manifested simultaneously with their deteriorating school performance, so they cannot be regarded as the cause of slow learning.

When considered from a cognitive point of view, the career of resistant learners looks enigmatic. We could find no credible predictors. The only hint appears to be a simultaneous deterioration in their motivational structures, which are essential for successful school work. Consequently, our next hypothesis was that perhaps there are children who show an unusual amount of psychosocial vulnerability when trying to learn under stressful conditions.

Motivational orientation and coping strategies affect the reading career from pre-school onwards

Are there any potent predictors of reading development other than those having a close conceptual and operational relationship with phonological awareness, e.g. verbal intelligence? Recent work suggests that beginning readers' motivational and coping tendencies may be such a factor. We wanted particularly to delineate the ways motivation interacts with the phonological awareness when the pupil's reading career is being shaped.

Motivation is no doubt an elusive explanatory concept. Sometimes it may be considered a cause of a behaviour, e.g. a child with no initial interest in school work and language tasks is likely to become a mediocre reader. Equally obvious is the possibility that poor motivation is a byproduct of negative learning experiences. In fact, our experimental work has provided preliminary evidence for three different ways in which motivational dispositions may interact with learning to read. First, children with similar initial motivational patterns show a diverging motivational development in parallel with diverging reading development. Second, children with similar phonological awareness in pre-school may develop vastly different reading careers which can be predicted on the basis of pre-school motivational patterns. Third, vulnerability as a learner can be predicted, i.e. the tendency to respond to situational cues ego defensively has its roots in pre-school motivational patterns.

Is it possible to show that mediocre school performance impairs pupils' motivation relative to that in pre-school (Poskiparta, E., Niemi, P., Lepola, J., Ahtola, A. and Laine, P., 2002)? The motivational development of pupils diagnosed as poor readers in grade 2 was traced from pre-school on. Two methods were used. First, researchers at pre-school age and classroom teachers in grades 1 and 2 rated the pupils' task, ego-defensive and socially dependent orientation. These ratings reflect a relatively permanent base level. Second, motivational vulnerability in stressful situations was diagnosed. This was done by means of an experimental situation that included performance obstacles. For example, the child had to compete with a superior adult in a Lego construction task, or was set a task made impossible by the absence of necessary building bricks. It turned out that pre-school motivation was fairly even across prospective good, average and poor readers, the only departure from that being the good readers' superior task orientation as rated by researchers. No group differences emerged in the pressure situations, indicating similar coping responses.

Perhaps not surprisingly, the situation looked very different in primary grades. Teacher ratings suggested uniformly that prospective poor readers were less task oriented, more ego defensive and socially dependent than both average and good readers. No reliable difference was observed between the last two groups. It is possible to argue, of course, that teachers' ratings are affected by their knowledge of the pupils' long-term performance in the classroom. Therefore, the play situations provide important converging information. As it turned out, there was no reliable difference between the prospective reading level groups at pre-school age. This held true for both the relaxed and the pressure situation, although, in the latter, task orientation decreased while ego defensiveness increased in all three groups. The picture was drastically changed in grades 1 and 2, with poor readers showing less task orientation and more ego defensiveness than average and good readers in both situations. What is more, this tendency was significantly enhanced in pressure situations.

Given that poor school success results in concomitant motivational setbacks, the possibility to predict such a development appears intriguing. The aforementioned study of Poskiparta et al. (2002) showed that motivational predispositions are evenly distributed in an unselected group of pre-schoolers. Salonen, Lepola and Niemi (1998) tackled the question of predictability by identifying motivationally extreme groups among the pre-school non-readers on the basis of teacher ratings. An original sample of 151 children was divided into quartiles according to the ratings. Four groups of eight children in each were identified: task oriented, socially dependent, ego defensive, and multiple non-task oriented. The last consisted of children with both social dependency and ego defensiveness. The selected children scored in the top quartile in a chosen motivational orientation, and in the bottom or lower middle quartile in the other two orientations. Would such extreme orientations be prognostic of motivational vulnerability and reading development? Pressure situations featuring competitive and impossible elements revealed that the task orientation of pre-school children with an initially high ego defensiveness collapsed (Figure 7.4). When under performance stress, they displayed task-oriented coping only about half the time. Needless to say, productive problem-solving becomes unlikely under such circumstances. Pre-school motivational disposition and coping patterns further predicted word recognition in grade 1, with $r = 0.51$ for initial task orientation and $r = -0.41$ for ego-defensive coping under stress. When pre-school phonological awareness ($r = 0.51$) was included in the prediction, initial task orientation still emerged as the strongest predictor. Together with phonological awareness, it explained 49% of total variance in grade 1 word recognition among the 32 pupils.

An intriguing question in view of the above findings is whether motivational factors predict reading development in primary grades when the initial level of phonological awareness is controlled for. Lepola, Salonen and Vauras (2000) started with the idea that there may be progressive reading careers,

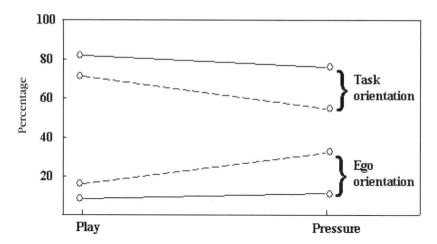

Figure 7.4. Percentage of task-oriented and ego-defensive coping behaviour as a function of performance context and high (dotted line) and low (solid line) initial ego-defensive orientation.

i.e. that children maintain their high position as readers or improve a low one as predicted by poor phonological awareness in pre-school. A regressive reading career would manifest itself as poor reading, in addition to low phonological awareness, or in spite of a high one, in pre-school. Good and poor reading were defined as being in the upper or lower third of word recognition scores, respectively, throughout grades 1 and 2. Good and poor initial levels were similarly defined with the scores of phonological aware-ness and verbal ability in pre-school. The results showed that a progressive reading career was associated with an increasing tendency to show more task orientation, together with less ego defensiveness, towards the end of grade 2. An opposite pattern emerged among pupils with a regressive reading career. Particularly impressive is the diverging development of the low–progressive group as opposed to the high–regressive one. For these two groups, the initial scores of phonological awareness were 3.2/40 and 16.2/40, whereas the final word-recognition scores in grade 2 were 315/400 and 172/400, respectively. Although each of these groups represented less than 10% of all pre-school non-readers, their diverging school careers strongly suggest that factors other than phonological awareness and verbal ability play a role in determining early reading development.

Unexpected reading failures

Usually pre-reading phonological awareness is a good predictor of reading acquisition in grade 1. However, at the end of grade 1, we encountered a group of pupils, about 8–10% of all, who were among the poorest decoders. In fact, they were at approximately the same level as the control group in grade 1, consisting of pupils with cognitive delays and receiving remedial teaching. Somewhat surprisingly, membership of this suddenly emerging group could not be predicted on the basis of their previous phonological awareness, which was close to average. Even their verbal ability was average and their listening comprehension above average. This group simply appears to be enigmatic, together with the group featuring a regressive reading career in spite of good initial phonological awareness.

It seems that there is a subgroup among poor readers whose problems have little to do with phonological awareness. Indeed, a literature search revealed one interesting possible explanation. Wolf (1997) writes persuasively about rate-disabled young readers. These are children whose reading difficulty emanates from slow and inaccurate naming instead of phonological processes (see also Lovett, 1987). Regrettably, our database did not include a measure of rapid naming. Fortunately, a contact with Hugh Catts of the University of Kansas was very helpful. He has collected longitudinal data on about 600 young readers, starting from pre-school age. The interesting group consisted of children belonging to the upper third in phonological awareness in kindergarten but falling to the lower third as decoders in primary grades. It was found that 9.5% of second graders and 6% of fourth graders satisfied these criteria, a frequency well in accordance with our observations. The only factor differentiating these children from others was their relatively poor performance on rapid naming with the mean z-score of second-grade poor decoders being −0.40 and that of fourth graders −0.66. Catts's result corroborates Wolf's hypothesis that there is a subgroup among poor readers who do not suffer from impaired phonological processing (Catts, personal communication; see also Ball, 1993).

Training in phonological awareness: useful but not salvation?

The temptation to regard phonological awareness as the decisive factor in beginning reading is well motivated. It is quite usual that components of it correlate with word recognition in grade 1 in the vicinity of 0.50. What is more, there is an abundance of positive training results, particularly favouring readers at risk. Some components of phonological awareness resemble reading proper, e.g. sound-blending tasks in a regular language such as Finnish are equivalent to 'reading by ear'. This makes the link to reading obvious, resulting in a strong prognosis. Against such a background it was rather disappointing to find that training gains tended to disappear during the following 2 years, at least in terms of reading fluency and accuracy. Before drawing conclusions, one potentially important point has to be made (Lundberg, personal communication).

Our intervention was carried out at the beginning of grade 1, in parallel with formal reading instruction. This may be an important difference. Gustafson, Samuelsson and Rönnberg (2000) observed, in their training study of fourth graders, that no less than half of the children showed little progress in reading in spite of gains in phonological awareness. Clearly, a replication featuring a pre-school intervention coupled with reading speed and accuracy measures is needed here. An additional prognostic factor may be the rate of acquisition of phonological awareness (Byrne, Fielding-Barnsley and Ashley, 2000), with a slow rate indicating little transfer to word reading.

However, even the most optimistic prognosis based on phonological awareness leaves approximately half of the variance in word recognition still unexplained. This fact calls for additional measures of prognostic value that do not correlate with phonological awareness. One such candidate is rapid automatic naming that has given impetus to the dual-deficit model (e.g. Wolf, 1997). We identified a group of problem readers at the end of grade 1 whose phonological awareness had been average in pre-school. Departing from Wolf's (1997) model, however, their comprehension processes were intact. A corresponding group could be identified in Kansas, USA with inferior naming speed, whereas phonological awareness was within normal range. Findings such as these suggest that rapid automatic naming should enter a prognosis of reading difficulty.

There is hardly any doubt about the importance of motivation and coping processes for beginning reading. The problem is rather one of adequate measuring. We suggest that a detailed analysis of coping responses under stressful situations has considerable diagnostic value. In fact, some subgroups show a dissociation between coping and initial phonological awareness, with inadequate coping processes apparently cancelling an expected favourable reading career. Such pupils are a prime example of resistant learners who seem to benefit only if cognitive training is coupled with motivational interventions (Lehtinen et al., 1995). Reading habits comprise an additional significant factor with parental preferences and beliefs probably playing an important role (e.g. Aunola et al., 2002).

A conclusion that is emerging is that, if essentially more than half of the variance in beginning reading is to be explained, phonological awareness does not account for it alone. Strong candidates for improving the prognosis are rapid automatic naming, rate of acquisition of phonological awareness and coping patterns under stress. Each of these can be diagnosed before formal teaching of reading, thus making it possible to discuss their eventual causal role in reading acquisition.

Acknowledgement

The research reported here was based on a longitudinal project (Decoding, Comprehension, and Motivation) conducted at the Centre for Learning Research at the University of Turku, Finland. It was supported by grants nos 4131 and 1071265 from the Council for Social Sciences Research, Academy of Finland, to the first author and Marja Vauras. The authors wish to thank the heads, teachers and children of 14 kindergarten and 4 primary schools in Turku, who unfortunately must remain anonymous.

References

Aunola, K., Nurmi, J.-E., Niemi, P., Lerkkanen, M.-K. and Rasku-Puttonen, H. (2002). Development of dynamics of reading skills, achievement strategies, and parental beliefs. *Reading Research Quarterly* in press.

Ball, E. (1993). Phonological awareness: What's important and to whom? *Reading and Writing: An Interdisciplinary Journal* **5**: 141–160.

Borstroem, I. and Elbro, C. (1997). Prevention of dyslexia in kindergarten. Effects of phoneme awareness training with children of dyslexic parents. In: Hulme, C. and Snowling, M. (eds), *Dyslexia: Biology, Cognition and Intervention*. London: Whurr, pp. 235–253.

Bryant, P., MacLean, M. and Bradley, L. (1990). Rhyme, language, and children's reading. *Applied Psycholinguistics* **11**: 237–252.

Bus, A. and van Ijzendoorn, M. (1999). Phonological awareness and early reading: A meta-analysis of experimental training studies. *Journal of Educational Psychology* **91**: 403–414.

Byrne, B., Fielding-Barnsley, R. and Ashley, L. (2000). Effects of preschool phoneme identity training after six years: Outcome level distinguished from rate of response. *Journal of Educational Psychology* **92**: 659–667.

Gustafson, S., Samuelsson, S. and Rönnberg, J. (2000). Why do some resist phonological intervention? A Swedish longitudinal study of poor readers in Grade 4. *Scandinavian Journal of Educational Research* **44**: 145–162.

Kinnunen, R., Vauras, M. and Niemi, P. (1998). Comprehension monitoring in beginning readers. *Scientific Studies of Reading* **2**: 353–375.

Lehtinen, E., Vauras, M., Salonen, P., Olkinuora, E. and Kinnunen, R. (1995). Long-term development of learning activity: Motivational, cognitive, and social interaction. *Educational Psychologist* **30**: 21–35.

Lepola, J., Salonen, P. and Vauras, M. (2000). The development of motivational orientations as a function of divergent reading careers from pre-school to the second grade. *Learning and Instruction* **10**: 153–177.

Lovett, M. (1987). A developmental approach to reading disability: Accuracy and speed criteria of normal and deficient reading skills. *Child Development* **58**: 234–260.

Lundberg, I. (1994). Reading difficulties can be predicted and prevented: A Scandinavian perspective on phonological awareness and reading. In: Hulme, C. and Snowling, M. (eds), *Reading Development and Dyslexia*. London: Whurr, pp. 180–199.

Lundberg, I., Frost, J. and Petersen, O.-P. (1988). Effects of an extensive program for stimulating phonological awareness in preschool children. *Reading Research Quarterly* **23**: 263-284.

Niemi, P., Poskiparta, E., Vauras, M. and Mäki, H. (1998). Reading and writing difficulties do not always occur as the researcher expects. *Scandinavian Journal of Psychology* **39**: 159-161.

Niemi, P., Kinnunen, R., Poskiparta, E. and Vauras, M. (1999). Do pre-school data predict resistance to treatment in phonological awareness, decoding and spelling? In: Lundberg, I., Toennessen, F.-E. and Austad, I. (eds), *Dyslexia: Advances in theory and practice*. Dordrecht, The Netherlands: Kluwer Academic Publishers b.v., pp. 245-254.

Niemi, P., Poskiparta, E. and Vauras, M. (2001). Benefits of training in linguistic awareness dissipate by grade 3? *Psychology: The Journal of the Hellenic Psychological Society* **8**: 330-337.

Olkinuora, E. and Salonen, P. (1992). Adaptation, motivational orientation and cognition in a subnormally performing child: A systemic perspective for training. In: Wong, B.E. (ed.), *Contemporary Intervention Research in Learning Disabilities: An international perspective*. New York: Springer, pp. 190-213.

Olofsson, Å. (1993). The relevance of phonological awareness in learning to read: Scandinavian longitudinal and quasi-experimental studies. In: Joshi, R. and Leong, C. (eds), *Reading Disabilities: Diagnosis and component processes*. Dordrecht, The Netherlands: Kluwer, pp. 185-198.

Olson, R., Wise, B., Ring, J. and Johnson, M. (1997). Computer-based remedial teaching in phoneme awareness and phonological decoding: Effects on the posttraining development of word recognition. *Scientific Studies of Reading* **1**: 235-253.

Petersen, D.K. (2001). What do you get if you add /mmm/ to ice? Training phoneme awareness in kindergarten. An intervention study with children of dyslexic parents. In: Badian, N. (ed.), *Preschool Prediction and Prevention of Reading Failure*. Timonium, MD: York Press, pp. 247-273.

Poskiparta, E., Niemi, P. and Vauras, M. (1999). Who benefits from training in linguistic awareness in the first grade and what components show training effects? *Journal of Learning Disabilities* **32**: 437-446, 456.

Poskiparta, E., Vauras, M. and Niemi, P. (1998). Promoting word recognition, spelling and reading comprehension skills in a computer-based training program in grade 2. In: Reitsma, P. and Verhoeven, L. (eds), *Problems and Interventions in Literacy Development*. Amsterdam: Kluwer, pp. 335-348.

Poskiparta, E., Niemi, P., Lepola, J., Ahtola, A. and Laine, P. (2002). Motivational-emotional vulnerability and difficulties in learning to read and spell (submitted).

Salonen, P., Lepola, J. and Niemi, P. (1998). The development of first graders' reading skill as a function of pre-school motivational orientation and phonemic awareness. *European Journal of Psychology of Education* **13**: 155-174.

Schneider, W. and Stengård, C. (eds) (1999). Inventory of European Longitudinal Studies of Reading and Spelling. COST A8 – Learning Disorders as a Barrier to Human Development (http://www.psychologie.uni-wuerzburg.de/cost/inventory.htm).

Schneider, W., Küspert, P., Roth, E., Vise, M. and Marx, H. (1997). Short- and long-term effects of training phonological awareness in kindergarten: Evidence from two German studies. *Journal of Experimental Child Psychology* **66**: 311-340.

Schneider, W., Ennemoser, M., Roth, E. and Küspert, P. (1999). Kindergarten prevention of dyslexia: Does training in phonological awareness work for everybody? *Journal of Learning Disabilities* **32**: 429–436.

Torgesen, J., Wagner, R. and Rashotte, C. (1994). Longitudinal studies of phonological processing and reading. *Journal of Reading Disabilities* **27**: 276–286.

Torgesen, J., Wagner, R. and Rashotte, C. (1997). Prevention and remediation of severe reading disabilities: Keeping the end in mind. *Scientific Studies of Reading* **1**: 217–234.

Wolf, M. (1997). A provisional, integrative account of phonological and naming-speed deficits in dyslexia: Implications for diagnosis and intervention. In: Blachman, B. (ed.), *Foundations of Reading Acquisition and Dyslexia: Implications for early intervention*. Mahwah, NJ: Erlbaum, pp. 67–92.

CHAPTER 8

Phoneme awareness and reading: from the old to the new millennium

RICHARD K. OLSON

Phonological awareness

The chapter starts with a review of some of the major things we have learned about phoneme awareness and reading development over the past 30 years. Then, new research programmes are discussed that hopefully further clarify the interrelationships of phoneme awareness, other cognitive skills, reading development, and their genetic and environmental aetiology.

Pioneering studies by the Liberman and the Haskins group in the USA (Liberman et al., 1974) and by Ingvar Lundberg and his colleagues in Sweden (Lundberg, Olofsson and Wall, 1980) emphasised the close interrelationships of children's ability to isolate explicitly and manipulate abstract phonemes in speech, their ability to develop an understanding of the alphabetic principle in reading and their ultimate reading success. The study by Lundberg, Olofsson and Wall was singled out for high praise in Wagner and Torgesen's (1987, p. 199) review of phonological processes and reading because the '. . . data represent a uniquely important contribution to our knowledge of empirical relations among measures of phonological awareness'.

The complex causal relationship between individual differences in phoneme awareness and reading has been clarified by two important lines of research. One involved the training of illiterate adults to read. The other involved the direct instruction of phoneme awareness in pre-readers. The combined outcome of these two lines of research revealed a bi-directional pattern of causation: learning to read promotes the development of phoneme awareness (Morais et al., 1979), and training in phoneme awareness before reading instruction promotes the later development of reading (Lundberg, Frost and Peterson, 1988). The latter study was particularly important in establishing a causal influence of phoneme awareness on later reading development, because an earlier study by Bradley and Bryant (1983) had found that only a non-significant trend for reading benefits from pre-schoolers' phonological training. Bradley and Bryant did show that pre-schoolers' phonological training *combined* with print yielded significant advantages for their later reading status. Lundberg, Frost and Peterson subsequently demonstrated the *specific* causal role of phoneme awareness *without* print instruction. This important result has been replicated in German-speaking children by Schneider et al. (1997), and in Swedish-speaking Finnish children by Kjeldsen, Niemi and Olofsson (2000).

The foregoing basic research on phoneme awareness was conducted during the course of vociferous arguments (primarily in the USA and the UK) about the best way to teach children to read in normal classrooms and in special education settings for disabled readers. On the one hand, it was argued, from the high correlation of phoneme awareness, phonological decoding of non-words and reading, that the direct teaching of phonological skills and the alphabetic principle is the best method. This view garnered additional support from surveys comparing the efficacy of classroom teaching methods which emphasised direct instruction of phonological skills for beginning readers, versus methods that placed greater emphasis on inductive learning of the alphabetic principle through reading practice. The instructional-methods surveys in the USA by Chall (1967), Bond and Dykstra (1967), Adams (1990), and most recently by the National Research Council (Snow, Burns and Griffin, 1998) and the National Reading Panel (2000, www.nationalreadingpanel.org) all concluded that explicit instruction in phonological skills leads to more rapid early growth in those skills and in reading.

Problems

There are two important caveats from the instructional-methods surveys. First, the greater benefits of direct instruction in phonological skills observed for beginning reading tended to diminish and sometimes disappear in the later grades. Second, direct-instruction benefits for reading comprehension were usually much smaller and also tended to disappear in the later grades. Although the data clearly supported the direct instruction of alphabetic skills in beginning readers, they also raised questions about why the early benefits tend to diminish, and why there is limited transfer to reading comprehension. Similar questions have been raised in a recent meta-analysis of studies on phonological-awareness training programmes, some with and some without print, in pre-school, kindergarten or first grade (Bus and van Ijzendoorn, 1999). Within a homogeneous subset of American studies with randomised or matched designs, there were significant short-term benefits for both phoneme awareness and word reading compared with no-treatment control groups. However, the significant long-term benefits for phoneme awareness over an average of 8 months across studies did not transfer to significant long-term benefits for word reading over an average 18-month interval. There were statistically significant long-term benefits for spelling and reading comprehension across the selected studies, but these effects were quite small. The authors argued that phonological training was clearly beneficial in the short term, but they were troubled by the non-significant long-term effects on word reading.

We have also been troubled by the lack of long-term transfer from better phonological skills to superior word reading, compared with accurate reading-practice control conditions. Our research has focused on the remediation of reading disabilities in the schools for 200 children in grades 2–5 who were below the local 10th percentile in word reading (Olson et al., 1997; Wise, Ring and Olson, 2000). The main features of our research design included random assignment of children to one of two treatment conditions, extensive pre-testing of reading, maths and phonological skills, training over about 50 half-hour sessions during the 4-month spring semester, and post-testing at the end of training, 1 year and 2 years later. The training was conducted in small groups of three to four students, each with their own computers, and one instructor. Students were taken out of their reading classes for the training sessions, thus displacing rather than supplementing their regular reading instruction.

The treatment conditions were designed to be as similar as possible, except in ways that would be informative about specific treatment effects from instruction in phoneme awareness and phonological decoding. One trainer in each of eight different schools worked with separate subject groups in both treatment conditions, thus controlling for any trainer or school confounders. Computers were employed to ensure compliance with the designed training contrasts, to increase individual support for error feedback while reading, and to record accurately critical training data. Trainers were carefully instructed and monitored to ensure that they carried out the two training programmes with equal levels of enthusiasm and structure. Thus, the critical difference between the training conditions was in their relative emphasis on phoneme awareness and phonological decoding instruction versus accurate reading in text and the use of comprehension strategies.

The 'phonological analysis' (PA) group spent about half their time in small group activities and computer exercises learning about phonemes through their association with articulatory motor movements (Lindamood and Lindamood, 1984), and the mapping of phonemes to graphemes of different unit sizes in reading and spelling exercises on the computer. Application of these trained phonological skills was subsequently encouraged while participants read stories on the computer. When they encountered difficult words in the stories, they used a mouse to highlight in different colours the onset-rime segments in one-syllable regular words or syllable segments in multisyllable words. They then attempted to pronounce and blend the highlighted segments to form the word, and asked the computer to pronounce the segments and word to check on their decoding accuracy. A multiple-choice comprehension question was presented after every 5–10 pages in the story, and a selection of the targeted words was presented in a recognition test on the computer at the end of the session.

The 'accurate reading in context' (ARC) group began their training in small-group sessions focused on the 'reciprocal teaching' of comprehension strategies (Palincsar and Brown, 1984), while accurately reading stories on and off the computer. In addition to training in comprehension strategies, the main training difference for the ARC group was in their amount of accurate computer-supported reading of stories and in the way they were trained to use the feedback from targeted words. The ARC group spent about twice as much time reading stories, and they were encouraged to use the story context along with initial letter sounds to help read difficult words that they had targeted. For half the ARC participants, the word segments were highlighted as in the PA condition's segmented feedback for targeted words, but there was no emphasis on sounding out the segments. For the other half of the ARC subjects, the words were highlighted but not segmented. (Segmentation did not matter for any of the ARC training effects.) Word-reading accuracy was equally emphasised in both the ARC and PA conditions.

At the end of training, gains in two measures of phoneme awareness and two measures of phonological decoding (non-word reading) were substantially greater in the PA group at all grade levels, and these training differences tended to be larger in the lower grades. Later follow-up tests revealed that the PA group had maintained a significant advantage in phonological decoding at 1 year, and a significant advantage in phoneme awareness 2 years after training ended. Unfortunately, and contrary to our strong hypothesis, the PA group's advantage in phoneme awareness and phonological decoding at the end of training and at follow-up tests was not broadly associated with an advantage for word reading, spelling or reading comprehension. The exception was that PA-trained children in grades 2 and 3 had a significant end-of-training advantage for gains on a standardised untimed test of word recognition, and on accuracy in untimed reading of previously targeted words from the stories, but these advantages were not found for those in grades 4 and 5. Moreover, the PA group showed a significant *deficit* compared with the ARC group at the end of training on an experimental measure of time-limited word recognition, wherein the words were presented for only 2 seconds. This deficit was strongest in the older children. However, both the PA group's advantage in untimed word recognition and their deficit in time-limited word recognition at the end of training disappeared in the 1- and 2-year follow-up tests.

Good and bad news

The good news from the study of Wise, Ring and Olson (2000) was that both the PA and ARC groups showed significant gains in word-reading standard scores, as well as greater standard-score gains in comparison to groups in other schools who remained in their regular reading classes (Wise, Ring and Olson, 1999). Both the ARC and PA programmes clearly fostered more rapid reading growth compared with regular classroom reading instruction in good schools, and their rates of growth per hour of training time in groups of three to four with computers in our reading *pull-out* study were comparable to those found in *supplementary* training studies that used one-on-one instruction with an expert tutor (reviewed by Torgesen et al., 2001).

The bad news from Wise, Ring and Olson (2000) is that the substantial improvement in PA children's phoneme awareness and phonological decoding only seemed to provide an advantage for the youngest poor readers in tests of word recognition where there was no time limit. The PA group's advantage in phonological decoding and phoneme awareness was maintained in follow-up tests, but the untimed word recognition advantage was apparent only during and immediately after the end of training.

We had expected that the PA group's superior phonological skills would transfer more broadly to word-reading accuracy and fluency, and to spelling and reading comprehension. We noted that poor readers typically show a unique deficit in phoneme awareness and phonological decoding that arguably causes their reading deficit (Rack, Snowling and Olson, 1992). Trained improvement in these skills was expected to have lasting advantages for reading growth, beyond that found from accurate reading in the ARC condition, by providing a 'self-teaching' mechanism for decoding and learning unfamiliar words (Share, 1995). Why did we fail to confirm our strong hypothesis?

We worked hard to avoid condition confounders with teacher skill and enthusiasm, time on task, overall accuracy in reading and non-random assignment of subjects that could have biased the results. (In spite of our efforts, there was some indication that our trainers had more confidence in the PA condition.) We considered two other reasons why we may have failed to find evidence for better long-term transfer to reading from the PA children's superior phonological skills.

The first reason would be apparent to many clinicians: the training time of only 25 hours may have been too short to realise unique long-term benefits from phonological training. Although we substantially improved our disabled readers' explicit phonological knowledge and accuracy in the outcome measures, we may not have sufficiently trained their 'automaticity' or speed in phonological processing (unfortunately, speed was not assessed). Without this speed or automaticity, PA children may not have been inclined or able to apply their greater explicit phonological knowledge to fluent reading processes after training ended. This hypothesis is the subject of several studies that are under way at the beginning of the new millennium (compare Wolf, 2001).

Regarding the need for longer training time, there is only one study we know of that included substantially longer training time with an experimental comparison of conditions similar to ours. Torgesen et al. (2001) individually trained 60 pupils in grades 3–6 with severe reading disabilities for a total of 67.5 hours over 2 months in one of two supplementary clinic programmes. At the end of training, their version of our PA condition led to significantly greater gains than their version of our ARC condition in phonological decoding, and smaller but significantly greater gains in rate and decoding-accuracy measures on a standardised paragraph reading test. However, there were *no* significant treatment differences on any of the eight different reading outcome measures 1 and 2 years after the end of training. The main point of the study was the very large gains made in *both* training conditions in standard scores on a number of measures, compared with the lack of growth in standard scores before training, and the maintenance of most gains in standard scores 1 and 2 years after intervention. Gains in reading accuracy were much stronger than gains in reading speed.

Overall, the results of Torgesen et al. (2001) provided clear evidence that intensive intervention can have lasting and positive benefits for disabled readers, counter to the assertion by Cossu (1999) that responses to reading intervention are negligible because of biological constraints. However, in spite of its longer and more intensive one-on-one training with expert reading therapists, this study did not find significantly greater long-term benefits for reading or spelling from a phonological training programme similar to our PA condition (Lindamood and Lindamood, 1984), when compared with a programme that had greater emphasis on accurate reading with less explicit phonological training.

A possible reason for the absence of long-term advantages from phonological training in both the Wise et al. (2000) and Torgesen et al. (2001) studies is that they began too late in the children's reading development. Perhaps phonological skills are more malleable before and in conjunction with beginning reading instruction. If trained early, they might be more likely to be effectively incorporated in later automatic reading processes in the later grades. Lundberg, Frost and Peterson (1988) found benefits from purely phonological training before reading instruction for later reading in unselected samples, and this benefit tended to be greatest in those children with the worst pre-test scores (Lundberg, 1994). Schneider et al. (1999) found a similar result when they analysed the lowest children in their replication of the study of Lundberg, Frost and Peterson (1988): the Schneider et al. (1997) training programme reduced the risk for reading disability in second grade for the lowest children at pre-test.

A larger body of research has combined phonological training with varying amounts of print training at the pre-school or kindergarten level, and then compared outcomes with children who did not receive any early instruction in phonology and print processing (Bradley and Bryant, 1983; Byrne and Fielding-Barnsley, 1991, 1995; Blachman et al., 1994; Hanson and Farrell, 1995; Borstrom and Elbro, 1997). These studies showed significant advantages from combined phonological and alphabetic training for reading in the early grades, and three studies showed small but significant follow-up advantages in the later grades as well (Bradley and Bryant, 1983; Byrne and Fielding-Barnsley, 1995; Hanson and Farrell, 1995). However, it is not entirely clear that these advantages were specifically caused by the phonological training component, as must have been the case in Lundberg, Frost and Peterson (1988), or whether the advantage could have come simply from getting early supplemental print instruction of any kind.

Perhaps a head start in reading improves long-term reading outcome when children move ahead of their peers in early reading instruction, view themselves as more competent readers and read more in later life (Hanson and Farrell, 1995), e.g. American children who are progressing more rapidly in early reading instruction are often separated into more advanced reading groups with higher expectations. This would certainly be a valuable outcome for those who were given early reading instruction before formal schooling, but it would not necessarily imply that phonological training was the uniquely beneficial component. It also raises the question of whether pre-school reading instruction should be given to all children, if its benefits are largely the result of the trained children's initial competitive advantage relative to other beginning readers. Reading instruction traditionally begins earlier for children in the USA and the UK, even in some pre-schools and kindergarten, but there is no indication that the USA and the UK have more advanced literacy development in the later grades, compared with Sweden, Finland, Germany and Austria, which have traditionally eschewed formal print instruction before age 7 (Lundberg, 1999).

Phonological training

Unique benefits

Returning to the question of unique benefits from early phonological training, two recent studies with children at risk for reading disabilities addressed this question by including print-instructed control groups without explicit phonological training. Schneider, Roth and Ennemoser (2000) compared reading and spelling outcomes at the end of grades 1 and 2 for children who were trained in daily 10- to 15-min sessions over 10 or 20 weeks. One group was trained for 20 weeks in phonological awareness (PA), a second group was trained for 10 weeks in phonological awareness and then 10 weeks in letter sounds (PA–LS), and a third group was trained only in the second 10-week block on letter sounds (LS). The last condition might be considered to be a less phonologically oriented beginning instruction with print.

For control purposes, it is unfortunate that this group received only half the instruction of the other groups, so this qualifies some of the group differences reported below. The PA and LS groups tended to perform similarly on post-training reading and spelling skills, so only the contrasts between the LS and PA–LS groups are addressed. These groups were not significantly different in word reading at the end of grade 1 or 2, although the PA–LS advantage in grade 2 fell just short of significance ($p = 0.06$), and there were no significant group differences in reading comprehension. However, the PA–LS group did have a significant advantage in spelling at the end of grades 1 and 2, a skill that Schneider, Roth and Ennemoser claim to be particularly important for academic success in German-speaking countries. Thus, the results of this reading-trained control study were mixed. The extra phonological training in the PA–LS group yielded significant advantages only in spelling, and this result may have been the result of the fact that the PA–LS group had twice the total amount of instruction compared with the LS group.

A second trained-control study starting with at-risk pre-readers in kindergarten has been conducted in the USA by Torgesen et al. (1999), with follow-up data in grades 3 and 4 reported by Torgesen (2000). The two conditions of greatest interest in this study were one that had greater emphasis on phonological awareness, beginning with phonological articulatory-based training similar to the Wise, Ring and Olson (2000) study, and a second 'embedded phonics' (EP) condition that had greater emphasis on learning about print–sound relationships in the context of reading activities. Both programmes started in the middle of kindergarten and extended through the second grade, including a total of 88 hours of supplementary one-on-one instruction. Participants were selected at the beginning of kindergarten to be in the lower 12% in phonological sensitivity and letter naming. They were then randomly assigned to the condition.

Torgesen et al. (1999) found very significant advantages for their PA group at the end of grades 1 and 2 on measures of phoneme awareness and phonological decoding skills. They found more modest but significant advantages in standardised measures of word reading, but not in standardised measures of spelling or reading comprehension. This pattern held up in further longitudinal assessments at the end of grades 3 and 4 (Torgesen, 2000). The lack of a significant PA advantage in reading comprehension was attributed to constraints from participants' generally low verbal IQ. It would be wonderful if 88 hours of tuition in basic phonological and reading skills would also boost verbal IQ, but this training is not likely to build the general vocabulary skills assessed in verbal IQ and that have a high correlation with reading comprehension.

At present, the Torgesen et al. (1999) study seems to provide the strongest support for a unique long-term advantage for both phonological *and* word-reading skills from phonologically based supplementary reading instruction in children at risk for reading disability. An early start, before and in conjunction with early reading instruction, may have been the key to this study's success in achieving long-term transfer. The remediation studies by Wise, Ring and Olson (2000) and Torgesen et al. (2001) with older children may have missed a critical period for integrating phonological processes and reading for long-term advantages. (Hopefully, new approaches in the new millennium will extend this critical period to older children.)

However, there were some aspects of the Torgesen et al. (1999) prevention study that suggest the need for further confirmation of their results. The favoured PA condition was developed and guided by experts from the Lindamood-Bell Corporation (Lindamood and Lindamood, 1984) with a strong financial stake in the success of their programme. The other non-commercial EP programme may not have had such strong support. In fact, the EP programme resulted in very modest differences in gains compared with a no-treatment control group. In addition, the EP programme had a significantly higher number of children who were referred for special education, compared with the no-treatment control or the PA group. It is hard to imagine that this could be a negative treatment effect from the EP programme, so it may have reflected some sort of sample bias that could have compromised the training effects for this group. It is very difficult to perform a training study with complete control over all potentially confounding variables. We should ultimately be guided by converging evidence from a number of studies. Hopefully, the advantage from early phonological training found in the Torgesen et al. (1999) study will be confirmed in future research.

Summary

In summary, the pattern of results from phonological training studies is complex. When training begins early, the benefits seem to be clearly present for word-reading skills in beginning reading, but most studies find that these benefits tend to diminish in the later grades. Phonologically based remediation for reading disabilities that begins in the later grades has generally failed to show unique long-term benefits when compared with remediation that emphasises accurate reading. We can hope that future research will show how improved and automated phonological skills can lead to greater long-term gains. To prepare for this research, we should reflect more deeply on possible reasons why phonological skills are so highly correlated with reading, but trained improvement in those skills has limited long-term benefits for reading.

One possible reason already considered is that improving accuracy in phonological processes typically assessed in our outcome measures is not enough. We may also need to make these skills more automated so that they can be incorporated in fluent reading.

A second possibility is that there is a more basic processing deficit that is at least partly responsible for the correlation between phoneme awareness and word reading, e.g. Tallal (2000), and others have argued that a specific rapid auditory–temporal processing deficit degrades the internal representation of phonemes and constrains the development of phoneme awareness. However, two recent studies have not found the specific deficit in rapid temporal processing reported by Tallal. Instead, Waber et al. (2001) and Nittrouer (1999) found processing deficits for auditory tone stimuli at *both* slow and rapid rates of presentation. Olson and Datta (2002) recently found a similar shared deficit for both slow (parvocellular) and rapid (magnocellular) processing of visual stimuli. Thus, although a specific deficit in rapid temporal processing in vision and audition is questioned by these recent results, the studies do show a modest general sensory processing deficit in children with reading disabilities.

Although a sensory basis for deficits in phoneme awareness is still controversial, there is evidence that disabled readers have deficits in the precision of their phonological representations for words. Elbro, Borstrom and Petersen (1998) have shown that children genetically at risk for dyslexia have less precise phonological representations for words, particularly for unstressed syllables, and this predicts later problems in phoneme awareness and reading. However, this does not explain why disabled readers' phoneme awareness can be much improved with intensive training, although the unique long-term benefit for reading is limited.

A third possibility is that there could be a general processing problem in disabled readers that constrains growth in phoneme awareness and other reading processes independently, and in different ways at different stages of reading development (Wesseling and Reitsma, 2000). Progress in slow but accurate reading at beginning alphabetic stages of learning may be more closely linked to children's explicit awareness of phonemes. Later fluent reading and spelling, particularly of a deep orthography such as English, may be more dependent on other processes that are also constrained by a deeper third factor, which is ultimately responsible for the correlation between early phoneme awareness and later reading. If a third factor does independently constrain growth in phoneme awareness and other reading-related skills, the remediation of deficits in phoneme awareness might not significantly diminish the constraints of that third factor on the other correlated reading skills. Scarborough (2001) has commented on a similar third-factor issue in the correlation between pre-school speech/language impairments and later reading problems:

> Preschool training that successfully ameliorates early speech/language impair-
> ments is not effective in reducing such children's risk for later reading problems,
> as it ought to be if those language weaknesses are a causal impediment to learning
> to read.

Challenges

A major challenge for the new millennium is to understand the nature of this third factor. One step in this direction has been taken by Byrne, Fielding-Barnsley and Ashley (2000). They followed up children in grade 5 who had been trained in pre-school on phoneme awareness of initial word sounds and their corresponding letters, accompanied by related pictures. A comparison group had practised classifying the same pictures without attention to the constituent phonemes or letters of the corresponding words (Byrne and Fielding-Barnsley, 1991). Although training time was modest at 6 hours over 12 sessions, the group trained on initial word sounds and print had a significant advantage at the end of grade 1 on non-word reading and a nearly significant advantage on a list of regular words (p = 0.06). In the grade 5 follow-up tests, the phonologically trained group was still significantly better in non-word reading, with an effect size of 0.34, and they were also significantly better in an experimental measure of regular and irregular word reading, with an effect size of 0.33. (The groups were not significantly different on the Woodcock Word Identification test or a spelling test.)

Byrne, Fielding-Barnsley and Ashley (2000) took two different views on grade 5 differences between the groups. On the one hand, the significant differences on two measures were remarkable with so little pre-school training ('the glass is half full'). On the other hand, the differences were quite small and inconsistent across measures, and some of the children in the phonologically trained group who had met the criterion by the end of training could be classified as reading disabled in grade 5 ('the glass is half empty'). After pondering these results, Byrne, Fielding-Barnsley and Ashley decided to look at two pre-school measures in order to understand the broad individual reading differences in their phonologically trained group. One measure was a reliable post-training measure of word initial phoneme identity. The other measure was the session of last error (SLE) out of 11 sessions, which gave an index of responsiveness to instruction. (Some children learned quickly in only a few sessions, whereas others took most or all of the training sessions to reach error-free performance.) The latter approach is reminiscent of 'dynamic testing' procedures which explore how well a child responds to increasing support in an assessment session (Spector, 1992; Grigorenko and Sternberg, 1998). A series of multiple regression analyses predicted grade 2 and grade 5 reading performance by first entering the post-training test of phoneme awareness, and then entering the 'dynamic' SLE measure in the second step. In grade 2, SLE accounted for more total variance than the phoneme awareness post-test on all measures, and particularly on reading and listening comprehension. In grade 5, the same was true of most measures of word and non-word reading.

Thus, the dynamic SLE assessment of learning rate for phoneme awareness in pre-school generally predicted later reading better than post-test phoneme awareness, even after the variance associated with the post-test was removed! This suggests the possibility of a general learning-rate factor that might account for untrained variance in phoneme awareness at early stages of reading development, and independently in other reading skills at later stages of development. These later stages might be characterised by the number of exposures needed to establish word-specific (orthographic) associations, and these might be little influenced by trained improvement in phoneme awareness. Of course this general learning parameter need not affect all aspects of intellectual function. There certainly are cases of large discrepancy between visuospatial skills and reading, or less commonly, between verbal IQ and reading. To account for the generally weak association between trained phonological skills and later reading, we need only to postulate learning-rate constraints in the parallel domains of phoneme awareness and fluent word recognition.

If there is a general learning-rate constraint that separately influences the learning of phoneme awareness and higher-level reading skills, what is its cause? In the new millennium, this question will be increasingly addressed at the biological level. It will be further examined with measures of brain activity, and through analyses of its genetic and environmental aetiology. We already know that there are strong genetic influences on deficits in phoneme awareness and word reading (Olson et al., 1989), and that the genetic aetiologies for deficits in phoneme awareness and word reading are largely caused by the same genes (Olson, Forsberg and Wise, 1994; Gayan and Olson, 2001). We even have evidence from disabled readers' DNA that important genes for deficits in phoneme awareness and reading are located in certain shared regions of the genome, with the strongest current support across studies for linkage on chromosome 6 (compare Gayan et al., 1999; Grigorenko et al., 2000). Other research in Norway and the UK has pointed to a region of chromosome 2. No doubt, there will be other important locations as well, suggesting varied genetic and environmental pathways to reading disability. Some of these pathways are likely to be shared with other disorders such as attention deficit hyperactivity disorder (ADHD) (Smith et al., 2001; Willcutt et al., 2002).

Finding the general locations of genes through linkage and association studies is the first step on a long road. Then we must find the actual gene, identify its related protein, and finally understand the complex role of that protein in brain development and function related to phoneme awareness and reading. This is a tall order for the new millennium, but the potential pay-off is huge! At present, we can profitably prescribe phoneme aware-ness training in beginning reading and lots of additional accurate reading practice for children who are slow in reading development. We can also begin to assess a child's genetic risk for reading disability and use this assessment to prescribe pre-school or earlier intervention. In the brave new world of the new millennium, direct genetic engineering and gene product manipulations may help avoid genetically based reading disabilities, allowing greater focus on the important environmental contributions to many reading disorders.

Along with the increasing emphasis on molecular genetics and physiolog-ical explorations of the brain, we will continue to conduct more searching behaviour–genetic studies on reading and related cognitive skills. The work of Byrne, Fielding-Barnsley and Ashley (2000) has led to a new international collaboration to assess individual differences dynamically in pre-school children's learning for phoneme awareness and relationships with other cognitive skills *before* they are contaminated by individual differences in reading. The genetic and environmental aetiology of these individual differ-ences will be explored through the comparison of identical and fraternal pre-school twins in the USA, Australia, and Norway, with the collaboration of Ingvar Lundberg's colleague Torleiv Høien and former student Stefan Samuelsson. The twins' reading development will then be followed at least through the second grade.

In conclusion, Ingvar Lundberg has been a guiding light through the last 20 years of research on phoneme awareness and reading development. It is clear that he is not finished, as evidenced by two new articles in the last issue of *Reading and Writing*. The reading field is fortunate that it can look forward to more of his careful and creative research on reading, and his legacy will grow into the new millennium with the excellent contributions of his lovingly mentored students.

References

Adams, M.J. (1990). *Beginning to Read: Thinking and learning about print*. Cambridge, MA: MIT Press.

Ball, E. and Blachman, B.A. (1991). Does phoneme awareness training in kindergarten make a difference in early word recognition and developmental spelling? *Reading Research Quarterly* **26**: 49–66.

Blachman, B., Ball, E., Black, S. and Tangle, D. (1994). Kindergarten teachers develop phoneme awareness in low-income, inner-city classrooms: Does it make a difference? *Reading and Writing: An Interdisciplinary Journal* **6**: 1–17.

Bond, G.L. and Dykstra, R. (1967). The cooperative research program in first-grade-reading instruction. *Reading Research Quarterly* **2**: 1–142.

Borstrom, I. and Elbro, C. (1997). Prevention of dyslexia in kindergarten: Effects of phoneme awareness training of children with dyslexic parents. In: Hulme, C. and Snowling, M. (eds), *Dyslexia: Biology, cognition, and intervention*. London: Whurr, pp. 235–253.

Bradley, L. and Bryant, P. (1983). Categorizing sounds and learning to read: A causal connection. *Nature* **301**: 419–421.

Bus, A.G. and van Ijzendoorn, M.H. (1999). Phonological awareness and early reading: A meta-analysis of experimental training studies. *Journal of Educational Psychology* **91**: 403–414.

Byrne, B. and Fielding-Barnsley, R. (1991). Evaluation of a program to teach phoneme awareness to young children. *Journal of Educational Psychology* **83**: 451–455.

Byrne, B. and Fielding-Barnsley, R. (1995). Evaluation of a program to teach phonemic awareness to young children: A 2- and 3-year follow-up and a new preschool trial. *Journal of Educational Psychology* **87**: 488–503.

Byrne, B., Fielding-Barnsley, R. and Ashley, L. (2000). Effects of preschool phoneme identity training after six years: Outcome level distinguished from rate of response. *Journal of Educational Psychology* **92**: 659–667.

Chall, J.S. (1967). *Learning to Read: The great debate*. New York: McGraw-Hill.

Cossu, G. (1999). Biological constraints on literacy acquisition. *Reading and Writing: An Interdisciplinary Journal* **11**: 213–237.

Elbro, C., Borstrom, I. and Petersen, D.K. (1998). Predicting dyslexia from kindergarten: The importance of distinctness of phonological representations of lexical items. *Reading Research Quarterly* **33**: 36–60.

Gayan, J. and Olson, R.K. (2001). Genetic and environmental influences on orthographic and phonological skills in children with reading disabilities. *Developmental Neuropsychology* **20**: 37–49.

Gayan, J., Smith, S.D., Cherny, S.S. et al. (1999). Large quantitative trait locus for specific language and reading deficits in chromosome 6p. *American Journal of Human Genetics* **64**: 157–164.

Grigorenko, E.L. and Sternberg, M.S. (1998). Dynamic testing. *Psychological Bulletin* **124**: 75–111.

Grigorenko, E.L., Wood, F.B., Meyer, M.S. and Pauls, D.L. (2000). Chromosome 6p influences on different dyslexia related cognitive processes: Further confirmation. *American Journal of Human Genetics* **66**: 715-723.

Hanson, R.A. and Farrell, D. (1995). The long-term effects on high school seniors of learning to read in Kindergarten. *Reading Research Quarterly* **30**: 908-933.

Kjeldsen, A., Niemi, P. and Olofsson, A. (2000). Does preschool training of phonological awareness promote the development of reading and spelling in school? Poster presented at the meeting of the Society for the Scientific Study of Reading, Stockholm, July 22, 2000.

Liberman, I.Y., Shankweiler, D., Fisher, F.W. and Carter, B. (1974). Explicit syllable and phoneme segmentation in the young child. *Journal of Experimental Child Psychology* **18**: 201-212.

Lindamood, C.H. and Lindamood, P.C. (1984). *Auditory Discrimination in Depth*. Austin, TX: PRO-ED, Inc.

Lundberg, I. (1994). Reading difficulties can be predicted and prevented: A Scandinavian perspective on phonological awareness and reading. In: Hulme, C. and Snowling, M. (eds), *Reading Development and Dyslexia*. London: Whurr, pp. 180-199.

Lundberg, I. (1999). Learning to read in Scandinavia. In Harris, M., Hatano, G. et al. (eds), *Learning to Read and Write: A cross-linguistic perspective*. New York: Cambridge University Press, pp. 157-172.

Lundberg, I., Frost, J. and Peterson, O. (1988). Effects of an extensive program for stimulating phonological awareness. *Reading Research Quarterly* **23**: 263-84.

Lundberg, I., Olofsson, A. and Wall, S. (1980). Reading and spelling skills in the first school years predicted from phonemic awareness skills in kindergarten. *Scandinavian Journal of Psychology* **21**: 159-173.

Morais, J., Cary, L., Alegria, J. and Bertelson, P. (1979). Does awareness of speech as a sequence of phonemes arise spontaneously? *Cognition* **7**: 323-331.

National Reading Panel (2000). Teaching children to read: An evidence-based assessment of the scientific research literature and its implications for reading instruction. Available at: www.Nationalreadingpanel.org/Publications/publications.htm

Nittrouer, S. (1999). Do temporal processing deficits cause phonological processing problems? *Journal of Speech, Hearing, and Language Research* **42**: 925-942.

Olson, R.K. and Datta, H. (2002). Visual-temporal processing in reading-disabled and normal twins. *Reading and Writing* **15**: 127-149.

Olson, R.K., Forsberg, H. and Wise, B. (1994). Genes, environment, and the development of orthographic skills. In: Berninger, V.W. (ed.), *The Varieties of Orthographic Knowledge I: Theoretical and developmental issues*. Dordrecht, The Netherlands: Kluwer Academic Publishers, pp. 27-71.

Olson, R.K., Wise, B., Conners, F., Rack, J. and Fulker, D. (1989). Specific deficits in component reading and language skills: Genetic and environmental influences. *Journal of Learning Disabilities* **22**: 339-348.

Olson, R.K., Wise, B.W., Ring, J. and Johnson, M. (1997). Computer-based remedial training in phoneme awareness and phonological decoding: Effects on the post-training development on word recognition. *Scientific Studies of Reading* **1**: 235-253.

Palincsar, A.S. and Brown, A.L. (1984). Reciprocal teaching of comprehension-fostering and comprehension-monitoring activity. *Cognition and Instruction* **2**: 117-175.

Rack, J.P., Snowling, M.J. and Olson, R.K. (1992). The nonword reading deficit in developmental dyslexia: A review. *Reading Research Quarterly* **27**: 28-53.

Share, D.L. (1995). Phonological recoding and self-teaching: Sine qua non of reading acquisition. *Cognition* **55**: 151-218.

Scarborough, H.S. (2001). Connecting early language and literacy to later reading (Dis) Abilities: Evidence, theory, and practice. In: Neuman, S. and Dickinson, D. (eds), *Handbook for Early Literacy Research*. New York: Guilford Press, pp. 97-110.

Schneider, W., Roth, E. and Ennemoser, M. (2000). Training phonological skills and letter knowledge in children at risk for dyslexia: A comparison of three kindergarten intervention programs. *Journal of Educational Psychology* **92**: 284-295.

Schneider, W., Kuspert, P. M., Roth, E., Vise, E. and Marx, H. (1997). Short and long term effects of training phonological awareness in kindergarten: Evidence from two German studies. *Journal of Experimental Child Psychology* **66**: 311-340.

Schneider, W., Emmroser, M., Roth, E. and Kuspert, P. (1999). Kindergarten prevention of dyslexia: Does training in phonological awareness work for everybody? *Journal of Learning Disabilities* **32**, 429-436.

Snow, C.E., Burns, M.S. and Griffin, P. (1998). *Preventing Reading Difficulties in Young Children*. Washington, DC: National Academy Press.

Smith, S.D., Willcutt, E., Pennington, B.F. et al. (2001). Investigations of the comorbidity of dyslexia and ADHD through linkage analyses. Presentation at the meeting of the British Dyslexia Association, York, April 18.

Spector, J.E. (1992). Predicting progress in beginning reading: Dynamic assessment of phoneme awareness. *Journal of Educational Psychology* **84**: 353-363.

Tallal, P. (2000). Experimental studies of language learning impairments: From research to remediation. In: Bishop, D.V.M. and Lawrence, B. (eds), *Speech and Language Impairments in Children: Causes, characteristics, intervention, and outcome*. Philadelphia, PA: Psychology Press/Taylor & Francis, pp. 131-155.

Torgesen, J.K. (2000). Follow-up results from successful early interventions. Presentation at the meeting of the International Dyslexia Association, Washington DC, November 8.

Torgesen, J.K., Wagner, R.K., Rashotte, C.A., Rose, E., Lindamood, P. and Conway, T. (1999). Preventing reading failure in young children with phonological processing disabilities: Group and individual responses to instruction. *Journal of Educational Psychology* **91**: 579-593.

Torgesen, J.K., Alexander, A.W., Wagner, R.K., Voeller, K., Conway, T. and Rose, E. (2001). Intensive remedial instruction for children with severe reading disabilities: Immediate and long-term outcomes from two instructional approaches. *Journal of Learning Disabilities* **34**: 33-58.

Waber, D.P., Weiler, M.D., Wolff, P.H. et al. (2001). Processing of rapid auditory stimuli in school-age children referred for evaluation of learning disorders. *Child Development* **72**: 37-49.

Wagner, R.K. and Torgesen, J.K. (1987). The nature of phonological processing and its causal role in the acquisition of reading skills. *Psychological Bulletin* **101**: 192-212.

Wesseling, R. and Reitsma, P. (2000). The transient role of explicit phonological recoding for reading acquisition. *Reading and Writing: An Interdisciplinary Journal* **13**: 313-336.

Willcutt, E.G., Pennington, B.F., Smith, S.D., Cardon, L.R., Gayán, J., Knopik, V.S., Olson, R.D. and De Fries, J.C. (2001). Quantitative trait locus for reading disability on chromosome 6p is pleiotropic for attention-deficit/hyperactivity disorder. *American Journal of Medical Genetics (Neuropsychiatric Genetics)* **114**: 260-268.

Wise, B.W., Ring, J. and Olson, R.K. (1999). Training phonological awareness with and without attention to articulation. *Journal of Experimental Child Psychology* **72**: 271–304.

Wise, B.W., Ring, J. and Olson, R.K. (2000). Individual differences in gains from computer-assisted remedial reading with more emphasis on phonological analysis or accurate reading in context. *Journal of Experimental Child Psychology* **77**: 197–235.

Wolf, M. (2001). Dyslexia, fluency, and intervention. Presentation at the meeting of the British Dyslexia Association, York, April 18.

CHAPTER 9

The reading rate deficit of German dyslexic children and surface dyslexia

HEINZ WIMMER AND HEINZ MAYRINGER

Dyslexia and orthography

There is a profound difference between what is understood as dyslexia in English-speaking countries and what is understood in countries with more regular orthographies, such as Germany – at least when it comes to diagnosis using reading tests. In the English-speaking world a dyslexic child is unable to read correctly many of the words that are read correctly by his or her peers. This is typically ascertained by graded word-reading tests. How long it takes the child to read a word correctly does not matter (Compton and Carlisle, 1994). In contrast, the typical German dyslexic child can read correctly more or less any German word, but does so in a slow, laborious manner (Klicpera and Schabmann, 1993; Wimmer, 1993). As a result of this, all everyday reading activities become a major burden. Obviously reading tests have to take into account reading time. In short, the English diagnosis of developmental dyslexia is based on impaired reading accuracy, whereas the diagnosis of dyslexia in more regular orthographies is based primarily on impaired reading speed.

How can the slow, but accurate, reading of German dyslexic children be explained in terms of proximal reading mechanisms? One possibility is that they are mainly suffering from surface dyslexia, which means that they have to rely on the slow, indirect sublexical route (mainly grapheme–phoneme coding), because of an impairment of the fast, direct lexical reading route. The latter requires orthographic memory representations of words. This explanation is based on the dual route model of visual word recognition that has influenced recent English-based attempts to subtype dyslexic children (Castles and Coltheart, 1993; Manis et al., 1996; Stanovich, Siegel and Gottardo, 1997).

An alternative explanation would follow from the assumption that a regular orthography such as German exerts little pressure to establish a lexical route for visual word recognition because the sublexical route reliably leads to correct recognition (e.g. Frost, 1998). Therefore, normal readers in the same way as dyslexic readers rely predominantly on the sublexical route. The difference between normal and dyslexic readers has simply to do with the speed of sublexical word processing. High sublexical speed may result from several components of sublexical visual word processing. It may be gained by fast activation of the phonemes associated with the graphemes of a given word, specifically when several graphemes are transformed in parallel (and not sequentially) into corresponding phonemes. Further speed may be gained by fast activation of appropriate phonological word representations or larger phonological segments of words (such as frequent syllables or rhymes).

The present study explored these different interpretations of the reading rate deficit of German dyslexic children in the following way. From a large sample of German-speaking children, who were tested at the beginning of the fourth year in school, we selected children in the lowest quartile on reading rate based on a combination of text and word list reading. The reading rate problem of these children was then related to impairments of the sublexical route (rate of non-word reading) and of the lexical route (foreign word reading and orthographic spelling). We first examined how impairments of the two routes allow discrimination between children with a reading rate problem and children without such a problem. We then explored within the rate-disabled group the occurrence of cases with single route impairments. The third question was whether and how any impairments of the two reading routes are related to verbal deficits which were assessed for the present sample at the beginning of school.

Studies

The slow readers of the present study came from a longitudinally traced sample of 296 German-speaking children who had already been tested at the beginning of grade 1 for precursors of reading difficulties. The present selection was based on the reading assessment of the whole sample in the early months of grade 4 (October and November). For the present purpose, we selected all children ($n = 73$) in the lowest quartile on a rate measure based on reading aloud a short simple story and two lists of compound words. Reading times for the story and each word list were taken separately. The story (57 words) included many high-frequency function words. The compound words of the two lists (11 items each) always joined at least two common morphemes (e.g. *Obststand* – fruitstand, *Selbstbedienung* – self-service). One would expect that a high reading rate for both the story and the two compound word lists would reflect to a major extent reliance on direct lexical word processing (based on memory representations for commonly occurring print words) and that – conversely – a low reading rate would reflect a poor orthographic memory and reliance on slow sublexical processing instead. The correlation between the reading times for each list was $r = 0.92$, the correlation between the combined reading time for the two lists and the text reading time was $r = 0.94$. As combined rate measure for the story and the two lists, Table 9.1 gives a syllable per minute score.

As evident from Table 9.1, the mean reading rate of our disabled group was low, only about half the rate of the rest of the sample. This low mean rate corresponds to a percentile of 11 within the distribution of the whole sample. Table 9.1 also shows that the combined accuracy score for the story and the word lists was close to perfect in our rate-disabled group. Reading refusals did not occur and misreadings tended to be minor deviations from the target (see Wimmer, 1993, for examples). As further evident from Table 9.1, the rate-disabled group was close to identical with the rest of the sample on age and non-verbal IQ, but included more boys.

Table 9.1 also shows the performance of the rate-disabled group for our assessments of sublexical and lexical route impairments. For the sublexical route children had to read aloud two lists (14 items each) of non-words (after a practice list). Time for each list was separately measured ($r = 0.95$). The non-words were intended to be difficult. Each contained two consonant

Table 9.1. Sublexical (non-word reading) and lexical measures (foreign word reading and spelling)

Measure	Rate disabled (n = 73) Mean (SD)	Control (n = 223) Mean (SD)
Text and compound word reading		
Speed (syllables/min)	105.76 (23.16)	189.31 (32.92)
Accuracy (%)	95.54 (4.39)	97.70 (2.50)
Non-word reading		
Speed (syllables/min)	32.84 (9.05)	56.40 (14.64)
Accuracy (%)	73.73 (14.67)	79.88 (13.86)
Foreign word reading (%)	67.53 (21.05)	88.70 (13.08)
Orthographic spelling (%)	60.23 (18.84)	76.89 (14.26)
Descriptive		
Age (months)	123.25 (5;21)	122.02 (4;90)
Non-verbal IQ (Raven)	98.75 (12.93)	101.28 (14.66)
Sex (girls/boys)	31/42	112/111

clusters and vowel graphemes often were digraphs or letters with diacritics (e.g. *Trümorp*). Furthermore, similarity with existing German words was avoided. Reading of these non-words can be seen as a demanding test for the sublexical route. Table 9.1 shows means for the combined score of syllables per minute and the combined accuracy score. For all further analyses we used only the rate score as a measure of sublexical word processing. The reason is that no single reading refusal occurred that might have led to artificially low reading times. Furthermore, nearly all the misreadings were minor deviations which should also have little effect on time. Examples of misreadings were: *Striegen* for *Strien*, *Trümprop* for *Trümorp*, *Strigecks* for *Sprigecks*. Also, there was no indication of a trade-off between accuracy and speed as higher error scores were not accompanied by lower reading times; in fact there was a tendency to the opposite: $r = 0.20$. It is also of relevance that – as evident from Table 9.1 – the non-word rate deficit of our rate-disabled group was much larger than the accuracy deficit.

Our assessment of lexical route deficits was based on two separate measures. One was reading aloud a list of 20 foreign, mostly English, words (e.g. *Clown*, *Cheeseburger*, *Walkman*). Children were instructed about the nature of these words and a list with examples was given before the test list. Instruction did not stress speed and reading time was not measured, because a pre-test showed quite a number of refusals. As shown by the examples, we selected words that are salient in a child's print environment, but it is equally important that the selected foreign words did not allow a correct pronunciation by sole reliance on German grapheme–phoneme correspondences. Therefore, correct reading can be assumed to depend on a representation of the print word in memory. Actually, as expected, about half of all misreadings were non-words resulting from misapplied German grapheme–phoneme rules (e.g. *Gameboy* read with a sounded letter e). As second lexical route assessment we used children's performance on a classroom spelling test with 35 critical words. The words were selected in such a way that simple phoneme–grapheme transcoding would not reliably result in the correct spelling. This is quite possible, because German is more regular in the reading direction than in the spelling direction. The orthographically correct spellings, therefore, reflect, in a direct way, the quality of the orthographic lexicon, which can be assumed also to be involved in the lexical processing in word recognition. Table 9.1 shows that on both lexical route measures the rate-disabled group scored lower than the control children.

Results

The first question posed at the start of the chapter was how impairments of the sublexical and the lexical route discriminate between children with a reading rate problem and children with no such problem. Some information on this question is provided by the finding that the sublexical route differences (non-word reading time) were more substantially associated with reading rate differences ($r = 0.77$), than lexical route differences ($r = 0.62$ [foreign word reading] and 0.59 [orthographic spelling]). More informative for the discrimination question is Table 9.2, which shows the percentages of rate-disabled and non-rate-disabled children below certain cut-off points for the two routes. For this analysis, the scores were converted to standard scores, with 0 as mean and 1 as standard deviation (based on the total sample of 296 children), and the two lexical measures were combined into a single one (correlation between the two was 0.61). Of particular interest for the question are the percentages of rate-disabled and non-rate-disabled children who scored below –0.5 (half a standard deviation below the total mean) or –1 (a full standard deviation below the mean) on lexical processing or on sublexical processing.

Table 9.2 shows that for these cut-off points, sublexical impairments discriminate better than lexical impairments between rate-disabled and non-rate-disabled children. The –0.5 cut-off for sublexical impairment correctly identifies close to 90% of the rate-disabled group and misidentifies only about 15% of the non-rate-disabled group. In contrast, the same cut-off for lexical impairment identifies only about 60% of the rate-disabled group. The cut-off at –1 also results in a substantial discriminatory advantage of the sublexical impairment over the lexical impairment. Only at lower cut-off points does the sublexical advantage vanish. It is evident that an impaired lexical route impairment cannot be a main cause of a reading rate impairment from the impressive finding that about a quarter of the rate-disabled children exhibited *above*-average lexical route performance (> 0 in Table 9.2).

The next question to examine is the relationship between sublexical and lexical impairments within the rate-disabled group. This question is not fully

Table 9.2. Cumulative percentages of rate-disabled children for different lower-end ranges on lexical processing and sublexical processing

Cut-off z score	Lexical processing		Sublexical processing	
	Rate disabled	Control	Rate disabled	Control
–2.0	15.1	1.3	4.1	0.0
–1.5	34.2	3.6	19.2	0.9
–1.0	43.8	6.7	57.5	5.8
–0.5	60.3	13.0	86.3	17.5
0.0	74.0	27.8	98.6	36.3

answered by the discriminatory advantage of sublexical impairments over lexical impairments. We used two cut-off z-scores for route impairment: -0.5 for selecting children with a route impairment that is at least mild and -1 for selecting children with a more severe impairment. The upper section of Table 9.3 shows the number of children for the resulting four combinations of route impairments. The important finding is the low number of rate-disabled children who exhibit a single lexical route impairment and the much higher number of children who exhibit a single sublexical route impairment. This was particularly the case for the subgroups resulting from the -0.5 cut-off (first row) with only eight children in the single lexical impairment subgroup, but 25 in the single sublexical impairment subgroup.

The lower section of Table 9.3 is relevant for the question of whether specific verbal deficits were associated with the different impairment patterns. The verbal measures shown in Table 9.3 were gathered in an individual testing session as part of the longitudinal study in the first 2 months after school entry. The vocabulary task elicited 39 words (minimally with three syllables, e.g. *elephant* or *astronaut*) by pictures or verbal descriptions. The phonological segmentation task required children to imitate the segmentation of 12 words modelled by the experimenter, e.g. the experimenter provided a segmentation of the type 'cat - /k/-/a/-/t/', and the child simply had to repeat the word and its segments. In the rapid automatized naming (RAN) task children had to name a random sequence (eight lines with four items each) of four repeatedly presented pictures. The time for naming the total sequence was measured. A full description of the phono-

Table 9.3. Number of rate-disabled children with different route impairment patterns (upper section) and means (SD) of verbal deficits for the subgroups with severe impairments

	Impairment pattern			
	No impairment	Single lexical	Single sublexical	Double impairment
Route impairments				
Mild (-0.5 cut-off)	4	6	25	38
Severe (-1 cut-off)	23	8	18	24
Verbal deficits (z-scores)				
Vocabulary	-0.19 (1.10)	-0.73* (0.80)	0.10 (0.71)	-0.87*** (1.09)
Phonological segmentation	-0.06 (0.97)	-0.80** (0.58)	0.13 (0.87)	-0.83*** (0.68)
Rapid naming	-0.39* (0.81)	-0.39* (0.46)	-0.63** (0.86)	-0.69*** (0.89)

$*p < 0.05$. $**p < 0.01$. $***p < 0.001$ one-tailed according to one-sample t-test for test value 0.

logical segmentation task and of the RAN task is given in Wimmer, Mayringer and Landerl (2000, Experiment 2). The means (z-scores) for the four subgroups resulting from the severe impairment classification are given in Table 9.3. As evident, phonological deficits (vocabulary and phonological segmentation) were limited to the subgroups with a lexical route impairment (single lexical and double impairment). A rapid naming deficit was shown mainly by the subgroups with a sublexical route impairment (single sublexical and double impairment), but in a mild form also by the two other subgroups. We should note in addition that the double impairment subgroup was the only one with a lower mean for non-verbal intelligence.

Conclusion

The overall pattern of results speaks against the general characterisation of the reading rate problem of German dyslexic children as surface dyslexia, i.e. that the rate-disabled children have to rely on the slow, indirect sublexical route, because of an impairment of the fast lexical route. The main evidence for this negative conclusion is that about 40% of the rate-disabled group showed lexical performance in the average range (above –0.5) and about 25% of the rate-disabled group showed even above-average lexical performance. Furthermore, only few children within the rate-disabled sample exhibited a single lexical impairment.

In contrast, the overall pattern of results speaks for the alternative interpretation that the difference between rate-disabled readers and normal readers has mainly to do with sublexical speed differences. For the whole sample, there was a higher correlation between reading rate and sublexical differences than between reading rate and lexical differences. More importantly, close to 90% of the rate-disabled sample exhibited a sublexical impairment that was at least mild (–0.5 criterion), but only about 60% exhibited such a lexical impairment. This primacy of sublexical differences is plausible under the assumption of a mandatory prelexical phase of phonological assembly in visual word recognition (e.g. Frost, 1998). It seems that the reading rate deficit of our rate-disabled children resulted mainly from this prelexical phonological assembly phase of word recognition. This interpretation is similar to one advanced in a previous publication (Wimmer, 1993), where German dyslexia was characterised as phonological speed dyslexia.

The presently found primacy of a sublexical speed impairment among German dyslexic children concurs at a general level with English-based subtyping studies which found a higher prevalence and a higher stability of the phonological dyslexic subtype than of the surface dyslexic subtype (Castles and Coltheart, 1993; Manis et al., 1996; Stanovich et al., 1997). However, there are important methodological differences as, for example, the English-based studies used impaired accuracy of non-word reading instead of impaired speed, as used in the present study. The present primacy of sublexical route impairments also concurs with the results of subtyping studies carried out with Spanish dyslexic children (Jiménez, 2000) and French dyslexic children (Sprenger-Charolles et al., 2000). These studies, as the present one, were based mainly on reading rate measures. This seems to be critical because a further French subtyping study based on reading accuracy led to a primacy of lexical route impairments (Genard et al., 1998).

A second main finding of the present study is that the different (dual-route-based) impairment patterns of our reading rate-disabled children were associated with different verbal deficit. The early vocabulary and phonological sensitivity deficits were clearly limited to the subgroups with a lexical impairment and did not extend to the subgroup with a single sublexical speed impairment. The latter subgroup showed an early rapid naming deficit only. This pattern was also found in prospective longitudinal studies from the authors' laboratory (Wimmer, Mayringer and Landerl, 2000) and is consistent with basic assumptions of the double deficit hypothesis of dyslexia proposed by Wolf and Bowers (1999). The phonological deficits of the lexical impairment groups is remarkable because it speaks against the position that orthographic memory entries are purely visual patterns. On the contrary, it suggests that multiple redundant associations to phonological entries play an important role in setting up orthographic memories (Ehri, 1992; Perfetti, 1992).

The early rapid naming deficit of the single sublexical impairment group is also important. It shows that slow access to phonology is already present before learning to read. Furthermore, it speaks of a general impairment in accessing phonology from visual stimuli. In the case of sublexical visual word recognition, the impaired access affects the phonemes associated with the letters. In the case of naming, the impaired access affects whole words associated with pictures. Recently, we found that the visual naming speed deficit apparently could not be reduced to slow visual processing (Wimmer and Mayringer, 2001). If this latter finding can be replicated and extended, then the conclusion would be that a certain version of the dominant phonological deficit explanation of dyslexia (e.g. Shaywitz, 1996) can be formulated for dyslexic children in more regular orthographies, who suffer primarily from a reading rate problem and not from a reading accuracy problem. This version may not specify the main underlying deficit as a phonological segmentation deficit – as done by the standard version propagated by the Haskins group in the 1970s (see Shankweiler, 1999). It may focus instead on speed deficits in accessing and assembling phonological structures.

Acknowledgement

Financial support for the research reported in this Chapter was provided by the Austrian Research Foundation (Grant No. P12481-SOZ).

References

Castles, A. and Coltheart, M. (1993). Varieties of developmental dyslexia. *Cognition* **47**, 149-180.

Compton, D.L. and Carlisle, J.F. (1994). Speed of word recognition as a distinguishing characteristic of reading disabilities. *Educational Psychology Review* **6**, 115-139.

Ehri, L.C. (1992). Reconceptualizing the development of sight word reading and its relationship to recoding. In: Gough, P.B., Ehri, L.C. and Treiman, R. (eds), *Reading Acquisition*. Hillsdale, NJ: Erlbaum, pp. 107-143.

Frost, R. (1998). Toward a strong phonological theory of visual word recognition: True issues and false trails. *Psychological Bulletin* **123**, 71-99.

Genard, N., Mousty, A., Content, J., Alegria, J., Leybaert, J. and Morais, J. (1998). Methods to establish subtypes of developmental dyslexia. In: Reitsma, P. and Verhoeven, L. (eds), *Problems and Interventions in Literacy Development*. Dordrecht: Kluwer Academic Publishers, pp. 163-176.

Jiménez, J.E (2000, July). Identifying subtypes among Spanish dyslexic children. Paper presented at the 27th International Congress of Psychology, Stockholm, Sweden.

Klicpera, C. and Schabmann, A. (1993). Do German-speaking children have a chance to overcome reading and spelling difficulties? A longitudinal survey from the second until the eighth grade. *European Journal of Psychology of Education* **8**, 307-323.

Manis, F.R., Seidenberg, M.S., Doi, L.M., McBride-Chang, C. and Petersen, A. (1996). On the basis of two subtypes of development dyslexia. *Cognition* **58**, 157-195.

Perfetti, C.A. (1992). The representation problem in reading acquisition. In: Gough, P.B., Ehri, L.C. and Treiman, R. (eds), *Reading Acquisition*. Hillsdale, NJ: Erlbaum, pp. 145-174.

Shankweiler, D. (1999). Words to meanings. *Scientific Studies of Reading* **3**: 113-127.

Shaywitz, S.E. (1996). Dyslexia. *Scientific American* **275**(5): 98-104.

Sprenger-Charolles, L., Colé, P., Serniclaes, W. and Lacert, P. (2000). On subtypes of developmental dyslexia: Evidence from processing time and accuracy scores. *Canadian Journal of Experimental Psychology* (Special Issue: Early literacy and early numeracy) **54**: 87-104.

Stanovich, K.E., Siegel, L.S. and Gottardo, A. (1997). Converging evidence for phonological and surface subtypes of reading disability. *Journal of Educational Psychology* **89**, 114-127.

Wimmer, H. (1993). Characteristics of developmental dyslexia in a regular writing system. *Applied Psycholinguistics* **14**, 1-33.

Wimmer, H. and Mayringer, H. (2001). Is the reading-rate problem of German dyslexic children caused by slow visual processes? In: Wolf, M. (ed.), *Dyslexia, Fluency and the Brain*. Timonium, MD: York Press.

Wimmer, H., Mayringer, H. and Landerl, K. (2000). The double-deficit hypothesis and difficulties in learning to read a regular orthography. *Journal of Educational Psychology* **92**: 668-680.

CHAPTER 10

Phonological processing in learning to read Chinese: in search of a framework

CHE KAN LEONG AND LI HAI TAN

There is now considerable evidence that phonological information processing skills, such as phonological awareness of sublexical units of phonemes, onsets and rimes, phonological memory and verbal information processing speed, are critical to learning to read alphabetic writing systems (Wagner and Torgesen, 1987; Adams, 1990; Goswami and Bryant, 1990; Høien et al., 1995; Share, 1995; Wagner et al., 1997). In this chapter we use the term 'phonological' to refer to the explicit awareness of the phonology of sublexical units, including suprasegmental elements of tones that have special significance in reading Chinese. We report two studies to examine the effects of phonological processing on reading Chinese words in Chinese children who speak Pu[3]tong[1]hua[4],[1] together with the effects of these tasks on reading English words by the same children as a comparison.

One important theoretical and practical question is: can a single theoretical framework explain the connection of phonological processing, reading development and dyslexia in different (alphabetic) writing systems? This was the question raised by Goswami (1999). She proposed that at least three kinds of evidence are needed to answer this question. One is the sequence of phonological development; the second is the nature of the phonological units predicting reading development in different linguistic environments; and the third is the phonological representation modulated by the transparency (shallowness) or opacity (depth) of the orthography (Frost and Katz, 1992). She further argues that making explicit the implicit phonological knowledge (epi-language) helps beginning readers and dyslexic readers to identify and produce different phonological units, and this 'phonological

---

[1] The numbers [1], [2], [3] and [4] inserted immediately after the main vowels of appropriate Chinese terms or names denote the first, second, third and fourth tones respectively in Pu[3] tong[1]hua[4] or Mandarin Chinese.

representations' hypothesis provides a unifying cognitive framework to explain reading development and dyslexia (Goswami, 2000). The present chapter is motivated by these proposals and related cumulative studies. We attempt to address the questions of the nature of phonological processing and the phonological units that are important in learning to read Chinese words, which are mainly meaning based but which also involve phonology as a constituent (Leong, 1997, 1999).

Phonological processing and Chinese word reading

There are many reasons for studying phonological processing and reading in Chinese. One reason is that, for any theory or model of reading to be fully explanatory, it should show the basic mechanisms common to writing systems and also specific to these systems. The other reason is that, as a morphosyllabic writing system (DeFrancis, 1989), Chinese has certain psycholinguistic characteristics, which differ from those of alphabetic writing systems. Each graphic symbol or character in Chinese is equivalent to the English syllable and occupies the same geometric space or GEON (see Leong, 1999). A word in Chinese consists predominantly of a combination of two characters and sometimes three or even four characters. As a result of the identical square-shaped configurations of the characters, certain information-processing features such as word length do not affect accurate and speedy identification of Chinese characters and words.

What is more important is that Chinese characters and words are mainly based on meaning, although in the evolution of the writing system there is considerable involvement of phonology. Leong (1997) has discussed three kinds of evidence to show the morphosyllabic nature in processing Chinese. One line of evidence is linguistic to explain the syllabic nature of Chinese, the other is psycholinguistic from studies of the 'slip of the tongue' phenomenon and the third is psychological. The third kind of evidence comes from a series of experimental studies with adult Chinese readers using different experimental techniques such as backward and forward masking and tongue twisters (Perfetti and Zhang, 1991, 1995; Perfetti, Zhang and Berent, 1992; Tan and Perfetti, 1998, 1999). Perfetti and his colleagues show that phonological processing is robust and activated rapidly and early in both single-character and two-character Chinese word identification. They also suggest that, as a constituent in visual word identification, phonological activation in Chinese has some unique features relative to English and other alphabetic writing systems.

The above important works in validating the 'universal phonological principle', proposed by Perfetti (Perfetti and Zhang, 1991, 1995), have been carried out under stringent experimental conditions and with adult Chinese readers. They all deal with phonological activation, rather than with phonological awareness in relation to reading development. What role does phonology play in Chinese children learning to read Chinese? What is the nature of this processing and what are the phonological units in making explicit what the children know implicitly from their speech? In addition, Chinese characters are visually complex and their accurate and rapid identification are likely also to entail a phonological to orthographic constituent and verbal memory, compared with the alphabetic English. These are some of the questions we attempt to answer. Next we turn to a succinct review of the relevant literature on phonological awareness pertaining to Chinese children.

Phonological awareness and learning to read Chinese

Much of the recent research on Chinese children's phonological awareness and reading is predicated on the prototypical study of Read et al. (1986), which is based on the logic of the Brussels group of Morais and Bertelson (Morais et al., 1979, 1986). The finding of Read et al. that there is a performance difference in a phoneme deletion or addition task of real and pseudo-English words by Chinese literate adults in Beijing, whether or not exposed to the Chinese phonetic or pin[1]yin[1] transliteration system, is generally replicated and refined in recent studies with Chinese children (Huang and Hanley, 1995; Hu and Catts, 1998; Hanley, Tzeng and Huang, 1999; Tao and Peng, 1999; McBride-Chang and Ho, 2000).

Huang and Hanley (1995) studied the effects of phonological awareness (rhyming and alliteration) of spoken words (the same tone for the Chinese items), English and Chinese phoneme deletion tasks, and visual skills (discrimination and pair associates) on the reading ability of 137 8-year-old primary school children in Taiwan, Hong Kong and the UK. One main result is that, when general ability and vocabulary were partialled out, the performance of the Chinese children on the phonological tasks did not relate significantly to their reading. Another main finding is that the performance of the Taiwanese children, who use a set of phonetic transcription symbols similar to pin[1]yin[1] and known as zhu[4]yin[1] fu[3]hao[4], was 'reminiscent' of the results of Read et al. (1986). The first finding of the role of the visual form of a word, more than phonological involvement, in reading Chinese was noted by Hanley, Tzeng and Huang (1999) as supporting the results of Ho and Bryant (1997), who found visual–perceptual skills in pre-school Hong Kong children predicting their first year reading. The second finding was taken to mean that awareness of phonetic symbols associated with the alphabetic English language facilitates phonemic awareness. Huang and Hanley (1995) and Hanley, Tzeng and Huang (1999, p. 191) suggest that learning the principle of an alphabetic script, as is the practice with beginning readers from Taiwan or from China, 'appears to exert an enormous effect on the subsequent reading behaviour and phonological awareness skills of Chinese children'.

Hu and Catts (1998) studied the reading performance of 50 Taiwanese first graders with measures of phonological awareness (phonetic contrasts of initial consonants and rimes with tones crossed orthogonally), phonological memory (repetition of bisyllabic pseudo-words spoken by the examiner), phonological retrieval (rapid automated naming of pictures of coloured animals) and visual memory of random visual shapes. Differing from the results of Huang and Hanley (1995), Hu and Catts did not find a contribution from their visual memory task to the variance of the children's reading of Chinese characters in their regression analyses, after adjusting for differences in reading familiar words printed in phonetic symbols. However, Hu and Catts found 'unique contributions' of phonological retrieval to reading familiar Chinese characters and of phonological awareness and phonological memory to reading less familiar words. These authors concluded that 'phono-logical processing skills and early reading ability is not specific to reading an alphabetic orthography' and that 'regardless of the particular structure of a language's orthography, phonological processing is intrinsic to children's reading acquisition' (Hu and Catts, 1998, p. 75).

More recently, McBride-Chang and Ho (2000) studied the phonological awareness (syllable or character deletion of two- or three-character Chinese words), speech perception and Chinese character recognition in 109 Hong Kong 3- and 4-year-old children. They found that syllable deletion and letter naming of the English alphabet contribute unique variance to character recog-nition, and that their reading or reading-related measures explained about 50% of the variation. This also begs the question of additional skills that should be considered, as the authors acknowledge. Tao and Peng (1999) studied the performance of a small number of grade 3, 4 and 5 'good' and 'poor' students in Beijing in several phonological processing tasks (judgement of speech–sound similarity, rhyme similarity and phoneme deletion, such as deleting the vowel glide /i/ from the rime part of the syllable /liang/). They found a progression of difficulty from the larger units of speech sounds as wholes through onsets and rimes, to the smaller units of phonemes, and there were significant differences between grades 3 and 5 and the good and poor readers.

Phonological processing as a constituent in Chinese word reading

In the succinct but fairly representative review of literature on phonological processing and reading development in Chinese, it is clear that there are two broad constructs with clusters of interrelated tasks to substantiate them. One cluster of tasks is associated with phonological awareness and generally requires the child to identify and manipulate phonological segments of different sizes within individual words such as syllables, intrasyllabic units of onsets, and rimes and phonemes. The other cluster of tasks is associated with verbal working memory, which requires the child to maintain and repeat phonological information in ordered sequence. These constructs and the tasks (with some variations) are based on sound theoretical grounds (e.g. Wagner and Torgesen, 1987) and have been found to be efficacious for caucasian people learning English.

For Chinese, one major issue is to clarify the nature of phonology as a constituent of Chinese word reading and the activation of the phonological form in representing meaning (Perfetti, 1998). In a critical examination of the manipulation of speech sounds as a precursor for reading Chinese, Leong (1997) argues forcefully that the analysis of Chinese speech sounds is paradigmatic, rather than segmental. The paradigmatic process is explained in terms of analogies made between members of a set of utterances sharing similar speech characteristics of rimes such as in *beak–peak* (Mattingly, 1987; Spencer, 1991). In terms of onset the analogy is with the English [dz] (*jar*), which is treated as a single segment rather than a succession of speech sounds. Leong further invokes linguists of the persuasion of Yuen Ren Chao (1968), Li Wang (1985) and Michael Halliday (1981) to buttress his argument for paradigmatic rather than segmental analysis in Chinese phonology. Halliday (1981) makes this clear: 'The phonology [for Chinese] remained a phonology of the syllable, always analyzed into initial [onset] and final [rime]' (p. 137, words in brackets added). Given this theoretical position of paradigmatic analysis as articulated by linguists and psycholinguistics, phoneme deletion for Chinese may be too fine grained and not readily grasped by beginning readers. Instead of asking children to delete phonemes, the analogous process should be deleting initials (onsets) and finals (rimes). A good example of paradigmaticity of Chinese phonology is shown as a succession of syllables such that the word *taxi* in Cantonese is segmented as /tek[1]-si[1]/, rather than /t/-/ae/-/k/-/s/-/i/ and *bus* as /ba[1]-shi[1]/.

There is another important linguistic feature in Chinese not shared by English. This is the suprasegmental element of tones, which represent a level of organisation above the segmental level. Tones in Chinese are defined in terms of the rhythmic rise and fall of pitch, or the pitch contour of the voiced part of the character, such that, if the initial is voiced, the tone begins with the initial and spreads over the whole syllable and, if the initial is voiceless, the tone is spread over the final only. Tones may also be differentiated by the timing of their rhythmic movements within a syllable (Shen and Lin, 1991). The four tones in Pu[3]tong[1]hua[4] are: ping[1] (*level* or *even*), shang[2] (*rising*), qu[3] (*going* or *departing*) and ru[4] (*entering*). It is noteworthy that some of the studies have included variations of tones in their research into phonological processing and Chinese word reading (e.g. Hu and Catts, 1998; McBride-Chang and Ho, 2000).

Two studies to test phonological processing and Chinese word reading

With the above theoretical position as background, we report two studies on phonological processing and Chinese word reading, carried out with one group of grade 4 and 5 students who speak Pu[3]tong[1]hua[4] in Beijing in May 1999, and another group of 180 grade 3, 4 and 5 Beijing students in May 2000. We predicated our investigation on the principle of paradigmatic analysis of Chinese within the broader context of integrating shape, speech sound and meaning in Chinese word reading. The broad aim was to explore the effect of phonological processing tasks (deletion of onsets and rimes, speech–sound repetition with tones crossed orthogonally, tongue twister repetition and working memory) on these children's reading of pseudo-words in Chinese and pseudo-words in English as surrogates of reading in these two writing systems.

There were two specific hypotheses covering the common and specific aspects of explicit speech analyses in relation to reading. The first hypothesis was that the reading of Chinese pseudo-words would be better predicted by the ability to repeat Chinese speech sounds with the same or different tones and the same or different onsets and rimes and related memory tasks, and less by deletion of onsets and rimes. The second hypothesis was that the reading of English pseudo-words would be better predicted by deletion of onsets and rimes (both Chinese and English), given that English is taught in Beijing schools only from grade 4 onward and with no training in phonemic awareness. A corollary of hypothesis 1 was that the children would perform better in repeating speech–sound segments with the same rime crossed with the same or different tones in their speech–sound repetition. As well, we were also interested in the performance of phonological processing tasks in different elementary grades.

The first hypothesis emphasising processing at the syllabic (morphemic) level was based on the character superiority effect (Sue and Liu, 1996) and the notion of 'constituency' that the activation of characters constituting words includes phonology, which serves an early cueing function in word identification (Tan and Perfetti, 1998). The second hypothesis stressing speech perception at the subsyllabic level of onsets and rimes was based on the 'large-unit-first' approach (Goswami and Bryant, 1990) in which Chinese children who begin to learn English in grade 4 would use analogies of onsets and rime more than the small units of phonemes. The corollary linked tonal features as part of phonological representation in distinguishing Chinese morphemes (Xu, 1991).

Study 1

The aim of study 1 was to explore the effects of some phonological processing tasks on Chinese word reading with English word reading as a comparison.

Participants

Participants consisted of 32 grade 4 students (19 boys and 13 girls) with a mean chronological age of 124.1 months and a standard deviation of 6.41 months, and 38 grade 5 students (16 boys and 22 girls) with a mean age of 133.1 months and a standard deviation of 4.43 months. These students all came from an 'average' elementary school in Beijing in terms of its location and the educational levels of the parents. Grades 4 and 5 were chosen because in Beijing English is taught only from grade 4 onward, and the inclusion of English reading would provide a foil to Chinese word reading.

Materials

The materials consisted of these specially designed tasks: Chinese pseudo-word reading, English pseudo-word reading, final or rime deletion, initial or onset deletion and speech–sound repetition. The Chinese pseudo-word reading task consisted of 72 two-character items with the characters all selected from the textbooks used for the grades. Each of the two characters comprising the pseudo-word was a real character but not in combination. The English pseudo-word reading task consisted of 67 three-, four-, five- and six-letter pronounceable non-words. For each of the deletion tasks 10 items were Chinese characters/words and 10 were English words (e.g. /t-ian/, /b-est/ for onset deletion and /m-ian/, /h-ide/ for rime deletion). For the speech–sound repetition task there were 20 sets of items with three conditions and four sound segments each: same onset, same rime and no segment all with same or different tones (one of the four sounds being a filler item to minimise ceiling and floor effects). Sample items of the tasks used are shown in the Figure 10.1. These tasks had all been tried out first on a small number of Beijing children and were found to be of suitable interest and level of difficulty.

Procedure

The reading and reading-related tasks were administered individually to the 70 children in their school by trained research assistants. The Chinese and English pseudo-word reading tasks were the only reading tasks where the children read from the printed pages. For the rime deletion, onset deletion the children first listened to each word spoken by the experimenters and uttered each speech sound after the appropriate deletion. For the

Chinese Pseudoword Reading (72 two-character items)

喊健   藏躲   炮喻   寂奔   偎瀑   瞎狹

English Pseudoword Reading (67 items for Grades 4 & 5 only)
orp   lun   stib   klat   slonk   plisk   wumber   biquid

Rime Deletion (10 items in Chinese, 10 in English)
mi   dao   mian   wet   hide   shirt

Onset Deletion (10 items in Chinese, 10 in English)
wo   xia   tian   kit   best   will

Speech-Sound Repetition (3 main condition : same onset, same rime,
no segment, all with same or different tones for total of 30 items)

yan[3]   zhun[3]   ye[3]   you[3]
man[1]   die[4]   chan[2]   zhan[3]
jian[4]   zong[1]   xiu[3]   mu[2]

Tongue Twister (3 sets of 2/3 sentences & 5 sets of 4 sentences)

四是四   si[4] shi[4] si[4]
十是十   shi[2] shi[4] shi[2]
十四是十四   shi[2] si[4] shi[4] shi[2] si[4]
四十是四十   si[4] shi[2] shi[4] si[4] shi[2]

Working Memory (Total of 13 sets of 2-, 3-, 4- & 5-sentences)

太陽射出強烈的光芒   The sun gives out bright light.
幫媽媽做一件難事   I help mom do a hard job.
問題：太陽放出甚麼樣的光芒？   [強烈]
詞語：光芒，難事

Figure 10.1 Sample items from different tasks.

speech–sound repetition task they first listened to the four characters spoken
in the appropriate tone(s) and then repeated them in the correct sequence.
Each task took between 3 and 8 minutes.

Results

The means and standard deviations of the tasks are given in Table 10.1 and
also shown in Figure 10.2. The intercorrelations are shown in Table 10.2.

Table 10.1. Means and standard deviations (in parentheses) for reading and reading-related tasks for grades 4 and 5 Beijing students

Grade	Chinese pseudo-word reading	English pseudo-word reading	Rime deletion	Onset deletion	Speech-sound repetition
4 (n = 32)	82.09 (38.27)	20.88 (14.74)	16.19 (2.99)	12.16 (4.03)	10.81 (2.73)
5 (n = 38)	83.63 (21.43)	30.61 (13.45)	17.26 (2.81)	13.97 (4.33)	11.00 (2.56)

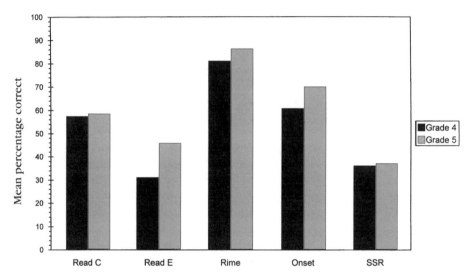

Figure 10.2. Mean percentage correct for reading and reading-related tasks for grade 4 and 5 Beijing students.

Table 10.2. Intercorrelations of reading and reading-related tasks for grades 4 and 5 Beijing students (total n = 70)

	Chinese pseudo-word reading (Read C)	English pseudo-word reading (Read E)	Rime deletion (Rime)	Onset deletion (Onset)	Speech-sound repetition (SSR)
Read C	1.000				
Read E	0.242*	1.000			
Rime	0.194*	0.307**	1.000		
Onset	0.182	0.507**	0.343**	1.000	
SSR	0.369**	0.286**	0.261*	0.222*	1.000

**Significant at 0.01 level; *significant at 0.05 level.

To test the hypotheses that differential phonological processing tasks would affect differentially Chinese pseudo-word reading and English pseudo-word reading, stepwise multiple regression analyses were carried out separately with reading as the criterion and the two deletion tasks and speech–sound repetition as predictors. For Chinese the significant predictor was speech–sound repetition with an R of 0.369 and an R^2 of 0.136 ($F[1, 68] = 10.69$, $p = 0.002$). For English it was onset deletion that was significant with an R of 0.507 and an R^2 of 0.257 ($F[1, 68] = 23.51$, $p = 0.000$) (R denotes multiple regression).

Discussion

Even with the modest multiple regression coefficients there was some evidence that pseudo-word reading in Chinese and pseudo-word reading in English were predicted differentially by different phonological processing tasks. Hypotheses 1 and 2 seem to be generally upheld. However, the very modest contribution to word reading suggests that additional phonological skills may be associated with reading Chinese and also English. A larger sample size would also yield more stable results. Study 2 was undertaken along these lines.

Study 2

Study 2 with expanded phonological processing tasks was undertaken in May 2000 in the same school in Beijing with 60 children in each of grades 3, 4 and 5, for a total of 180 children. The aim was to replicate and extend the first study.

Participants

There were 60 grade 3 children (31 boys and 29 girls) and their mean chronological age was 113.1 months with a standard deviation of 7.53 months, 60 grade 4 children (32 boys and 28 girls) with a mean age of 123.1 months and a standard deviation of 4.31 months, and 60 grade 5 children (34 boys and 26 girls) with a mean age of 135.1 months and a standard deviation of 6.81 months. Grades 4 and 5 were selected for the same reasons as in study 1 and grade 3 was added because this may be a transition grade in which children's reading skills may become more automatic compared with lower grades.

Materials

The same tasks (Chinese pseudo-word reading, English pseudo-word reading, rime deletion, onset deletion, speech–sound repetition) as used in study 1 were refined and used in study 2. For speech–sound repetition 10 more sets were added to make a total of 30 sets of items. Two more phonological and memory tasks shown to relate to word reading were added. One was a

Chinese tongue-twister task with three sets of two or three short sentences and five sets of four short sentences; the other was a verbal working memory task. This Chinese tongue-twister task was based on the logic and the finding (Zhang and Perfetti, 1993, experiment 1) that automatic phonological coding applies to both Chinese and English word reading. The tongue twisters were designed with sets of non-segmental phonemes such as alveolar fricatives (/s/ and /z/), alveolar stops (/t/ and /d/), and bilabial and velar stops (/b/ and /p/; /g/ and /k/). The verbal working memory task consisted of a total of 13 sets of two, three, four and five sentences, all unrelated in meaning and selected from the appropriate textbooks. The verbal working memory task has been shown to be predictive of reading in English (Swanson, 1992). In addition, the Standard Raven's Progressive Matrices Chinese version (Raven, 1987) was administered. Both parents also indicated their level of education (completion of secondary school, university or higher education). Raven's would provide an index of general ability of the students and the parents' educational level might have some bearing on their children's Chinese and/or English word-reading performance.

Procedure

The procedure was similar to that of study 1 with each phonological and memory task taking about 10 minutes. For the tongue-twister task, the child listened to each set of sentences and repeated the characters/words in the correct order with the correct speech sound and tone. For the working memory task, the child listened to each set of semantically unrelated sentences spoken at an even pace by the experimenter. After the oral presentation of each doublet, triplet, quartet and quintet set of sentences, the students were asked to answer one comprehension question and to say the very last word of each of the sentences in that set. The total testing time for all the tasks for each child was about 45 minutes.

Results

The means and standard deviations of the performance on the tasks for the total group of 180 children are given in Table 10.3 and Figure 10.3. As English is not taught until grade 4, Tables 10.4 and 10.5 show, respectively, the intercorrelations of reading and reading-related tasks for grades 3, 4 and 5 and grades 4 and 5, respectively.

Similar to study 1, stepwise multiple regression analyses were carried out separately for Chinese and English pseudo-word reading to test the hypothesis that differential phonological processing tasks would affect such performance. These predictor variables were used to predict Chinese pseudo-word reading: rime deletion, onset deletion, speech–sound repetition, tongue

Table 10.3. Means and standard deviations (in parentheses) for reading and reading-related tasks for grades 3, 4 and 5 Beijing students (n = 180)

Grade	Chinese pseudo-word reading	English pseudo-word reading	Rime deletion	Onset deletion	Speech–sound repetition	Tongue twister	Working memory	Raven's Progressive Matrices
3 (n = 60)	108.75 (21.17)		17.87 (1.85)	12.38 (4.15)	23.45 (4.10)	11.48 (3.27)	22.48 (12.57)	43.07 (9.04)
4 (n = 60)	117.80 (16.79)	20.23 (14.62)	18.28 (1.78)	14.67 (4.04)	25.68 (3.53)	13.08 (3.23)	24.58 (10.27)	44.37 (8.74)
5 (n = 60)	105.90 (28.64)	20.75 (17.51)	17.85 (1.89)	14.17 (4.39)	24.82 (3.44)	12.88 (3.01)	27.27 (10.75)	45.10 (6.62)
Total (n = 180)	110.82 (23.17)	20.49 (16.06)	18.00 (1.84)	13.74 (4.29)	24.65 (3.79)	12.48 (3.23)	24.77 (11.35)	44.18 (8.20)

Table 10.4. Intercorrelations of reading and reading-related tasks for grades 3, 4 and 5 Beijing students (total n = 180)

	Chinese pseudo-word reading (Read C)	Rime deletion (Rime)	Onset deletion (Onset)	Speech–sound repetition (SSR)	Tongue twister (TT)	Working memory (WM)	Raven's Progressive Matrices (Raven)	Chronological age (CA)	Parents' educational level (PEL)
Read C	1.000								
Rime	0.039	1.000							
Onset	0.354**	0.203**	1.000						
SSR	0.427**	-0.021	0.438**	1.000					
TT	0.392**	0.141*	0.410**	0.420**	1.000				
WM	0.377**	0.200**	0.211**	0.345**	0.534**	1.000			
Raven	0.298**	0.072	0.288**	0.303**	0.295**	0.259**	1.000		
CA	-0.098	-0.008	0.062	0.049	0.087	0.181**	0.091	1.000	
PEL	0.230**	0.091	0.193**	0.230**	0.206**	0.156*	0.221**	-0.044	1.000

**Significant at 0.01 level; *significant at 0.05 level.

Table 10.5. Intercorrelations of reading and reading-related tasks for grades 4 and 5 Beijing students (total n = 120)

	Chinese pseudo-word reading (Read E)	Rime deletion (Rime)	Onset deletion (Onset)	Speech-sound repetition (SSR)	Tongue twister (TT)	Working memory (WM)	Raven's Progressive Matrices (Raven)	Chronological age (CA)	Parents' educational level (PEL)
Read E	1.000								
Rime	0.337**	1.000							
Onset	0.472**	0.187*	1.000						
SSR	0.266**	-0.018	0.471**	1.000					
TT	0.282**	0.112	0.404**	0.410**	1.000				
WM	0.315**	0.222**	0.299**	0.316**	0.568**	1.000			
Raven	0.277**	0.105	0.458**	0.318**	0.342**	0.303**	1.000		
CA	-0.010	-0.054	-0.180	-0.181*	-0.144	0.086	-0.012	1.000	
PEL	0.022	-0.048	0.131	0.233**	0.058	0.070	0.103	-0.144	1.000

**Significant at 0.01 level; *significant at 0.05 level.

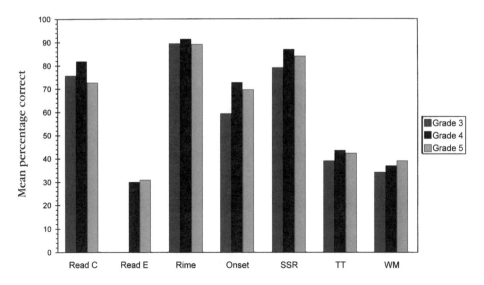

Figure 10.3. Mean percentage correct for reading and reading-related tasks for grade 3, 4 and 5 Beijing students.

twister, verbal working memory, Raven's Progressive Matrices, age and parents' educational level. The speech–sound repetition task was the most predictive with an R of 0.427 and an R^2 of 0.182 ($F[1, 178] = 39.685$, $p = 0.000$). This contribution was followed by verbal working memory with an r change of 0.06, onset deletion with another R change of 0.028 and chronological age with a further R change of 0.029. Thus the total contribution to the variance from speech–sound repetition (18%), working memory (6%), onset deletion (3%) and age (3%) was 30%. In comparison, English pseudo-word reading for the 120 grade 4 and 5 students with the same predictor variables was predicted by onset deletion with an R of 0.472 and R^2 of 0.223 ($F[1, 118] = 33.82$, $p = 0.000$). Rime deletion added another 0.064 to the variation with a total R of 0.536 and an R^2 of 0.287 for a total R^2 of 0.287.

As speech–sound repetition was shown to be the most predictive of Chinese pseudo-word reading this task was further analysed in a 3 (grade) × 3 (condition: same onset, same rime, no segment) ANOVA (analysis of variance) with the last factor repeated. There was a significant between-factor difference for grade ($F[2, 177] = 5.513$, $p = 0.005$). Pairwise comparison showed there was a significant difference between the performance of grades 3 and 4, 3 and 5 but not between grades 4 and 5. The overall condition factor was significant ($F[2, 354] = 10.909$, $p = 0.000$). Students were generally more accurate in repeating those speech–sound segments with the same onset, collapsing tones. Pairwise comparisons showed significant differences between the same onset and same rime conditions (F = 1, 177) = 21.986, p = 0.000) and between the same onset and no segment conditions (F[1, 177] = 11.454, p = 0.001), but not between the same-rime and no-segment conditions. There was no grade × condition interaction. Performance of the students by grade in the three conditions of the speech–sound repetition task is shown in Figure 10.4.

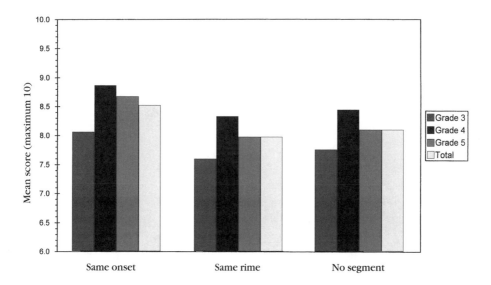

Figure 10.4. Speech–sound perception by onset, rime and segment for grade 3, 4 and 5 Beijing students.

To examine the results of the predictive efficacy for Chinese and English pseudo-word reading further, the best predictors from the multiple regression analyses were used in discriminant function analyses with subgroups of 'good' and 'poor' readers. These were defined as those students scoring plus or minus 1 SD (standard deviation) on the performance of Chinese of English pseudo-word reading tasks. For Chinese pseudo-word reading, the predictor variables of speech–sound repetition, working memory, onset deletion and chronological age correctly classified 15 of the 18 or 83.3% of the good readers and 20 of the 21 or 95.2% of the poor readers. For English pseudo-word reading, onset deletion and rime deletion correctly classified 23 of the 25 or 92.0% of the good readers and 14 of the 18 or 77.8% of the poor readers. The details are shown in Table 10.6.

Table 10.6. Discriminant function analyses

Classification accuracy for grades 3, 4 and 5 good and poor readers on Chinese pseudo-word reading[a]

Actual group	n	Predicted group			
		Good		Poor	
Good	18	15	(83.3%)	3	(16.7%)
Poor	21	1	(4.8%)	20	(95.2%)

Classification accuracy for grades 4 and 5 good and poor readers on English pseudo-word reading[b]

Actual group	n	Predicted group			
		Good		Poor	
Good	25	23	(92.0%)	2	(8.0%)
Poor	18	4	(22.2%)	14	(77.8%)

[a]Predictor variables: speech–sound repetition, working memory, onset deletion, chronological age.
[b]Predictor variables: onset deletion, rime deletion.

Discussion

Study 2 provided further evidence that Chinese pseudo-word reading and English pseudo-word reading were predicted differentially by different phonological processing tasks. Hypothesis 1 and hypothesis 2 were upheld. In reading Chinese words, phonological processing at the syllable or morpheme level is important together with involvement of verbal working or short-term memory, as shown by the moderate predictive value of the speech–sound repetition task. In comparison, for Chinese students learning English for the first and second years, processing of large units of onsets and rimes at the subsyllabic level is important. This explains the contribution of the onset and rime deletion tasks to the variance. In addition, the corollary to hypothesis 1 that better performance of repeating speech–sound segments with the same rime would be better than repeating those with the same onset was upheld. The general age trend in the phonological processing and reading tasks is expected except that the grade 4 students were performing just as well as, if not better than, the grade 5 students in many of the tasks. It is not clear if this is the result of some sampling bias or the need for more discriminating tasks or both.

General discussion and implications

In this investigation we set out to clarify the nature of phonological processing in Chinese word reading. Study 2, with an expanded and refined battery of phonological processing tasks and a larger sample size, replicates and supports the findings of study 1. Taken together, the results generally uphold the two hypotheses and the corollary. Word reading of the morpho-syllabic Chinese requires accurate perception and repetition of segments of speech sounds with tones crossed orthogonally – more than other phonological skills. Word reading of the alphabetic English for beginning Chinese readers revolves around the processing of the large speech units of onsets and rimes first. These hypotheses are borne out by the regression analyses. The moderate contributions by the predictor variables suggest that phonology is one of the interrelated constituents in processing Chinese words and that there are other constituents such as orthographic knowledge, including sensitivity to the internal structure of characters (Tan and Perfetti, 1998).

Our results generally support those of Hu and Catts (1998). Whereas Hu and Catts found it easier for their 50 Taiwanese first graders to delete the 'initial consonant', we found the performance of our Beijing third to fifth graders to be better in rime deletion than onset deletion. This same pattern was further observed in the speech–sound repetition task when the children were required to repeat the sets of four characters or syllables spoken by the experimenters with the same rimes with same or different tones. Our finding of better performance in rime deletion supports that of the paper-and-pencil results found by Bertelson, Chen and de Gelder (1997) in their preliminary study with their adult Hong Kong, Taiwan and Beijing participants.

There are linguistic and psycholinguistic reasons why rime deletion might be slightly easier for students learning Chinese and English. In 'addressing' Chinese speech sounds of individual characters, the most important constituents are the main vowel in the rime part of the character and the tone alternation, which is applied to the main vowel. As examples, the rime part of the syllable *mian* (see Addendum) is /-ian/, of which /i/ is generally classified as a medial glide and /a/ is the main vowel or peak with /n/ as the 'ending' or coda. In this hierarchical structure of rime consisting of medial glide, main vowel (peak) and ending (coda), the main vowel is a necessary and sufficient phonological element, even if the other two phonetic elements may not be present. There are some examples to show the necessary and sufficient constituency of the main vowel: /iao[1]/ meaning *hip*, /bao[1]/ meaning *paper* or *to announce*, /ku[3]/ meaning *bitter* and /u[3]/ meaning *five*. As rime and especially the embedded main vowel are a necessary and sufficient constituent in any character heard or written, students may get more practice in both perceiving and producing vowel sounds. Moreover, there is less rapid change in the formant transition for vowels than there is for consonants and consonant clusters, and vowels are generally acoustically longer than consonants There is another reason in terms of the audibility of phonetic segments. According to the 'sonority principle', there is a tendency for the sonority of the segments to increase from stops as the least sonorous through fricatives, nasals, liquids, glides and vowels as the most sonorous (Kiparsky, 1979). As a result of this, the rime segment is more sonorous, more marked and much preferred than the onset segment. All these phonetic and acoustic characteristics play a role in the deletion of rimes and onsets. In addition to main vowels the other important constituent in the phonology of Chinese characters is the four tones in Pu[3]tong[1]hua[4]. These suprasegmental tonal elements are critical in providing meaning in the context of the extremely extensive homophony of Chinese characters.

Our use of the onset and rime deletion tasks and the results obtained suggest that the role of onsets and rimes in reading development and developmental dyslexia in Chinese should be studied further. Whereas some earlier studies might have emphasised the role of the segmental phoneme deletion and substitution based on notions from alphabetic languages, we have provided some evidence that it is the paradigmatic aspects of Chinese speech sound that should be the locus of phonological processing in Chinese word reading (see also Tao and Peng, 1999). We consider this to be important both theoretically and practically. Theoretically, the results provide some psychological evidence to support the linguistic notions articulated by Chao (1968), Wang (1985) and Halliday (1981), as discussed earlier and as explained in Leong (1997). Practically, the approach to using larger linguistic units of onsets and rimes rather than the smaller units of phonemes is where learning to read English should begin for Chinese children, although not where it should end.

Phonological representations in a cross-linguistic framework

Our work highlighting the main vowel in the rime part of the Chinese character and the involvement of speech–sound segment retrieval and repetition also points to phonological processing skills common to language systems and modulated by them. These common and specific 'phonological representations' investigated cross-linguistically (Goswami, 2000) should further advance our knowledge of reading development and developmental dyslexia in the coming years.

Two lines of studies may be cited to buttress this argument of the common and specific phonological representations from quite different linguistic systems. Shimron (1993) suggested that the role of Hebrew vowels in identifying Hebrew words is complementary and may even be secondary to that of other linguistic cues. This is because the Semitic Hebrew alphabet is largely consonantal and the 'mothers of reading' and the diacritical marks signifying the five basic vowels provide a systematic and unambiguous vowel system (Shimron, 1993). Decoding Hebrew words is relatively direct and straightforward in comparison with English. This suggestion by Shimron must be interpreted in the context that phonological processing is still the *sine qua non* in learning Hebrew, and that the identity and order of letters and letter clusters (orthographic knowledge) must be amalgamated with this 'self-teaching' device for children learning to read Hebrew (Share, 1999).

In some contrast to the alphabetic Hebrew and English, speech segmentation of the Japanese *kana* syllabary by Japanese children is first based on the syllable and later on the subsyllabic rhythmic timing device of *mora* (e.g. the word *kureyon*, segmented into ku/re/yon/, being syllable based and, into ku/re/yo/n/, being *mora* based) through an intermediate phase of a mixture of syllable-based and *mora*-based segmentation as reading develops (Inagaki, Hatano and Otake, 2000). This finding by Inagaki, Hatano and Otake (2000) supports the earlier study by Otake et al. (1993). Otake et al. found that adult Japanese listeners' response patterns of the rhythmic Japanese *kana* is based on moraic segmentation, at least for the most common CV *mora* structure and the nasal coda N. These authors also suggested the possibility that their adult participants might produce their moraic response patterns via an orthographic representation. However, Otake et al. emphasised that 'a mora-based code seems to be easy and natural for listeners to use' (p. 275). The main argument here, just as in the study by Inagaki, Hatano and Otake (2000), of young Japanese children, is that the phonological explanation of moraic segmentation finds a parallel in the syllabic segmentation in French and the stress segmentation in English, in that the *mora*, syllable and stress are all units of rhythm in the three respective languages.

What the present study with Chinese children, and the Hebrew (Shimron, 1993; Share, 1999) and Japanese studies (Otake et al., 1993; Inagaki, Hatano and Otake, 2000), have shown is that listeners'/readers' segmentation of spoken characters/words is related to procedures constrained by the phonological characteristics of their language and writing systems. To the extent that Chinese word reading is paradigmatic and not so much segmental, and relies on lexical tones to disambiguate decontextualised character reading, perceiving and retrieving speech sounds with appropriate tones is critical and verbal memory also plays a part. These results are shown in both study 1 and study 2. What is also important is that phonological processing in the visual identification of Chinese characters and words is robust and is activated early, or 'at lexicality' (Tan and Perfetti, 1998). To the extent that beginning readers of English in Beijing have not been taught phonemic awareness skills, they have to rely on larger speech units such as onsets and rimes to address phonology in English pseudo-word reading. These results are obtained in both studies. We can thus claim with some confidence that further studies with more refined phonological processing tasks and with the addition of orthographic processing tasks should explain more of the variance of word reading in Chinese. Furthermore, phonological processing skills develop over time as children acquire literacy. From grade 3 onwards, Chinese children are functionally aware of the roles of the phonetic and semantic radicals in single and compound characters and should be encouraged to use this knowledge and that of speech sounds in developing reading (Shu and Anderson, 1999).

Going beyond the cognitive level to understand reading and developmental dyslexia in Chinese

Although phonological processing modulated by psycholinguistic considerations of different language systems provides a locus of learning to read, a much more powerful framework should link the cognitive, behavioural and biological levels, especially for neurodevelopmental disorders such as dyslexia (Frith, 1999). It is possible that the brain holds much, if not most, of the answers to human language processing and this 'causal modelling' linking the different levels should provide the focus for both reading research and practice in the coming years.

There are good reasons to believe that such linkage should delineate more clearly the basic architecture of different language systems and specific and interrelated domains within each system. A good example in the realm of Chinese is the functional magnetic resonance imaging (fMRI) study by Chee, Tan and Thiel (1999) of Mandarin and English single-word processing. Chee, Tan and Thiel studied 24 fluently bilingual (English and Chinese) Singaporean subjects using fMRI when the participants performed word generation in each language. They found that common cortical areas are activated for both languages in the prefrontal, temporal and parietal regions, and also the supplementary motor areas. They suggested that Brodmann's area 37 might be a convergence area for symbolic representation. Brodmann's area 37 and the left frontal operculum have also been shown to be in common for picture naming, colour naming, letter naming and reading in English, with appropriate control of the baseline data (Price and Friston, 1997). Tan et al. (2000) also used fMRI to study brain activation in the processing of Chinese characters and words. They found involvement of frontal (Brodmann's areas 9, 46 and 47) and temporal Brodmann's area 37 cortices and right lateralisation of visual systems (Brodmann's areas 17–19), parietal lobe (Brodmann's area 3) and the cerebellum. These researchers point out that Brodmann's area 9, a cortical region in the left frontal lobe, is much less or hardly active in reading alphabetic languages, including English. The results of Tan et al. suggest that reading Chinese also involves cortical regions relevant to semantic and ortho-graphic processing. In all these recent brain imaging studies a main concern should be the relationship between the cognitive tasks and experimental designs and the architecture of the language faculty.

Coda

Data from fMRI and other studies further validate the macro-models of literacy based on social, cultural, psychological and neurological contexts as proposed by Lundberg and Høien (1991) and of intervention for dyslexia as delineated by Høien and Lundberg (2000). In celebrating the cumulative achievement of Ingvar Lundberg, it may be appropriate to invoke the summary statement of Stanovich (1988, p. 7) on phonemic awareness and reading as a converging success in cognitive psychology: '. . . isolating a theoretically intriguing process, link the process to the performance of a real-world task of critical importance, and show that the efficacy of the process in question can be brought under experimental control.' Phonemic awareness and phonological processing are but one of the main areas that Lundberg has contributed to our understanding of language processing and literacy devel-opment. There is yet more to come from Ingvar Lundberg on literacy and cognition in the new millennium.

Acknowledgement

The first author would like to thank the Social Sciences and Humanities Research Council of Canada, the Department of Educational Psychology and the Hong Kong Institute of Educational Research, and the Chinese University of Hong Kong for their assistance. The studies were undertaken during his lecture visits to Hong Kong. He thanks Dr K.T. Hau and Dr Leslie Lo of CUHK. He also thanks the Swedish Council for Research in the Humanities and Social Sciences and the Swedish Council for Social Research for making possible his participation in the Symposium. The second author has been assisted by the Research Grants Council of the University Grants Committee, Hong Kong in this investigation and other studies and would like to express his apprecia-tion. Both authors are grateful to the Principal, the Director of Language Studies, and the teachers and students of Yuquan Primary School in Beijing for their participation in their investigation

References

Adams, M.J. (1990). *Beginning to Read: Thinking and learning about print*. Cambridge, MA: MIT Press.

Bertelson, P., Chen, H.-C. and de Gelder, B. (1997). Explicit speech analysis and orthographic experience in Chinese readers. In: Chen, H.-C. (ed.), *Cognitive Processing of Chinese and Related Asian Languages*. Hong Kong: The Chinese University of Hong Kong Press, pp. 27–46.

Chao, Y.R. (1968). *A Grammar of Spoken Chinese*. Berkeley, CA: University of California Press.

Chee, M.W.L., Tan, E.W.L. and Thiel, L. (1999). Mandarin and English single word processing studied with functional magnetic resonance imaging. *Journal of Neuroscience* **19**: 3050–3056.

DeFrancis, J. (1989). *Visible Speech: The diverse oneness of writing systems*. Honolulu: University of Hawaii Press.

Frith, U. (1999). Paradoxes in the definition of dyslexia. *Dyslexia* **5**: 192–214.

Frost, R. and Katz, L. eds (1992). *Orthography, Phonology, Morphology, and Meaning*. Amsterdam: North-Holland.

Goswami, U. (1999). Towards a theoretical framework for understanding reading development and dyslexia in different orthographies. In: Lundberg, I., Tønnessen, F.E. and Austad, I. (eds), *Dyslexia: Advances in theory and practice*. Dordrecht: Kluwer Academic Publishers, pp. 101–116.

Goswami, U. (2000). Phonological representations, reading development and dyslexia: Towards a cross-linguistic theoretical framework. *Dyslexia* **6**: 133–151.

Goswami, U. and Bryant, P.E. (1990). *Phonological Skills and Learning to Read*. Hillsdale, NJ: Lawrence Erlbaum.

Halliday, M.A.K. (1981). The origin and early development of Chinese phonological theory. In: Asher, R.E. and Henderson, E.J.A. (eds), *Towards a History of Phonetics*. Edinburgh: Edinburgh University Press, pp. 123–140.

Hanley, J.R., Tzeng, O. and Huang, H.S. (1999). Learning to read Chinese. In: Harris, M. and Hatano, G. (eds), *Learning to Read and Write: A cross-linguistic perspective*. Cambridge: Cambridge University Press, pp. 173–195.

Ho, C.S.-H. and Bryant, P. (1997). Learning to read Chinese beyond the logographic phase. *Reading Research Quarterly* **32**: 279–289.

Høien, T. and Lundberg, I. (2000). *Dyslexia: From theory to intervention*. Dordrecht: Kluwer Academic Publishers.

Høien, T., Lundberg, I., Stanovich, K. and Bjaalid, I.-K. (1995). Components of phonological awareness. *Reading and Writing: An Interdisciplinary Journal* **7**: 1–18.

Hu, C.-F. and Catts, H.W. (1998). The role of phonological processing in early reading ability: What we can learn from Chinese. *Scientific Studies of Reading* **2**: 55–79.

Huang, H.S. and Hanley, J.R. (1995). Phonological awareness and visual skills in learning to read Chinese and English. *Cognition* **54**: 73–98.

Inagaki, K., Hatano, G. and Otake, T. (2000). The effect of kana literacy acquisition on the speech segmentation unit used by Japanese young children. *Journal of Experimental Child Psychology* **75**: 70–91.

Kiparsky, P. (1979). Metrical structure assignment is cyclic. *Linguistic Inquiry* **10**: 421–441.

Leong, C.K. (1997). Paradigmatic analysis of Chinese word reading: Research findings and classroom practices. In: Leong, C.K. and Joshi, R.M. (eds), *Cross-language Studies of Learning to Read and Spell: Phonological and orthographic processing*. Dordrecht: Kluwer Academic Publishers, pp. 379–417.

Leong, C.K. (1999). What can we learn from dyslexia in Chinese? In: Lundberg, I., Tønnessen, F.E. and Austad, I. (eds), *Dyslexia: Advances in theory and practice*. Dordrecht: Kluwer Academic Publishers, pp. 117–139.

Lundberg, I. and Høien, T., eds (1991). *Literacy in a World of Change: Perspectives on reading and reading disability*. Stavanger: Centre for Reading Research.

Mattingly, I.G. (1987). Morphological structure and segmental awareness. *Cahiers de Psychologie Cognitive* 7: 488–493.

McBride-Chang, C. and Ho, C.S.-H. (2000). Developmental issues in Chinese children's character acquisition. *Journal of Educational Psychology* 92: 50–55.

Morais, J., Bertelson, P., Cary, L. and Alegria, J. (1986). Literacy training and speech segmentation. *Cognition* 24: 45–64.

Morais, J., Cary, L., Alegria, J. and Bertelson, P. (1979). Does awareness of speech as a sequence of phones arise spontaneously? *Cognition* 7: 323–331.

Otake, T., Hatano, G., Cutler, A. and Mehler, J. (1993). Mora or syllable? Speech segmentation in Japanese. *Journal of Memory and Language* 32: 258–278.

Perfetti, C.A. (1998). Two basic questions about reading and learning to read. In: Reitsma, P. and Verhoeven, L. (eds), *Problems and Interventions in Literacy Development*. Mahwah, NJ: Kluwer Academic Publishers, pp. 15–47.

Perfetti, C.A. and Zhang, S. (1991). Phonological processes in reading Chinese characters. *Journal of Experimental Psychology: Learning, Memory and Cognition* 17: 633–643.

Perfetti, C.A. and Zhang, S. (1995). Very early phonological activation in Chinese reading. *Journal of Experimental Psychology: Learning, Memory and Cognition* 21: 24–33.

Perfetti, C.A., Zhang, S. and Berent, I. (1992). Reading in English and Chinese: Evidence for a 'universal' phonological principle. In: Frost, R. and Katz, L. (eds), *Orthography, Phonology, Morphology and Meaning*. Amsterdam: North-Holland, pp. 227–248.

Price, C.J. and Friston, K.J. (1997). Cognitive conjunctions: A new approach to brain activation experiments. *NeuroImage* 5: 261–270.

Raven, J.C. (1987). *Manual for Raven's Progressive Matrices and Vocabulary Scales*, Section 3, *Standard Progressive Matrices*. London: H.K. Lewis.

Read, C., Zhang, Y.-F., Nie, H.-Y. and Ding, B.-Q. (1986). The ability to manipulate speech sounds depends on knowing alphabetic writing. *Cognition* 24: 31–44.

Share, D.L. (1995). Phonological recoding and self-teaching: Sine qua non of reading acquisition. *Cognition* 55: 151–218.

Share, D.L. (1999). Phonological recoding and orthographic learning: A direct test of the self-teaching hypothesis. *Journal of Experimental Child Psychology* 72: 95–129.

Shen, X.S. and Lin, M. (1991). A perceptual study of Mandarin tones 2 and 3. *Language and Speech* 34: 145–156.

Shimron, J. (1993). The role of vowels in reading: A review of studies of English and Hebrew. *Psychological Bulletin* 114: 52–67.

Shu, H. and Anderson, R.C. (1999). Learning to read Chinese: The development of metalinguistic awareness. In: Wang, J., Inhoff, A.W. and Chen, H.-C. (eds), *Reading Chinese Script: A cognitive analysis*. Mahwah, NJ: Lawrence Erlbaum, pp. 1–18.

Spencer, A. (1991). *Morphological Theory: An introduction to word structure in generative grammar.* Oxford: Blackwell.

Stanovich, K.E. (ed.) (1988). *Children's Reading and the Development of Phonological Awareness.* Detroit, MI: Wayne State University Press.

Sue, I.-R. and Liu, I.M. (1996). Word and character superiority effects in Chinese. *Chinese Journal of Psychology* **38**: 11–30 [in Chinese].

Swanson, H.L. (1992). Generality and modifiability of working memory among skilled and less skilled readers. *Journal of Educational Psychology* **84**: 473–488.

Tan, L.H. and Perfetti, C.A. (1998). Phonological codes as early sources of constraint in Chinese word identification: A review of current discoveries and theoretical accounts. In: Leong, C.K. and Tamaoka, K. (eds), *Cognitive Processing of the Chinese and the Japanese Languages.* Dordrecht: Kluwer Academic Publishers, pp. 11–46.

Tan, L.H. and Perfetti, C.A. (1999). Phonological activation in visual identification of Chinese two-character words. *Journal of Experimental Psychology: Learning, Memory, and Cognition* **25**: 382–393.

Tan, L.H., Spinks, J.A., Gao, J.-H., Liu, H.-L., Perfetti, C.A., Xiong, J., Stofer, K.A., Pu, Y., Liu, Y. and Fox, P.T. (2000). Brain activation in the processing of Chinese characters and words: A functional MRI study. *Human Brain Mapping* **10**: 16–27.

Tao, J. and Peng, D.-L. (1999). Chinese phonological awareness of children and the difference between good and poor readers. *Acta Psychologica Sinica* **31**: 60-68 [in Chinese].

Wagner, R.K. and Torgesen, J.K. (1987). The nature of phonological processing and its causal role in the acquisition of reading skills. *Psychological Bulletin* **101**: 192–212.

Wagner, R.K., Torgesen, J.K., Rashotte, C.A., Hecht, S.A., Barker, T.A., Burgess, S.R., Donahue, J. and Garon, T. (1997). Changing relations between phonological processing abilities and word-level reading as children develop from beginning to fluent readers: A five-year longitudinal study. *Developmental Psychology* **33**: 468–479.

Wang, L. (1985). *Modern Chinese Grammar.* Beijing: Shangwu Yinshuguan [in Chinese].

Xu, Y. (1991). Depth of phonological recoding in short-term memory. *Memory and Cognition* **19**: 263–273.

Zhang, S. and Perfetti, C.A. (1993). The tongue-twister effect in reading Chinese. *Journal of Experimental Psychology: Learning, Memory, and Cognition* **19**: 1082–1093.

CHAPTER 11

Twenty years of phonological deficits: Lundberg's sample revisited

ÅKE OLOFSSON

The persistence of phonological deficits

Psychologists and other scientists have been studying dyslexia for over 100 years now. During this time reading has been awarded the position of probably the most important human skill and a cornerstone of all modern educational systems. From this it follows that in the new millennium reading difficulties and dyslexia run the risk of becoming an even more severe handicap for the individual and a high-priced problem for society. The last millennium ended with an outburst of dyslexia research, resulting not in a clear definition of dyslexia, but in a consensus that dyslexia is basically a verbal processing problem and, more specifically, a problem related to the phonological aspects of language processing (see, for example, Snowling, 2000). It has recently been shown that phonological problems tend to persist in adults with childhood reading problems, even when the adults' reading skill is within normal range (Felton, Naylor and Wood, 1990; Bruck, 1992; Snowling et al., 1997; Olofsson, 1999; Snowling, 2000). Many dyslexic adults seem to circumvent most of their problems with word decoding by relying more on context and top-down processing. Compensating people with dyslexia tend, in the long run, to develop a qualitatively different word-decoding ability with less specific orthographic knowledge and persisting deficits in lower level decoding and spelling skills. This chapter reports on phonological processing and word-decoding abilities in a sample of adults with a history of dyslexia. The sample was identified (Lundberg, 1985) on the basis of their reading problems in the early school years, 20 years earlier, and is here compared with both their original control group and a new sample of university students with dyslexia.

Paulesu et al. (1996) found phonological deficits in five compensating dyslexic adults in comparison to a control group. The dyslexic adults had normal reading skills (even in non-word reading) and their identification as people with dyslexia was based on well-documented reading problems in their earlier school years. Despite their normal reading ability, they still showed weaknesses on phoneme deletion and production of spoonerisms. Bruck (1992) correspondingly found that the phonological problems continued in adults with childhood reading problems, even when their reading skill was within the normal range. Thus, the reading development of the poor readers was not associated with phonological awareness in the same way as it is in normal readers. Similar results were reported by Felton, Naylor and Wood (1990) in a long-term follow-up study with 115 adults who had reading problems in school. They found that the adults scored lower than age-matched controls on pseudo-word reading, phonological awareness and naming. Snowling et al. (1997) also found residual deficits in phoneme awareness and in non-word reading in adults with dyslexia. Similar results were also reported by Pennington et al. (1990), Lefly and Pennington (1991) and Elbro, Nielsen and Petersen (1994).

The overall impression from the above studies is that dyslexic children can make progress in reading acquisition but, nevertheless, their difficulties in pseudo-word reading, phonological awareness and rapid naming persist. The importance of phonological variables also holds for samples of university students independent of whether they have been tested for dyslexia in childhood (Hanley, 1997) or diagnosed at university level (Everatt, 1997). Even in a selected sample of successful people with dyslexia, Fink (1998) found evidence for specific deficits in lower level decoding and spelling skills.

A sample revisited

The present study revisited a sample of childhood dyslexics and their control group, collected by Lundberg almost 20 years ago, and compared them to a recently collected sample of undergraduate students with dyslexia. Olofsson (1999) reported follow-up data on the Lundberg sample finding persisting deficits in most of the phonological processing and word decoding variables. These children diagnosed with dyslexia were also found to have a different educational history; they had chosen school subjects and programmes that demand lower levels of reading skill and thus do not meet the entrance requirements for many university programs. None of those diagnosed with dyslexia in childhood had taken any university courses and had no such plans for the future either. In the present chapter those diagnosed with dyslexia in childhood are compared with a sample of undergraduate students with dyslexia, i.e. a sample with a very different educational history, and the question is how these groups differ on reading and phonological processing variables.

Groups and tests

Three groups of adults were tested. The first group included adults who were diagnosed in childhood as dyslexic (20 years earlier); the selection criteria were based on the discrepancy between Raven's matrices (non-verbal intelligence – Raven, 1960) and poor word recognition and/or spelling on two consecutive test occasions 6 months apart (see Lundberg, 1985, for details). Participants in the second group were recruited via the Special Needs Office at the University of Umeå and consisted of first-year and second-year students from both the natural and the social sciences. The third group, which served as a control group, was selected from the same primary schools as the dyslexic group but had normal reading ability.

In the original Lundberg study the groups consisted of 46 dyslexic and 44 control children. About half of the subjects could be found and they received a questionnaire. This questionnaire had questions about their school history, educational background, social status, job, reading habits and future plans. Twenty-five of these individuals (10 dyslexic and 15 controls) agreed to participate in additional testing. With respect to childhood variables there were no statistical differences between the missing cases and the ones found in the current subsample. Thus, there was no evidence for any selection bias in the recovered sample.

Participants

Dyslexic adults

These consisted of 15 Swedish adults (13 men and 2 women), mean age 27, who were diagnosed as having dyslexia when they were 8 years old. Originally, 705 pupils from the area of Umeå were screened and 49 of these were defined as stable underachievers according to the criteria mentioned above. Three pupils were excluded in order to assure that the children's reading difficulties were not associated with social, emotional, cultural, educational or medical factors, thus leaving 38 boys and 8 girls. (For more details, see Lundberg, 1985.) A total of 15 participants completed the questionnaire and 10 of these participated in additional testing.

Dyslexic undergraduates

These consisted of seven adults (four men and three women), mean age 23, from Umeå University who were referred via the Student Needs Office. Four of them had been advised by their university student counsellor to take a reading test and the other three asked for a test on their own initiative. None of the students had a formal diagnosis of dyslexia but they all experienced various study problems in high school and at university.

Normal adults

These consisted of 22 adults (20 men and 2 women), mean age 27, who were taken from the same schools as the dyslexic adults. All 22 participants completed the questionnaire and 15 of them participated in a testing session.

Tests

Spelling

The spelling test was constructed to give a quick and 'non-offensive' measure of spelling knowledge of the Swedish j sound. Eight low-frequency one- and two-syllable words with regular spelling of the j sound were used. Swedish spelling generally represents the j sound with the letters j, g or i. The j sound can also be represented by the letter clusters hj and lj. In Swedish, a strict rule-based spelling of the j sound would give approximately 20% spelling errors. The following words were used: *Sorg* [grief], *bälg* [bellows], (/j/ in final position after a consonant in one-syllable words); *gärs* [ruff, (fish)], *gös* [pike, perch], *gyro* [gyro] (/j/ in initial position before a front vowel); *juvel* [jewel], *pjäs* [theatre, play], *miljö* [milieu] (otherwise spelled with j). The number of spelling errors was scored and the maximum score was 6.

Vocabulary

This task was adopted from a similar Danish task used by Elbro, Nielsen and Peterson (1994). The participants were given a word and asked to choose a synonym from three alternative words. The alternatives (all real words) were chosen in order to maximise the phonological similarity between them. The childhood dyslexia group and the normal group received the written form of the task but for the group of university level individuals with dyslexia the words were presented orally. Accordingly, the comparison of the results must be made with great caution. The number of correct items was scored and the maximum score was 19.

Digit naming speed

The test is similar to the digit naming task used by Snowling et al. (1997). The participants read aloud twice a list of 50 randomly ordered digits. The mean reading time in seconds was measured. Typically, only few errors were made on this task. The inter-list correlation was 0.80.

Initial phoneme analysis

The participants were asked to say aloud the first sound (phoneme) of an orally presented word. The following words were used (the first sound is given in parenthesis): *grönt* [g], *sluss* [s], *knä* [k], *gäst* [j], *chips* [ç], *kväll* [k]. The number of correctly identified sounds was scored, giving a maximum score of 6.

Sound deletion

The participants were asked to repeat a word but without a given sound, e.g. 'Say stop, but without /p/'. The following words were used (the sound to be deleted is given in parenthesis): *skval* (k), *skrot* (r), *skolk* (l), *vits* (t), *snits* (s), *sparv* (v), *stoft* (t), *stoft* (f). The sound deletion also gave a common word as a result. For two of the items the to-be-deleted phoneme was present in two positions in the word. For these two words, both solutions (deletions) were scored as correct, even when the resulting word was a pseudo-word. The number of successful responses was scored, giving 8 as the maximum score.

Phonological coding in word recognition

This task was a paper-and-pencil Swedish adaptation of the computerised phonological coding task used by Olson et al. (1994). The task was to decide, and underline with a pencil, which one of three or four pseudo-words is a pseudo-homophone of a real word, i.e. 'sounds' like a real word. There were four lists of 20 lines, each line consisting of three or four word alternatives. Subjects were given 2 minutes to complete the task. The score was the number of words correctly chosen minus the number of wrong choices. The number of errors was very low, most of the participants making no errors. The maximum score was 80.

Orthographic coding in word recognition

This task is a Swedish adaptation of the computerised orthographic coding task used by Olson et al. (1994). The participant had to underline the true word in true word–pseudo-homophone pairs. Stimuli were presented on 6 lists of 20 pairs each. The phonological codes for the pairs were identical so that both the word and its pseudo-homophone would be pronounced in the same way in Swedish. Thus, in order to give a correct response the reader must use word-specific orthographic knowledge. The score was the number of correctly chosen words in 2 minutes minus the number of wrong choices. Errors were more common than in the phonological coding task. Only one-third of the participants made no errors. The maximum score was 120.

Word decoding

For this task the participant had to read silently 'chains' of words that were concatenated by deletion of the inter-word blank space. Each chain consisted of two to four words, randomly ordered, and the reader had to mark each word boundary with a pencil. The chains were constructed so that there was no ambiguity regarding the boundary location and the chains consisted of a large proportion of high-frequency words. The number of correctly marked chains in 3 minutes minus the number of errors was scored. Maximum score was 120 (see Jacobson, 1995, for a similar measure).

Proofreading

The participants' task was to read a simple text with 289 words in 22 sentences and to underline every word that was misspelt. The text contained 35 common Swedish homophones (compare *there*, *their*, in English) which in the present context were misspelt, i.e. the wrong word in the homophone pair was used in the text. The score was computed as the number of detected misspellings in 2.5 minutes minus the number of incorrect choices.

Reading comprehension

The test consisted of two texts, each written on a standard page and with a difficulty level corresponding to the texts in daily newspapers. For each text there were two multiple-choice questions. The first had four alternatives and the participants were asked to select an appropriate headline for the text. The second consisted of six statements related to the text and the reader had to select those statements that were true according to the text – four of the statements were true, one was an inference, two were paraphrases and one was identical to the text. The erroneous alternatives included one highly plausible statement that was not mentioned in the text and a statement in which one word had been replaced by a word with an opposite meaning.

Visuomotor figure chains

This test was a non-verbal visuomotor task which was, in some aspects, analogous to the word-decoding (word chain) task above. Eighty 'chains' made by 8 to 14 small figures (generated by a computer font) were presented in two columns on three pages. Within each chain there were two positions where the same figure (character) was repeated. The task was to find and mark each position where the figure was doubled. The number of correctly marked chains in 90 seconds was scored. Maximum score was 80.

Questionnaire and interview

A 60-item questionnaire was given to the childhood dyslexia group and to the control group: 24 items were questions about the participant's educational history; 11 concerned the participant's preferences for different school subjects; and 20 were questions about the participant's current activities and behaviours. The remaining items concerned the current family status and occupation. Both rating scales and yes–no answers were used. For the group of undergraduate students with dyslexia the corresponding information was collected in a personal interview.

Procedures

The participants were tested individually in a quiet room at the university; one individual was tested in his office. The testing was completed in a single session of approximately 1 hour, allowing for breaks between the blocks.

Main findings

First, the results from the testing session are reported and thereafter the interview and questionnaire data are shortly described.

The comparison of group means in Table 11.1 shows that there are differences between the group means on all variables except for reading comprehension and the visuomotor test. For word-decoding errors the difference just failed to reach significance but, as can be seen in Table 11.1, both the F value and the effect size (η^2) are substantial and the power of this analysis was as low as 0.56. Post-hoc tests (at the 0.05 level) were done for all variables with significant F values, and there was no difference between the two dyslexic groups on spelling errors, phonological coding and proofreading. The same pattern of superiority for the group without dyslexia also seemed to hold for the vocabulary variable, although here the test form was different for the dyslexic undergraduates, so that the only certain conclusion that can be drawn is that those whose dyslexia was diagnosed in childhood scored lower than the control group. All three groups differed significantly from each other on digit naming speed and orthographic coding, and the undergraduate students with dyslexia had the lowest result on both tests. The dyslexic undergraduates were slow on word decoding but they differed significantly only from the control group.

For the two phonological awareness tests, Table 11.1 shows a totally different pattern with the dyslexic undergraduates; they outperformed those diagnosed with dyslexia in childhood on the initial phoneme analysis variable, as well as on the sound deletion test, where they in fact scored higher than both the other groups.

The means and effect sizes given in Table 11.1 reveal that there were salient problems for both dyslexic groups on the two measures of orthographic knowledge: the orthographic coding and the proofreading test. A similar large effect was also found for the digit naming test.

The results from the questionnaire and the interviews showed no differences between the groups regarding their family status, social relationships and a variety of general competencies (e.g. a driver's licence or a completed military service). The occupational status was different for the childhood

Table 11.1. Mean scores, standard deviations (SD), F-values and effect size for two groups of adults with dyslexia and a group of adults with no history of reading problems

Variable	Childhood dyslexic[a] Mean (SD)	Dyslexic undergraduate[b] Mean (SD)	Normal[c] Mean (SD)	F	η^2
Spelling	2 (1.33)	2 (1.29)	0.73 (0.88)	5.02*	0.26
Vocabulary[d]	13.5 (2.8)	12.8 (2.2)	17.4 (1.7)	13.8***	0.50
Digit naming speed	18.3 (2.7)	22.4 (5.4)	15.4 (2.2)	11.1***	0.43
Initial phoneme analysis	1.9 (2.1)	5.3 (0.76)	4.6 (2.2)	7.74**	0.35
Sound deletion	4.1 (1.6)	6.0 (1.29)	4.9 (1.5)	3.34*	0.19
Phonological coding	11.0 (10.0)	12 (2.9)	23.1 (10.5)	6.04**	0.30
Orthographic coding	68.6 (20.5)	42.5 (19.3)	87.6 (19.6)	11.4***	0.45
Word decoding (chains)					
speed	44.8 (18.3)	40.3 (16.0)	57.8 (13.4)	3.57*	0.20
errors	1.7 (1.25)	1.3 (0.95)	0.73 (0.70)	NS (3.16)	(0.18)
Proofreading	11.9 (8.7)	8.8 (4.3)	24.4 (9.0)	10.4***	0.44
Reading comprehension	7.2 (1.8)	7.2 (2.2)	8.1 (2.0)	NS	
Visual motor figure chains	38.6 (6.4)	34.7 (7.5)	38.7 (8.5)	NS	

For all F tests the degree of freedom is 2/28 or 2/29.
[a]n = 10.
[b]n = 7.
[c]n = 15.
[d]For this variable a partially different testing procedure is used for the group of university students with dyslexia (see the description in the method part).
*p < 0.05. **p < 0.01. ***p < 0.001.

dyslexic group compared with the control group; the latter consisted of 10 university students whereas those whose dyslexia was diagnosed in childhood were all employees or self-employed. The groups also differed clearly in their educational history and their future plans for university courses. Those who were diagnosed with dyslexia in childhood had avoided advanced theoretical programmes and instead chosen more practical programmes. The educational background of the undergraduates with dyslexia was more like the background of the control group, although all of the dyslexic undergraduates reported that they had to struggle through their high school programmes. The group with childhood dyslexia reported fewer courses in Swedish and more low-level courses in mathematics. Some of those diagnosed with dyslexia in childhood also stated that they chose courses that they believed made lower demands for reading and spelling, although there were other courses in which they were more interested. However, the awareness of what their decision was based on did not arise until several years later.

The frequency of using an encyclopaedia or a dictionary differed greatly between the groups. The dyslexic adults seemed to dislike the process of using a dictionary where words are listed in alphabetical order.

Many participants in both dyslexic groups had vague and imprecise memories from their early educational history. A common picture even among those diagnosed with dyslexia in childhood was that their dyslexic problems had been discovered as late as in high school or college. Several of the dyslexic undergraduates remembered having a 'hard time in school' or 'a struggle', but they did not recall that they had been given an explanation or a diagnosis of dyslexia. In many cases these vague problems had already been present from the start of school. Three of the participants in the control group remembered having problems with reading acquisition and two others reported that they had had some speech therapy.

Conclusions

The results of this study are consistent with theories of a general phonological deficit in dyslexia. There were clear and persisting problems in tasks involving phonological processing in reading as well as in naming, and for those diagnosed with dyslexia in childhood also a low level of phonological awareness. Even more salient deficits were, however, found in tasks demanding advanced levels of orthographic processing. Thus, the findings here do not support the earlier view that dyslexic adults have almost normal word-recognition skill but persisting spelling problems (Miles, 1993). In addition to the documented phonological deficit, there were also weaknesses in orthographic processing which showed up when the task was demanding.

The undergraduates with dyslexia show very similar results to those whose dyslexia was diagnosed in childhood, with the exception of the phonological awareness tests where they scored better than the controls in sound deletion. This finding illustrates the dissociation between metaphonological development and reading skill described by Bruck (1992) in a different way (see also Paulesu et al., 1996). It seems that it takes some dyslexic individuals 10–15 years of reading and spelling to develop phonological awareness. Although they have participated in normal educational programmes quite successfully, they still suffer from specific word-decoding problems.

When comparing those diagnosed with dyslexia in childhood with their controls, Olofsson (1999) found that for the word-decoding test ('word chains'), the difference in speed (number of correct solutions in 3 minutes) was not statistically significant, although the direction of the difference between the sample means was in favour of the control group. Although the dyslexic individuals did not differ significantly from the controls in the number of items judged correctly, they made significantly more errors in this task. It is likely that there is a trade-off between errors and speed in this test, and thus a plausible explanation would be that dyslexic individuals 'pay' for their speed with a higher error rate. The dyslexic undergraduates in the present study appear to be slower but more accurate in word decoding than those whose dyslexia is diagnosed in childhood. It could be that these two groups of dyslexic individuals may use different compensation strategies. This difference in compensation strategy could be caused by their different educational experiences.

The present result is in line with a view of Goulandris, Snowling and Walker (2000) that compensating dyslexic individuals use relatively more higher-order language skills, context and top-down processing and, in the long run, achieve a less-developed word-decoding ability and less specific knowledge of orthography.

If orthographic processing is learned through reading and spelling these latter group differences may be a result of the dyslexic adult's lack of practice. On the other hand, the effect sizes and their current decoding status seem to indicate that these readers have developed a reading skill that is qualitatively different from normal readers. The low level of orthographic knowledge among the dyslexic university students also makes the lack-of-practice explanation less plausible. These students are active readers and enrolled in high-school and college programmes demanding substantial levels of reading. It is more likely that their phonological deficit hinders the development of orthographic knowledge (compare Share, 1995).

The dyslexic undergraduates did remarkably well on the phonological awareness tasks but those whose dyslexia was diagnosed in childhood did not. This discrepancy may be explained by two of the differences between the groups. First, the undergraduates might receive more practice in phonological decoding because they read and study more actively than those whose dyslexia was diagnosed in childhood, and it might be that in doing more advanced reading (studying) they are in fact engaged in detailed phonological coding. Second, the undergraduates were given support and special training much later in life and could perhaps benefit more from this training than those who are given the training earlier and who have less-developed metacognitive level.

Our results also showed that those whose dyslexia was diagnosed in childhood went through the educational system apparently avoiding reading and language studies, and today belong to a group that do not meet the requirements for university studies. But the performance of those whose dyslexia was diagnosed in childhood was very similar to the dyslexic undergraduates on practically all variables and both groups did well on everyday reading tasks. The groups were also similar on the vocabulary test, which may indicate that the dyslexic undergraduates have not benefited fully from their higher educational level. However, as the test format was not identical for the vocabulary tests, we have to treat this finding with great caution.

When comparing these two groups of dyslexic individuals it is tempting to conclude that those whose dyslexia was diagnosed in childhood also have the qualities necessary to studies at university level, although because they are aware of their poor reading they do not take the opportunity. The dyslexic individuals in the Lundberg sample still have phonological problems and difficulties in advanced word decoding and spelling, but their reading speed and reading comprehension are adequate for studies at university level. On the one hand, their level of phonological awareness is lower than that of the dyslexic undergraduates but, on the other, their reading speed is faster.

During school the great majority of children with early reading problems seem to develop sufficient reading and compensation skills to become fairly good everyday readers. However, in order to access the educational system of the new millennium these individuals also need motivational support and treatment against low self-esteem and perceived self-efficacy (see the discussion of secondary symptoms in Rack, 1997).

The present small sample of dyslexic undergraduates is selected in several ways and hence it follows that the results may be affected by so-called selection effects. First, these dyslexic individuals went to college: all of them struggled through high school; some did not fully reach their goals but some of them were very successful. Second, they continue their struggle at the university but now they seek help. There might be a population of students with similar pre-college background as the present sample but with even more positive outcome. These students could then be described as 'fully compensating dyslexic individuals' and they do not need to see the student counsellor and therefore there is no way to know about them and, accordingly, these fully compensating individuals are not present in research literature on adult dyslexia. Another shortcoming with dyslexia research on adult samples, illustrated by the present findings, is the low reliability of the self-reported early results, treatment and diagnosis. More research on adult dyslexia is still needed and the research should include longitudinal studies that could illuminate the developmental course of dyslexia.

Acknowledgement

The study was supported by grant F0395/96 from the Swedish Council for Research in the Humanities and Social Sciences (HSFR).

References

Bruck, M. (1992). Persistence of dyslexics' phonological awareness deficits. *Developmental Psychology* **28**: 874–886.

Elbro, C., Nielsen, I. and Petersen, D.K. (1994). Dyslexia in adults: Evidence for deficits in non-word reading and in the phonological representation of lexical items. *Annals of Dyslexia* **44**: 205–226.

Everatt, J. (1997). The abilities and disabilities associated with adult developmental dyslexia. *Journal of Research in Reading* **20**: 13–21.

Felton, R.H., Naylor, C.E. and Wood, F.B. (1990). Neuropsychological profile of adult dyslexics. *Brain and Language* **39**: 485–497.

Fink, R.P. (1998). Literacy development in successful men and women with dyslexia. *Annals of Dyslexia* **48**: 311–346.

Goulandris, N., Snowling, M. and Walker, I. (2000). Is dyslexia a form of specific language impairment? A comparison of dyslexic and language impaired children as adolescents. *Annals of Dyslexia* **50**: 103–120.

Hanley, M. (1997). Reading and spelling impairments in undergraduate students with developmental dyslexia. *Journal of Research in Reading* **20**: 23–30.

Jacobson, C. (1995). Word recognition index (WRI) as a quick screening marker of dyslexia. *Irish Journal of Psychology* **16**: 260–266.

Lefly, D. and Pennington, B. (1991). Spelling errors and reading fluency in compensated adult dyslexics. *Annals of Dyslexia* **41**: 143–162.

Lundberg, I. (1985). Longitudinal studies of reading and reading difficulties in Sweden. In: MacKinnon, G.E. and Waller, T.G. (eds), *Reading Research: Advances in theory and practice*. New York: Academic Press, pp. 65–105.

Miles, T.R. (1993). *Dyslexia: The pattern of difficulties*, 2nd edn. London: Whurr.

Olofsson, Å. (1999). Early reading problems: A follow up 20 years later. In: Lundberg ,I., Tønnessen, F.E. and Austad, I. (eds), *Dyslexia: Advances in theory and practice*. Dordrecht: Kluwer, pp. 197–206.

Olson, R.K., Forsberg, H., Wise, B. and Rack, J. (1994). Measurement of word recognition, orthographic and phonological skills. In: Lyon, G.R. (ed.), *Frames of Reference for the Assessment of Learning Disabilities: New views on measurement issues*. Baltimore, MD: Paul H. Brookes, pp. 243–277.

Paulesu, E., Frith, U., Snowling, M., Gallagher, A., Morton, J., Frackowiak, R.S.J. and Frith, C.D. (1996). Is developmental dyslexia a disconnection syndrome? Evidence from PET scanning. *Brain* **119**: 143–157.

Pennington, B.F., van Orden, G.C., Smith, S.D., Green, P.A. and Haith, M.M. (1990). Phonological processing skills and deficits in adult dyslexics. *Child Development* **61**: 1753–1778.

Rack, J. (1997). Issues in the assessment of developmental dyslexia in adults: theoretical and applied perspectives. *Journal of Research in Reading* **20**: 66–76.

Raven, J.C. (1960). *Guide to the Standard Progressive Matrices. Sets A, B, C, D, and E.* London: Lewis.

Share, D.L. (1995). Phonological recoding and self-teaching: Sine qua non of reading acquisition. *Cognition* **55**: 151–218.

Snowling, M.J. (2000). *Dyslexia*, 2nd edn. Oxford: Blackwell.

Snowling, M., Nation, K., Moxham, P., Gallager, A. and Frith, U. (1997). Phonological processing skills of dyslexic students in higher education: a preliminary report. *Journal of Research in Reading* **20**: 31–41.

CHAPTER 12

Neuromagnetic correlates of impaired reading in developmental dyslexia

PÄIVI HELENIUS AND RIITTA SALMELIN

In developmental dyslexia the acquisition of reading and writing is disturbed and dyslexic individuals remain slow readers even as adults. Development of functional imaging techniques has made it possible to map the cortical organisation of reading in dyslexic and fluent readers from the late 1980s (Hynd et al., 1987; Rumsey et al., 1987; Petersen et al., 1988). Lack of temporal resolution has, however, complicated both the identification of activation related to specific aspects of written word processing, such as orthographic, phonological or semantic analysis, and the identification of the earliest stage of reading-related neural events, where dyslexic reading deviates from the normal pattern of reading-related brain activation. Electroencephalographic (EEG) studies of reading shed further light on certain critical time windows during which event-related brain potentials (ERPs) seem to discriminate between fluent and dyslexic readers (Brandeis, Vitacco and Steinhausen, 1994).

The distinction of spatially and temporally overlapping activation patterns based on ERPs is, however, complicated, and rarely done. Thus, the underlying neural substrate of abnormal reading in dyslexia has remained elusive: which subprocesses of reading are affected and how dyslexia is manifested in the functional organisation of reading have remained undecided. Magnetoencephalography (MEG) is based on detecting magnetic fields associated with cortical activation (for reviews, see Hämäläineni et al., 1993; Lounasmaa et al., 1996). This method provides millisecond temporal resolution combined with reasonable spatial accuracy of a few millimetres. This combination makes MEG an ideal tool for studying developmental disorders in which differences in cortical activation between impaired and non-impaired individuals may be quite subtle. Using three different paradigms, we have investigated the cortical dynamics of fluent and impaired reading using the Neuromag-122 whole-head neuromagnetometer (Ahonen et al., 1993).

Word and non-word processing in non-impaired and dyslexic readers revealed by MEG

In the study of Salmelin et al. (1996) the spatiotemporal resolution of MEG was used for the first time to investigate reading in non-impaired and dyslexic individuals. Thus, we used as stimuli words and pseudo-words that could be expected to engage both lexical and sublexical routes of reading (see, for example, Coltheart, 1978; Coltheart et al., 1993). The stimuli were seven- to eight-letter Finnish abstract and concrete words, orthographically legal pseudo-words, and random letter strings constructed by scrambling the letters in the real words. Each category contained 100 stimuli which were presented once every 3 seconds for 300 ms. Participants were instructed to say a rarely occurring word '*kirahvi*' (giraffe) aloud when it appeared. Responses to these control stimuli were not included in the averages.

Six dyslexic readers and eight non-impaired readers participated in the study. We found differences in the activation of three brain areas in dyslexic compared with control adults in viewing words and non-words. The lower occipitotemporal border in the left hemisphere was not activated between 100 and 200 ms after stimulus presentation in dyslexic participants, contrary to controls (L1 in Figure 12.1a). Further, most controls had activation in the left temporal area, either in or near the vicinity of Wernicke's area (L2 in Figure 12.1b), peaking between 200 and 600 ms after word presentation. None of the dyslexic participants had activation in the left temporal cortex between 200 and 400 ms. The third difference was discovered in Broca's area, where four dyslexic participants, but none of the controls, showed activation between 200 and 400 ms after word onset (L3 in Figure 12.1b).

Systematic differences were not detected between concrete and abstract real words or pseudo-words and random letter strings. However, the cortical processing of words compared with non-words differed in at least one cortical area in six of eight controls and in half of the dyslexic participants. In the controls, sources differentiating between words and non-words were most consistently found in the left temporoparietal area and the differences typically emerged between 350 and 400 ms after stimulus onset. In dyslexic participants the temporal pattern and spatial distribution of sources differentiating between words and non-words was comparable to the pattern found in controls.

Conclusions of the word/non-word study

Earlier haemodynamic studies had found increased level of blood flow during reading in dyslexic compared with non-impaired adults in the bilateral inferior occipital areas (Gross-Glenn et al., 1991). In the study of Salmelin et al. (1996), however, left inferior occipitotemporal cortex activation, peaking

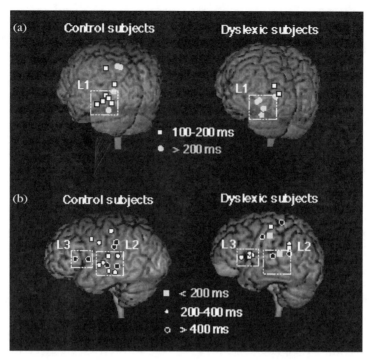

Figure 12.1. Responses to words and non-words in control (left) and dyslexic subjects (right) in (a) posterior and (b) anterior left hemisphere regions. Dashed rectangles indicate statistically significant differences between groups. L1 refers to left inferior occipitotemporal region, L2 to Wernicke's area and L3 to Broca's area. (Modified from Salmelin et al. 1996.)

between 100 and 200 ms after stimulus onset in controls, was not detectable in dyslexic readers.

Earlier intracranial studies had indicated that words and pseudo-words, but not objects, elicit activation in bilateral inferior occipitotemporal areas around 200 ms after stimulus onset (Nobre, Allison and McCarthy, 1994). Later, Puce et al. (1996) reported letter-string-specific changes in blood flow in the left inferior occipitotemporal area. As the signals were elicited by both words and non-words, but not by objects, this activation probably reflects prelexical, orthographic letter processing. The locations and timing of letter-string-specific responses agree with the occipitotemporal signals in our study. In the present study, objects were not presented and, thus, possible letter-string specificity of the signal could not be determined with certainty; the spatiotemporal behaviour, however, strongly supports this role. According to this interpretation, dyslexic individuals are already impaired in visual word recognition at this early prelexical stage.

Differences between dyslexic and non-impaired readers were also detected during later time periods near classic language regions. In controls activation peaked between 200 and 400 ms after stimulus onset around Wernicke's area, whereas in dyslexic readers left temporal areas remained practically silent. Both grapheme-to-phoneme conversion and phonological word-form activation have been suggested as recruiting left temporoparietal areas (Howard et al., 1992; Rumsey et al., 1997). Earlier studies in dyslexic readers had indicated that rhyming of auditorily presented words and visually presented letters fail to engage left temporoparietal areas in dyslexic readers as strongly as in controls (Rumsey et al., 1992; Paulesu, Frith and Frackowiak, 1993). According to these findings, the reduced activation in Wernicke's area might reflect inefficient phonological processing during reading. But, as Wernicke's area is classically associated with word comprehension, the difference between groups could be explained equally well in terms of delayed or reduced level of semantic activation.

Broca's area was activated between 200 and 400 ms in most dyslexic readers but in none of the controls. One interpretation for this finding could be differences in reading strategies: Broca's area has been classically associated with speech production and, thus, dyslexic participants, in order to compensate for the defective visual word recognition, could be engaged in top-down processing, i.e. trying to guess the word. On the other hand, activation in Broca's area might reflect grapheme-to-phoneme conversion (Pugh et al., 1996; Rumsey et al., 1997; Shaywitz et al., 1998). Accordingly, dyslexic readers might be relatively more engaged in sublexical word recognition, leading to an increased level of activation in Broca's area.

Semantic cortical activation in non-impaired and dyslexic readers

Our first MEG study of reading revealed clear differences between control and dyslexic readers in the activation of left hemisphere brain areas. The functional relevance of these differences could not be determined with certainty. The following MEG studies were thus targeted to dissociate different levels of visual word recognition. In our next studies, semantic processing was investigated in non-reading-impaired (Helenius et al., 1998) and dyslexic individuals (Helenius et al., 1999a).

Four types of sentences were used: in the probable condition the sentences ended with expected high probability words; in the rare endings the most probable last words were replaced by semantically appropriate words that were of low probability; in the anomalous endings, semantically totally inappropriate endings were used to replace the expected endings; and in the phonologically related endings sentence-final words were semantically inappropriate to the sentence context, but the word shared its initial phonemes and graphemes with the expected endings (Connolly, Phillips and Forbes, 1995). In ERP studies, presentation of anomalous sentence-final words has been reported to evoke a negative deflection peaking around 400 ms after word presentation (Kutas and Hillyard, 1980). There were 100 sentences in each category. Participants were instructed to concentrate on the meaning of the sentences.

The stimuli were sentences presented visually one word at a time. The duration of one word was 330 ms and a 750-ms gap was inserted between the words of the sentences. A longer gap followed the end of each sentence. The total number of different sentences was 400.

We measured responses from ten non-reading-impaired adults and eight dyslexic individuals. Together with the MEG measurement, EEG signals were recorded at Fz, Cz and Pz. If the strength of activation in a given cortical area differed statistically significantly between anomalous and probable endings, this area was considered to be involved in sentence comprehension. In controls the cortical structures implicated most consistently with compre-hension were located in the left superior temporal cortex (Figure 12.2a, left). Final words inappropriate to the sentence context evoked enduring activa-tion, starting around 230 ms and lasting up to 600 ms after word onset (Figure 12.2a, right). Rare endings produced weaker activation which termi-nated earlier. The probable sentence-final words totally failed to activate this region. After the culmination point of the response to the rare final words at around 350 ms, the activation elicited by the anomalous and phonologically related final words continued to increase, although the waveforms started to diverge, with the activation evoked by the phonological endings lagging behind the waveform related to anomalous endings by approximately 35 ms. Latency of left temporal cortex activation (at 50% maximum) in the phono-logically related ($r = 0.89$) and anomalous ($r = 0.84$) conditions correlated significantly with word-recognition speed, as can be expected assuming that both measures are closely related to the speed at which the meaning of the word can be accessed.

With a resemblance to the pattern described in normal readers, cortical activation sensitive to the semantic appropriateness of the sentence-final words was most consistently found in the left superior temporal cortex in dyslexic readers (Figure 12.2b, left). Thus, at the anatomical level, there were no clear differences between the groups. However, the time behaviour of the responses to unexpected sentence endings (rare, phonologically related and anomalous) was different in dyslexic compared with control readers (Figure 12.2b, right). The activation sensitive to word meaning within a sentence context began about 100 ms later in dyslexic readers than in controls, and was significantly weaker. In addition, in contrast to controls who exhibited

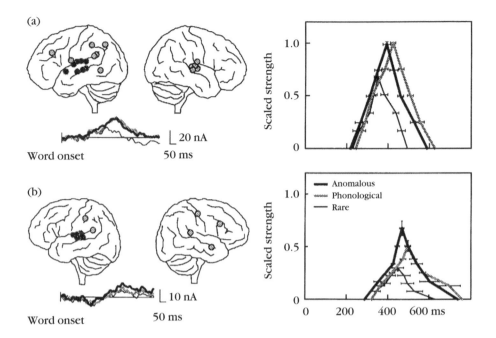

Figure 12.2. Left: cortical areas sensitive to semantic congruity in (a) control and (b) dyslexic readers. Most consistently semantic activation was found in the left superotemporal cortex and the centre of this activation across different individuals is shown with black dots; example of the time course of activation in one individual is given below. Right: averaged time course of the left temporal activation in (a) controls and (b) dyslexic participants for the three unexpected endings, scaled with respect to the phonological condition. (Modified from Helenius et al. 1999a.)

equally strong activation to both semantically incongruous sentence types, dyslexic readers showed significantly weaker activation as a response to phonologically related endings than totally anomalous endings. The most posterior ERP channel (Pz) also detected the delayed peak amplitude of the N400 response.

When the number of sources activated during sentence reading irrespective of their sensitivity to the experimental manipulation was compared between the two groups, no statistically significant differences were discovered anywhere in the brain. In the left inferior occipitotemporal area, however, only three of eight dyslexic readers had a source peaking within the first 300 ms after stimulus onset whereas eight of the ten controls had a source in this area. Further, the ERPs between 150 and 350 ms were different in the two groups: dyslexic readers seemed to lack a negative deflection peaking at 200 ms in controls.

Conclusions of the semantic experiments

In normal adults the activity of several cortical areas was modulated by the semantic appropriateness of the sentence-final words but most often semantic activation was found in the left superior temporal cortex. The relatively late (> 200 ms post-word onset) beginning of the activation suggests postlexical analysis (Balota and Chumbley, 1985). As the phonologically correct beginnings did not delay the onset of the activation either, it seems likely that fluent readers were recognising words in larger units than single letters or groups consisting of a few letters. Based on the distinct time courses of the responses to the word categories, the cortical activation probably reflects two partly overlapping semantic stages, the first interval (250–350 ms) mainly dominated by analysis of word meaning and the later phase (350–600 ms) by integration of the word into the sentence context. The cortical networks involved in these processes were spatially indistinguishable. The location of semantic activation in the left temporal cortex, within or in the immediate vicinity of Wernicke's area, is in accordance with both lesion studies and some recent neuroimaging studies, suggesting that Wernicke's area maintains semantic associations (Geschwind, 1970; Hart and Gordon, 1990; Pugh et al., 1996; Fiez, 1997). This prominent lateral temporal semantic activation had not been earlier emphasised in intracranial N400 recordings (McCarthy et al., 1995; Nobre and McCarthy, 1995).

The dyslexic readers displayed the same clear lateralisation of semantically sensitive brain activation to the left superior temporal cortex as normal readers. However, both timing and strength of activation differed between the two groups. Previous ERP studies have reported delayed N400 peak amplitudes during reading in dyslexic participants which is in line with our observations (Brandeis, Vitacco and Steinhausen, 1994). As a result of difficulties in separating activation patterns arising in different brain areas using ERPs, the delayed onset of the activation had not been discovered earlier. It seems that, in dyslexic readers the pre-semantic processing levels were already affected, as was suggested by the study of Salmelin et al. (1996), resulting in delayed beginning of semantic activation. The reduced strength of the semantically sensitive activation in dyslexic participants indicates that the conceptual network was activated less synchronously or engaged a smaller number of neurons in dyslexic readers than in controls. Earlier neuroimaging studies have not attempted to dissociate semantic processing in dyslexic readers. However, a reduced level of activation in the left temporal area during reading has been reported (Rumsey et al., 1997; Shaywitz et al., 1998).

In contrast to controls, the dyslexic readers showed clearly weaker responses to words that shared their initial letters with the expected words than to totally unexpected semantically anomalous words. This finding suggests that word-recognition strategies could be different in dyslexic readers: whereas controls perceived a word as a whole, dyslexic readers may have relied more on sublexical word recognition and occasionally mistook a word with correct initial graphemes for the one they had expected. As a consequence, the overall level of activation was reduced. Detailed behavioural data of the reading styles of dyslexic adults do not exist, but by applying the present paradigm this question could be further elucidated.

Dissociating feature analysis and letter-string processing in dyslexic and non-impaired readers

As the studies of both Salmelin et al. (1996) and Helenius et al. (1999a) indicated that differences between dyslexic readers and controls might arise relatively early, i.e. before 250 ms, in the next two studies these early stages of visual word recognition were studied in detail. In Tarkiainen et al. (1999), we used stimulus degradation which is known to delay word recognition. Thus, if a given brain area is involved in visual word recognition, it should show sensitivity to this manipulation (delayed or reduced response). Non-letter control stimuli were included to reveal the possible letter-string preference of the signals. In a subsequent study by Helenius et al. (1999b), letter-string-specific signals were also recorded in dyslexic readers to reveal whether differences can be detected at the first letter-string-specific stage of word recognition or even earlier during visual feature analysis.

The stimuli were (1) noise patches, (2) noise patches with embedded dark-grey single letters or symbols, (3) noise patches with embedded two-letter syllables or two-item symbol strings or (4) noise patches with embedded four-letter words or four-item symbol strings (Figure 12.3). Each condition (1–4) contained stimuli with four levels of Gaussian noise. At noise level 0, no noise was present, and the patches were evenly grey. At noise levels 8, 16 and 24,

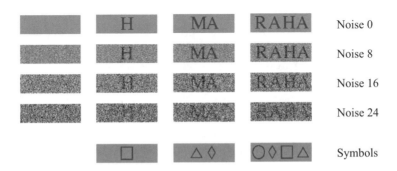

Figure 12.3. Examples of the stimuli used in the letter-string experiment. (Modified from Tarkiainen et al. 1999.)

increasing amounts of noise were added by allowing the pixels to change their colour in black–white scale at three probability levels. When letter strings were embedded in the noise patches, the luminance of their pixels was also allowed to vary. Symbol strings were presented only at noise level 0. We used 50 different four-letter Finnish nouns, 25 syllables and 25 letters. In the dyslexic readers only conditions (1) and (4) were included. The stimuli were presented once every 2 s and the display duration was 60 ms. Participants were asked to pay attention to the stimuli and in conditions (2–4) they were asked to say aloud the stimuli they had just seen when prompted by a question mark.

We measured 12 non-reading-impaired adults and 10 dyslexic readers. In 11 of 12 controls, activated areas were detected in posterior brain regions that were sensitive to word degradation (stronger or earlier response to noiseless words than to the most heavily degraded words) and to word-likeness of the stimulus (stronger or earlier response to noiseless words than to symbol strings). As is evident from Figure 12.4a, the letter-string-specific responses of the controls were strongly left lateralised, concentrating to the inferior occipi-totemporal border (11 sources in 10 individuals). This activation typically peaked around 145 ms for clear words, and about 10 ms later for heavily degraded words and for symbol strings. The letter-string-specific responses were equally strong to all visible words (noise 0, 8 and 16) and were reduced by about 30% to heavily degraded words (noise 24) and to symbol strings. Further, the responses peaked earlier to words containing little or no noise (noise 0, 8) than to more heavily degraded words or symbol strings. The responses were also stronger to visible than to heavily degraded syllables or two-item symbol strings. However, for the single letters degradation seemed to play no role, either in response strengths or latencies (Figure 12.4b and c).

Degradation had almost an opposite effect on the early activation of poste-rior occipital areas preceding the lateral occipitotemporal letter-string-specific responses. In 9 controls, 16 sources had weaker responses to noiseless patches than to noise patches at the next noise level 8, peaking within 130 ms of word onset. These sources were distributed along the ventral visual stream, bordering on visual area V1 and extending as far later-ally as visual area V4 (Figure 12.5a). For all stimulus conditions (0 to four-item strings), the response strengths monotonically increased with increasing noise level (Figure 12.5b). Further, for the noiseless letter and symbol strings the strength of the responses systematically increased with increasing number of items in the strings. Degradation increases the frequency of local luminance contrast borders, and thus the number of visual features. Therefore, posterior occipital areas are likely to be involved in visual feature analysis.

In line with the patterns reported for the controls, dyslexic participants had activation in the posterior occipital areas, increasing in strength with

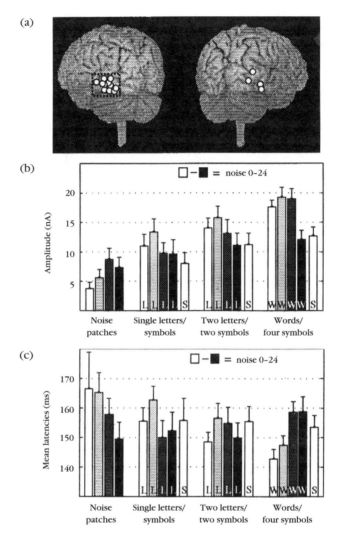

Figure 12.4. (a) The location of activity showing preference to letter-string stimuli up to 180 ms after stimulus onset in controls. Activation was concentrated in the left inferior occipitotemporal cortex (dashed rectangle). (b) Mean (+ SEM) strength and (c) peak latency of the letter-string-specific responses. (Modified from Tarkiainen et al. 1999.)

increasing noise level. The number of controls (nine individuals) and dyslexic participants (seven individuals) who had at least one source of activation involved in visual feature analysis (statistically significantly stronger responses to the noisiest patches than to noiseless patches) did not differ between the groups. Nor were statistically significant differences discovered in the overall number of sources (21 in control and 11 in dyslexic partici-

(a)   (b)

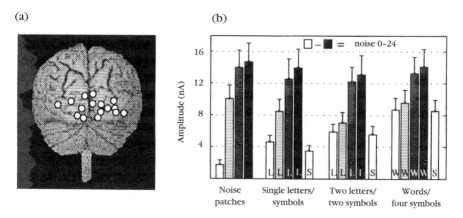

Figure 12.5. (a) The location of activity involved in visual feature analysis up to 130 ms after stimulus onset in controls. (b) Mean (+ SEM) strength of activation involved in visual feature analysis. (Modified from Tarkiainen et al. 1999.)

pants) (Figure 12.6a). In addition, the response latencies or amplitudes did not differ between the groups.

The letter-string-specific responses at the left inferior occipitotemporal border, invariably found in ten controls, were detected in only two dyslexic participants (dashed rectangles in Figure 12.6b). In two dyslexic individuals letter-string-specific sources were located more than two standard deviations more posterior in the left medial occipital area. One dyslexic individual had two letter-string-specific responses in the right hemisphere. In addition, the overall strength of these letter-string-specific responses was reduced in dyslexic participants compared with the mean source strength of all letter-string-specific responses in controls (Figure 12.6b).

Conclusions of the letter-string experiments

The study of Tarkiainen et al. (1999) revealed that the strength of activation in the bilateral posteromedial occipital areas increased with increasing noise level. When noise level was low, the activation increased with an increasing number of visual items in the images. The level of activation did not differentiate between words and symbols. This pattern of activation clearly suggests involvement of medial occipital areas in object-invariant visual feature analysis. The activation peaked around 100 ms after word onset. Earlier neuroimaging studies reported increased activation of posteromedial occipital areas for scrambled images (Puce et al., 1996; Grill-Spector et al., 1998) or when noise was added to the images (Malach et al., 1995), in line with the present results. Both manipulations increase the number of local luminance contrast borders, and thus the number of visual features.

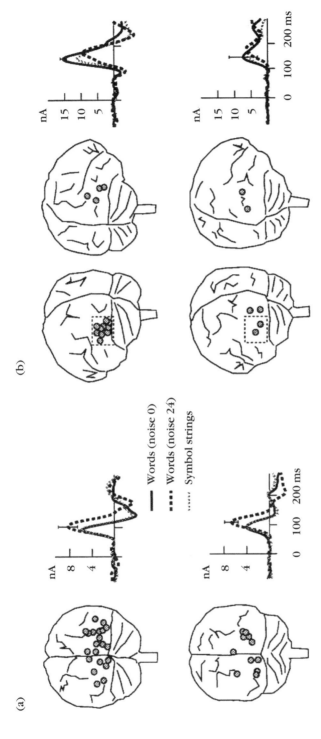

Figure 12.6. The location and time behaviour of all sources of activation involved in visual feature analysis in control (a, upper row) and dyslexic participants (a, lower row). The location and mean time behaviour of all sources specifically involved in letter-string analysis in controls (b, upper row) and dyslexic readers (b, lower row). Contrary to the control group, only two dyslexic readers had letter-string-specific responses in the left inferior occipitotemporal cortex (dashed rectangles). (Modified from Helenius et al. 1999b.)

The time course of this activation around 100 ms after stimulus onset is in agreement with a previous intracranial study (Allison et al., 1994). No differences were detected between non-impaired and dyslexic readers in this early stage of visual word recognition, characterised by object non-specific visual feature analysis.

Clear differences were, however, detected between dyslexic and fluent readers during prelexical orthographic word processing: the letter-string-specific responses, prominent in the left occipitotemporal area in controls, were mostly undetectable in dyslexic participants. The earlier and stronger responses to words than to equally long symbol strings confirmed the letter-string-specific role of the responses. Further, as the degradation influenced the response strengths to both words and syllables, this activation is likely to be prelexical (as was also suggested by equally strong responses to words and non-words in this same area by Salmelin et al., 1996). The location (Puce et al., 1996) and timing (Nobre, Allison and McCarthy, 1994) of letter-string-specific responses are in accordance with earlier neuroimaging studies. The reduced activation in the occipitotemporal area in dyslexic participants agrees further with our earlier findings (Salmelin et al., 1996; Helenius et al., 1999a), as well as two recent functional magnetic resonance imaging (fMRI) studies (Rumsey et al., 1997; Shaywitz et al., 1998) and a positron emission tomography (PET) study (Brunswick et al., 1999).

Summary of the neuromagnetic findings in dyslexic and non-impaired readers

The MEG studies were successful in dissociating distinct subprocesses of reading in dyslexic and non-reading-impaired individuals. Cortical signals reflecting processing of visual features of the words originated in the bilateral posteromedial occipital area, peaking around 100 ms. These early signals were similar between dyslexic individuals and controls. Prelexical orthographic analysis took place in the left occipitotemporal border around 150 ms after word onset. During this stage, the first differences between dyslexic and fluent readers emerged: in dyslexic readers the left occipitotemporal activation between 100 and 200 ms was mostly undetectable. The subsequent postlexical semantic activation, recruiting neural populations of the left superior temporal lobe between 250 and 600 ms after word onset, was delayed in dyslexic readers.

Future goals

As literacy is a relatively new skill or even lacking in certain human cultures, brain structures genetically devoted to reading are unlikely to exist. During reading, acquisition processes shared with other cognitive operations, such as speech processing or object recognition, are probably utilised instead. Later, as the reading skills develop and become automated, neural populations might become specialised for the execution of certain reading-related operations. The occipitotemporal area, involved in prelexical word processing, as well as the superior temporal cortex, involved in semantic processing, might well contain neural populations that develop their functional role in word recognition relatively late in life. In dyslexic readers functional development could be disturbed, especially in the occipitotemporal area, which would account for the reduced level of activation in this area during reading. Thus, the reasons underlying difficulties in acquiring automated reading would also be responsible for the functional underdevelopment of certain brain structures.

Phonemic skills at pre-school age predict later success in reading (Lundberg, Olofsson and Wall, 1980) and phonological processing deficits are thus far the only identified causal correlations of reading difficulties (Bradley and Bryant, 1983). However, more basic auditory deficits as well as magnocellular visual defects might also contribute to dyslexia. Although the parvocellular stream is mainly engaged in visual object and word processing, the magnocellular pathway might contribute to some aspects of reading such as letter-position encoding (Cornelissen et al., 1998). In the future, it would be of great importance to characterise auditory word processing in dyslexia and the relative contribution of, for example, auditory, phonological and visual factors on the cortical organisation of visual word recognition in children learning to read.

References

Ahonen, A.I., Hämäläinen, M.S., Kajola, M.J. et al. (1993). 122-channel SQUID instrument for investigating the magnetic signals from the human brain. *Physica Scripta* **T49**: 198–205.

Allison, T., McCarthy, G., Nobre, A., Puce, A. and Belger, A. (1994). Human extrastriate visual cortex and the perception of faces, words, numbers, and colors. *Cerebral Cortex* **5**: 544–554.

Balota, D.A. and Chumbley, J.I. (1985). The locus of word-frequency effects in the pronunciation task: Lexical access and/or production? *Journal of Memory and Language* **24**: 89–106.

Bradley, L. and Bryant, P.E. (1983). Categorizing sounds and learning to read – a causal connection. *Nature* **301**: 419–421.

Brandeis, D., Vitacco, D. and Steinhausen, H.-C. (1994). Mapping brain electric microstates in dyslexic children during reading. *Acta Paedopsychiatrica* 239–247.

Brunswick, N., McCrory, E., Price, C.J., Frith, C.D. and Frith, U. (1999). Explicit and implicit processing of words and pseudowords by adult developmental dyslexics: A search for Wernicke's Wortschatz? *Brain* **122**: 1901–1917.

Coltheart, M. (1978). Lexical access in simple reading tasks. In: Underwood, G. (ed.), *Strategies of Information Processing*. New York: Academic Press, pp. 151-216.

Coltheart, M., Curtis, B., Atkins, P. and Haller, M. (1993). Models of reading aloud: Dual-route and parallel-distributed-processing approaches. *Psychological Review* 100: 589-608.

Connolly, J.F., Phillips, N.A. and Forbes, K.A.K. (1995). The effects of phonological and semantic features of sentence-ending words on visual event-related brain potentials. *Electroencephalography and Clinical Neurophysiology* 94: 276-287.

Cornelissen, P.L., Hansen, P.C., Hutton, J.L., Evangelinou, V. and Stein, J.F. (1998). Magnocellular visual function and children's single word reading. *Vision Research* 38: 471-482.

Fiez, J.A. (1997). Phonology, semantics, and the role of the left inferior prefrontal cortex. *Human Brain Mapping* 5: 79-83.

Geschwind, N. (1970). The organization of language and the brain. *Science* 170: 940-944.

Grill-Spector, K., Kushnir, T., Hendler, T., Edelman, S., Itzchak, Y. and Malach, R. (1998). A sequence of object-processing stages revealed by fMRI in the human occipital lobe. *Human Brain Mapping* 6: 316-328.

Gross-Glenn, K., Duara, R., Barker, W.W. et al. (1991). Positron emission tomographic studies during serial word-reading by normal and dyslexic adults. *Journal of Clinical and Experimental Neuropsychology* 13: 531-544.

Hämäläinen, M., Hari, R., Ilmoniemi, R.J., Knuutila, J. and Lounasmaa, O.V. (1993). Magnetoencephalography: theory, instrumentation, and applications to noninvasive studies of the working human brain. *Reviews of Modern Physics* 65: 413-497.

Hart, J. and Gordon, B. (1990). Delineation of single-word semantic comprehension deficit in aphasia, with anatomical correlation. *Annals of Neurology* 27: 226-231.

Helenius, P., Salmelin, R., Service, E. and Connolly, J. (1998). Distinct time courses of word and context comprehension in the left temporal cortex. *Brain* 121: 1133-1142.

Helenius, P., Salmelin, R., Service, E. and Connolly, J. (1999a). Semantic cortical activation in dyslexic readers. *Journal of Cognitive Neuroscience* 11: 535-550.

Helenius, P., Tarkiainen, A., Cornelissen, P., Hansen, P.C. and Salmelin, R. (1999b). Dissociation of normal feature analysis and deficient processing of letter-strings in dyslexic adults. *Cerebral Cortex* 9: 476-483.

Howard, D., Patterson, K., Wise, R. et al. (1992). The cortical localization of the lexicons. *Brain* 115: 1769-1782.

Hynd, G.W., Hynd, C.R., Sullivan, H.G. and Kingsbury, T.B. (1987). rCBF in developmental dyslexia: activation during reading in a surface and deep dyslexia. *Journal of Reading Disability* 20: 294-300.

Kutas, M. and Hillyard, S.A. (1980). Reading senseless sentences: brain potentials reflect semantic incongruity. *Science* 207: 203-205.

Lounasmaa, O.V., Hämäläinen, M., Hari, R. and Salmelin, R. (1996). Information processing in the human brain: magnetoencephalographic approach. *Proceedings of the National Academy of Sciences of the USA* 93: 8809-8815.

Lundberg, I., Olofsson, A. and Wall, S. (1980). Reading and spelling skills in the first school years predicted from phonemic awareness skills in kindergarten. *Scandinavian Journal of Psychology* 980: 159-173.

McCarthy, G., Nobre, A.C., Bentin, S. and Spencer, D.D. (1995). Language-related field potentials in the anterior-medial temporal lobe: I. Intracranial distribution and neural generators. *Journal of Neuroscience* 15: 1080-1089.

Malach, R., Reppas, J.B., Benson, R.R. et al. (1995). Object-related activity revealed by functional magnetic resonance imaging in human occipital cortex. *Proceedings of the National Academy of Sciences of the USA* **92**: 8135-8139.

Nobre, A.C. and McCarthy, G. (1995). Language-related field potentials in the anterior-medial temporal lobe: II. Effects of word type and semantic priming. *Journal of Neuroscience* **15**: 1090-1098.

Nobre, A.C., Allison, T. and McCarthy, G. (1994). Word recognition in the human inferior temporal lobe. *Nature* **372**: 260-263.

Paulesu, E., Frith, C.D. and Frackowiak, R.S.J. (1993). The neural correlates of the verbal component of working memory. *Nature* **362**: 342-345.

Petersen, S.E., Fox, P.T., Posner, M.I., Mintun, M. and Raichle, M.E. (1988). Positron emission tomographic studies of the cortical anatomy of single-word processing. *Nature* **331**: 585-589.

Puce, A., Allison, T., Asgari, M., Gore, J.C. and McCarthy, G. (1996). Differential sensitivity of human visual cortex to faces, letterstrings, and textures: A functional magnetic resonance imaging study. *Journal of Neuroscience* **16**: 5205-5215.

Pugh, K.R., Shaywitz, B.A., Shaywitz, S.E. et al. (1996). Cerebral organization of component processes in reading. *Brain* **119**: 1221-1238.

Rumsey, J.M., Berman, K.F., Denckla, M.B., Hamburger, S.D., Kruesi, M.J. and Weinberger, D.R. (1987). Regional cerebral blood flow in severe developmental dyslexia. *Archives of Neurology* **44**: 1144-1150.

Rumsey, J.M., Andreason, P., Zametkin, A.J. et al. (1992). Failure to activate the left temporoparietal cortex in dyslexia. *Archives of Neurology* **49**: 527-534.

Rumsey, J.M., Nace, K., Donohue, B., Wise, D., Maisog, J. and Andreason, P. (1997). A positron emission tomographic study of impaired word recognition and phonological processing in dyslexic men. *Archives of Neurology* **54**: 562-573.

Salmelin, R., Service, E., Kiesilä, P., Uutela, K. and Salonen, O. (1996). Impaired visual word processing in dyslexia revealed with magnetoencephalography. *Annals of Neurology* **40**: 157-162.

Shaywitz, S.E., Shaywitz, B.A., Pugh, K.R. et al. (1998). Functional disruption in the organization of the brain for reading in dyslexia. *Proceedings of the National Academy of Sciences of the USA* **95**: 2636-2641.

Tarkiainen, A., Helenius, P., Hansen, P.C., Cornelissen, P.L. and Salmelin, R. (1999). Dynamics of letter string perception in the human occipitotemporal cortex. *Brain* **122**: 2119-2132.

CHAPTER 13

Culture, the brain and dyslexia

UTA FRITH

One hundred years of dyslexia research: what have we learned?

After a turbulent history which swerved from recognising dyslexia as a neurologically based disorder to reviling the very concept of dyslexia, most researchers and practitioners now agree that dyslexia is not a figment of the imagination. They generally agree on the kind of disorder that dyslexia appears to be, namely, a developmental disorder of genetic origin with a neurological basis. The arguments that dyslexia is just a social construct rather than a natural entity are no longer worth attacking, so thoroughly have they lost their ground. However, many questions remain to be answered. On the one hand, research in genetics and brain anatomy and function in dyslexia of the last few decades has provided many clues to the complex causes of the disorder; on the other, behavioural research has shown that dyslexia is highly variable in its manifestations and may need to be split into many subtypes. It is perhaps for these reasons that we are still lacking an unequivocal definition of the disorder.

No genetic marker has been found that can be used as a basis for a quick, objective and early diagnosis, and until the phenotype is appropriately speci-fied, genetic markers remain an impossible aim. What of the use of brain anatomy and functional brain imaging? Again a major stumbling block is the identification of the phenotype. Nevertheless, these techniques are robust enough to demonstrate significant group differences in both brain structure and function. They are not suitable, however, for defining and identifying individual cases. Thus, the consensus about the nature of dyslexia is still somewhat precarious. One of the hotly debated points is whether dyslexia is a condition that makes reading and reading-related skills qualitatively different from normal, or whether it is simply the tail end of a normally distributed continuum of skills. The implication of the continuity view is that dyslexia may not be a separate entity and not necessarily a disorder – merely a normal variation. The implication of the category view is that dyslexia is a separate entity and a disorder.

The diagnosis of dyslexia is made on the basis of behavioural criteria, and these criteria remain arbitrary. Behavioural criteria are by their very nature biased towards the continuity assumption. Scores on reading and related diagnostic tests are normally distributed. The tests are designed that way. Criteria are then set up to specify a certain cut-off point on test scores. This then captures the lowest scoring individuals, be it 1 or 2 standard deviations below the mean for the population norms. Low scores on critical tests may raise the suspicion of dyslexia, but they do not define it. After all, low scores can be obtained for a variety of reasons, e.g. a child may have been inadvertently tested on a reading test that is not in his native language. To avoid errors of diagnosis, exclusion criteria have to be specified. One of the most common reasons for low scores on an educational achievement test is low IQ and, for this reason, an individual's score on a reading or spelling test needs to be seen in relation to the individual's IQ. This results in the famous discrepancy definition of dyslexia, which again depends on arbitrary cut-off points. How far below the expected level should an individual's reading score lie in order to indicate dyslexia?

Carefully formulated exclusion criteria may take care of errors of wrongly diagnosing a child as dyslexic. On the other hand, they do nothing to avoid the opposite error: missing a diagnosis when it should be given. This happens not infrequently. With good remedial teaching over a number of years children qualify less and less for the discrepancy diagnosis. Yet they have not lost the problem and continue to have trouble with written language. They simply pass the diagnostic tests that have eventually become insensitive. Different tests have to be applied at different ages with the undesirable consequence that different sets of criteria are needed. If different ages need different criteria, then the problem is even more acute when we compare individuals in different countries with different educational standards and different writing systems. Is dyslexia to be redefined at each age? Is dyslexia to be redefined in each language? Surely, a highly unsatisfactory state of affairs.

A way out of this impasse is to take into account not only the behavioural level for the definition of dyslexia, but also the cognitive and biological level, as well as their interaction with environmental factors (Frith, 1999). The framework suggested by this approach is referred to as a three-level framework and a visual notation to indicate these levels has proved useful (Morton and Frith, 1995). Figure 13.1 shows the basic outline of this framework which can be applied to all developmental disorders of biological origin.

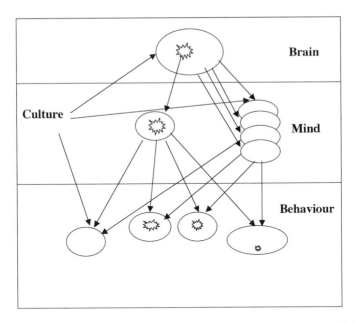

Figure 13.1. The three-level framework for causal modelling of developmental disorders.

Cultural factors interact with internal factors at each of the three levels (brain, mind, behaviour). Here the flash-point symbol indicates a biological abnormality, that impacts on a single cognitive component, leaving other components intact. At the behavioural level, varying degrees of impairment are shown on several tests. The variability is the result of the interaction of the different cognitive and cultural factors. In one test, the furthest left in Figure 13.1, compensation, resulting from both cultural factors and other internal factors, was so successful as to obliterate any sign of the underlying fault. The resulting picture is only confusing if the behavioural level is considered in isolation. Taking into account all levels simultaneously allows the conceptualisation of a developmental disorder with variable manifestations, such as dyslexia.

The notation is helpful in allowing us to see the chameleon-like nature of dyslexic signs without losing sight of the disorder itself. First, the notation indicates that the behavioural measures are influenced by a large number of factors, divided here roughly into those that are internal and those that are external to the individual, e.g. some internal factors that affect test performance have to do with a particular underlying cognitive deficit, which will manifest itself differently in performance at different ages. Other internal factors have to do with cognitive components that are intact and might act as compensatory forces. The effects of external factors can also be seen as having either negative or positive effects on performance. Those cultural influences provided through expert teaching and transparent orthography would have a beneficial effect. The cultural influences that arise from a poor attitude to literacy, or those arising from a complex orthography, would have a detrimental effect. The notation shows that behavioural data – for example, a test score on a reading test – are far from being a direct and pure index of an underlying cognitive function, but rather a remote and noisy reflection. When we consider causes of dyslexia, the notation of the three-level framework makes explicit that there are interactions between genetic and environmental factors, thus making obsolete discussions of nature versus nurture, and pointing to complex rather than simple causes. The diagram in Figure 13.1 can easily be expanded to add more than one presumed biological, cognitive or environmental cause.

The notation also allows differences and similarities between the two sides of the dyslexia debate to become more explicit – the category versus continuity view. Continuity is always present at the behavioural level, but not necessarily at the cognitive and biological levels. On the category view, the assumption is that at the biological and cognitive level qualitative abnormalities would be detected. These can perhaps be understood as faulty or even missing components. On the continuity view, the assumption would be that there are no qualitative abnormalities at any level. In particular, critical cognitive components and their anatomical substrates would be the same as in normal readers, but functioning less well. Clearly, the arguments for and against these two views can be resolved only when we have better knowledge of the underlying components and their function. What the notation makes clear is that the debate cannot be decided merely on the basis of behavioural data.

The following section considers the potentially strong effects on reading, both negative and positive, that are associated with the writing system adopted in different European languages. It focuses mainly on a comparison between Italian, which enjoys a highly transparent orthography, and English, which is infamous for its complex and even contrary use of the alphabetic code. The effects are considered first on normal reading skill, and then on dyslexia. If there are differences in the transparency of the writing system, we should expect that this would affect highly skilled readers as well as those whose reading is impaired. The size of the effect should enable us to gauge the contribution of cultural factors on the variable manifestations of dyslexia. This would help us to form a more comprehensive picture of the disorder and to indicate to what extent we can generalise findings from one language to the other. In other words, we can ask whether the chameleon changes its colours or whether it becomes quite a different animal.

Orthographic conventions in alphabetic scripts

Cultural factors form part of the social context of which the individual is a part. A good example is the language an individual speaks and the writing system that is offered to render this language visible. The writing system and how it is taught depend on the intense interaction of many individuals over many generations. The result is more like a work of art than a simple and rational code. The translation between spoken and written form in all languages tends to contain ambiguities and inconsistencies, but more so in some languages than in others.

What are the main problems for rendering speech visible in an alphabetic system? Perhaps the most obvious is that there are too few letters in the alphabet for the number of phonemes in most European languages. One way round this would be to invent additional letters, but this is rare. In fact, diacritic marks are favoured, rather than novel symbols, to amplify the number of vowels, e.g. in Scandinavian or German orthographies. Could one alphabet, i.e. one comprehensive set of vowels and consonants, serve for all European languages and would it be practicable? Yes and no. The International Phonetic Alphabet (IPA, revised 1993) has symbols for 58 consonants, 27 vowels, 15 other consonant sounds and several dozen diacritics to specify the exact pronunciation of speech sounds. It works for specialists, but, clearly, learning and using such a comprehensive system is not easy. Furthermore, for ordinary communication, the surface features of pronunciation are less important than their meaning. Should one choose different phonetic symbols for slightly different accents? Sometimes this is important, e.g. when attempting to render a dialect. Sometimes surface features are distracting when underlying meaning is to be conveyed. Moreover, alphabetic decoding is cumbersome and it may be more efficient to recognise familiar syllables and words from well-rehearsed spelling patterns.

An important factor in the apparent perversity of orthographies is the independent development of written and spoken language. Changes in spoken language can occur very rapidly and seemingly without the control of schoolteachers and pedants. Yesterday's slang is today's conventional speech. Schoolteachers and pedants, on the other hand, can exert a considerable amount of control over writing patterns. History tells us that written language also changes but very slowly, with a tendency to lag behind changes in spoken language. The spellings of many words in English used to be quite phonetically accurate renderings of their spoken forms, but their pronunciation has changed beyond recognition, resulting in silent letters. Orthography appears to need formal intervention to codify change. This was seen in the recent spelling reform of German, which took many years of debate to put into effect. More radical spelling reforms happen from time to time, often coinciding with radical political change. The rejection of Danish spelling in the newly formed Norwegian State in the nineteenth century is a good example.

Clearly, factors outside language play a role. Political views may dictate adoption of certain spellings or use of specific graphemes. Thus, in the construction of national identity, the writing system has often served an important purpose, distinguishing one nation from another, e.g. the Ukrainian form of the Cyrillic letter for the sound /I/ differs from the one used in standard Russian. Plain practicalities also play their role. In German orthography, the ss now replaces the grapheme ß, a form long used in Swiss orthography and by international keyboard operators.

Of course, there are also factors that influence discrepancies between spoken and written language, which are inherent in the language itself. The sound system of a language and its orthography are not independent, e.g. the important role of syllable stress in English, Dutch and German creates schwa vowels and consequent clustering of consonants. This is very different in languages that are not stress dependent, such as French, Spanish and Italian. Here different syllables of a word obtain more or less equal stress. As in this case the vowels retain the same length, the vowel sounds remain constant and can be related very reliably to the corresponding graphemes.

It is not only the phonology of a language that plays a role in spelling, but also the morphology. The individual components of word stem and affixes are very clear in Italian. Here, gender is marked, plural is marked very explicitly and so is the tense in verbs. Likewise, the structure of word compounds using prepositions for verbs, or forming new nouns, is highly rule governed and expressed equally in phonological and orthographic forms. Marking morphological relationships in English is often more transparent in writing than in speaking, e.g. the relationship between muscle and muscular is shown in the spelling, but is not marked when speaking. In the case of past tense, the ending -ed trumps the pronunciation /t/ (jumped). In German, the relationship of vowels is retained in singular and plural form (*Rad – Räder*), although the phonological form changes, and this is reflected in the Umlaut.

English spelling, just like traditional European architecture, is rich and varied. Even if you are a highly skilled reader, it is possible to encounter a novel word, say a place name, and not know how to pronounce it, just as it is possible to encounter a building in a novel style built with unconventional materials. 'Chiltern Hills' might be the name of a house with no number, which is not situated on a hill. It is an individual name that has to be learnt individually. This sort of problem might be found in other countries too, but hardly in terms of unique spelling patterns. In Italian, Spanish, Finnish or Hungarian, the expectation is that you would be able to pronounce and make sense of a new name. These languages have in common a high degree of transparency of phonology, morphology and orthography. If all these factors work in the same direction, one might presume that learning the orthography is indeed child's play. The analogy with architecture suggests that they are more akin to a rationally planned city-scape. Here 13th Street naturally comes after 12th Street, and here ideal materials are present for building and result in essentially similar structures. To take the architectural metaphor a step further, certain words in English are like ancient monuments with preservation orders: their spelling, although irregular, is remembered lovingly.

What does the persistence of idiosyncratic spelling tell us? The human brain is geared towards remembering names, places and spelling as individual objects. Learning does not depend on the existence of transparent rules. Of course, it is helpful, especially in the learning phase, when clear and generalisable rules exist. However, at a later stage, there is apparently a tempting short cut. It is easy to recognise a familiar word as a 'well-loved' individual with its own particular sound, meaning and spelling. This short cut seems to be used even in those transparent languages where it is strictly speaking unnecessary, and where learning is made easy by a simple code that can be used again and again. We know that here too there is a so-called lexicality effect, i.e. familiar words are recognised faster than unfamiliar nonsense words. One fact about the difficulties of dyslexic readers is that they take a long time to learn to connect sound, meaning and letters of a word. Consequently they take a long time to set up their orthographic lexicon. This, in turn, sets them back in using the short cut. In a complex orthography, this is also disastrous for non-words, which do not have a lexical entry. This is because it is often essential to consult the lexicon for the sound of parts of their spelling patterns to decide between alternative pronunciations.

As, in language, nothing is fixed forever (Aitchison, 1981), it would be foolish to imagine that a single and enlarged alphabet could permanently solve the problems of consistency and transparency of all alphabetic scripts. Interestingly, however, the consistency of orthography differs in such a way that it is possible to conduct a natural experiment. We can observe the effects of consistency on the learning of reading and writing, and in particular the effects on those children who are at risk for dyslexia.

The impact of different orthographic conventions on word recognition

The alphabetic writing system used for European languages has been developed over centuries and adapted to the varying demands of different languages. This means that learning to read and to write in different

European countries is a very different experience for young children starting school. Some children will have an easy time and quickly become versed in the translation of spoken and written language; others will have a hard time and may need many years to acquire facility in reading and spelling. Where does that leave dyslexic children who are already at risk for difficulties in learning to read and write? There is reason to believe that it will be even more difficult for these children to become literate in writing systems where spelling-to-sound inconsistencies abound than in those where a limited set of transparent rules governs the translations. In this sense some languages/ writing systems are supportive or 'therapeutic' for dyslexic individuals, but others aggravate the burden (Lindgren, De Renzi and Richman, 1985).

A particularly good contrast is shown between highly regular orthographies, such as Italian, and English, which is known to be highly inconsistent and irregular. In Italy most children learn to read within the same time span over the first year of schooling (Cossu, 1999). Only a small number of children, about 5%, were found to be struggling longer and had some difficulties up to 2 years after school entry. Even these children were eventually able to accurately read and write any word that was presented to them. This result is similar to results from young German readers (Frith, Wimmer and Landerl, 1998; Wimmer, Landerl and Frith, 1999). Here the acquisition of reading and spelling also takes 1 year for the vast majority of children, with a proportion of strugglers who catch up later and a further smaller proportion of dyslexic children who show difficulties with the accurate decoding of words and their spelling even 5 years later.

Given that acquisition of written language differs in young children, what about differences in adults? With Eraldo Paulesu and a team of Italian researchers we compared adult skilled readers, namely university students (Paulesu et al. 2000). Clearly, a gross measure such as reading accuracy would not have been suitable, because ceiling effects would be expected with this population. Instead we used naming latencies. Words were selected that were all bisyllabic and extremely common in both languages. In English, moreover, they were judged as having regular spelling. The Italian readers read the Italian words; the English readers read the English words. The two sets of bisyllabic words were turned into non-words by the simple rule of changing internal vowels or consonants. These non-words, whether derived from English or Italian, were given to both the Italian and the English readers, who were instructed to pronounce these non-words in their own phonology.

The two language groups differed markedly in their naming latencies. The Italian readers were faster at reading any of the stimuli. They were faster even at reading the non-words that were derived from English words and were in their spelling very unlike Italian words. Of course, they were slowed down in this condition relative to their reading non-words derived from Italian words.

The English readers, on the other hand, were slower to recognise all stimuli, but they took no longer to read the Italian-derived non-words than the English-derived non-words. It seemed that English readers made no allowance for potentially greater transparency of grapheme-to-phoneme mappings in one set than the other.

Suppose that English readers are handling more rules simultaneously and, just as in the architectural metaphor, they have to remember many different individual entities. Just as for English architecture, the English language has always freely incorporated foreign words of different origins, including French (bouquet), Irish (Sean), Scottish (loch) and Indian (gymkhana). Their sound is adapted to the English tongue, but their written form is more or less preserved. The many types of words require mastery even of a large set of stimuli and a disregard for consistency. This should have the effect of increased processing time and slower naming speed.

The behavioural results showed strong effects of orthographic systems. The system determines the processing load imposed by print and the facility with which words are recognised. Learning to read and write in different alphabetic writing systems is different and seems to train up different processing strategies. It is not surprising that the optimal system for Italian is not the same as the optimal system for English. Does this difference have a basis in the brain? Is the word-recognition system of the brain shaped differently by orthography? Would different resources be allocated to different aspects of word recognition in the two languages?

We expected that English readers would show more activation in those language areas of the left hemisphere that are apparently specialised for orthographic identity, relative to areas that are specialised for grapheme–phoneme mapping. The hypothesis is that, in order to pronounce a word or non-word correctly, they need to process orthographic patterns extensively in addition to alphabetic decoding. This was indeed confirmed in two experiments involving positron emission tomography (PET) scans in which participants, either English or Italian, were exposed to print. In one experiment they read aloud simple words; in the other, they saw the words but did not read them. Instead they carried out a visual feature detection task using the paradigm of Price, Wise and Frackowiak (1996).

The results for both experiments were analysed together and were clear-cut: the same reading system was activated in both languages/orthographies, but with subtle differences in the weighting of two of its components. Based on work by Démonet and colleagues (1992) and Price and colleagues (1997), these components are interpretable as relating to phonological and semantic aspects of reading respectively. The component known from other experiments to be involved in tasks of phoneme–grapheme conversion, and situated in the left superotemporal regions, was more important in Italian.

The component known from other experiments to be involved with individual word naming, and situated in the left posteroinferior temporal gyrus, was more important in English. This latter area, Brodmann's area 37, has been seen to be activated in tasks where it is important to distinguish individual objects and to retrieve their names (Price, Wise and Frackowiak, 1996). This area could conceivably act as a gateway to the names of words from their orthographic pattern. It is easy to see why this region is of particular importance in English orthography. As in our metaphor with different types of architecture, skilled readers recognise words as individual objects. Just as buildings have names, so can abstract orthographic patterns. In each case the individual pattern has become familiar and is individually recognisable from its critical features. In the case of words, these features are spelling patterns.

The other component of word recognition, the translation of phonemes to graphemes, is thought to be a necessary part of word recognition in English as well as in Italian. In Italian, however, it appears to be of greater importance. This makes sense, because it will automatically lead to the correct word name. Italian readers show greater activation of the corresponding region than English readers do.

Implications for dyslexia

Do Italian and English dyslexic individuals differ in their brain activation patterns? Using exactly the same PET scan paradigms, English dyslexic individuals differ from normal readers in activating less of the posterior inferotemporal cortex (Brodmann's area 37), the area most associated with individual naming (Brunswick et al., 1999). Would this be true also for Italian dyslexic individuals? A recent study has investigated this question using the same procedure as that used with normal skilled readers (Paulesu et al., 2001).

The results showed that Italian and English dyslexic individuals were very similar to each other, and both differed from normal readers by reduced activation in the posterior inferotemporal region (Brodmann's area 37). This was despite very different behavioural findings which suggested that Italian dyslexic individuals were far more accurate and faster than English ones. Nevertheless, when dyslexic individuals were compared with their respective peers in each country, the same significant differences appeared. Italian dyslexic individuals were just as impaired relative to their peers in accuracy and speed of reading (words as well as non-words) as English dyslexic individuals were relative to theirs. The same applied to a small battery of phonological tests. Italians with dyslexia were slower at reading digits, slower at forming spoonerisms and poorer at short-term memory for words and digits than their peers.

The results indicate that, despite cultural variation, the underlying deficit in dyslexia is the same in the two languages. Very similar conclusions were drawn for German- and English-speaking dyslexic children by Landerl, Wimmer and Frith (1997). Only the behavioural manifestations differ, showing a more benign picture in more transparent orthographies. This can explain the difference in prevalence estimates of dyslexia, which are based on the severity of the reading disorder relative to IQ. Italian-speaking dyslexic individuals can achieve a high degree of reading and spelling accuracy. Nevertheless, as the comparison between dyslexic individuals and their language peers shows, dyslexia is a handicap even in a language with transparent and consistent phonology and orthography.

From a neurophysiological point of view, dyslexia reflects the same processing abnormality in Italian and English. What inferences can we draw from this remarkably clear result? We can conclude that dyslexia is the same disorder in the two languages. Moreover, the results are consistent with the disconnection hypothesis of dyslexia. They point less to a circumscribed deficit in phoneme segmentation, and/or a grapheme-to-phoneme translation problem, than to a deficit in retrieving word or syllable sounds from orthographic patterns.

The suggestion is that the main bottleneck for the Italian and the English dyslexic reader is the same, namely, securely learning the associations of orthographic pattern, meaning and word name. This is the process most closely associated with the posterior inferotemporal region, which is abnormally underactivated in dyslexic individuals. It is underactivated perhaps because it receives less input as a result of fewer connections from one component of the language-processing system to the other. This problem has a less serious consequence for the Italian dyslexic reader, because he or she can arrive at a word name by the alphabetic code used in a piecemeal fashion. However, the English dyslexic reader is more seriously disadvantaged than the Italian dyslexic reader in a cross-country comparison. This is because the alphabetic code is not sufficiently reliable to provide an alternative solution to the problem of lexical look-up.

Conclusions

The interaction of brain, mind and culture is a fascinating subject and has aroused much speculation. However, remarkably little hard evidence has been produced to support the claim that culture can shape brain function. The work related here begins to fill this gap in our knowledge. The example of dyslexia is instructive in that it shows how a neurologically based disorder can have different manifestations in different languages, and can lead to a very different degree of burden for the individual and society. Culture shapes not only the primary symptoms of this disorder but also brings its own remedies for compensatory learning. These remedies are particularly clear in Italian, but much more difficult in English. This mirrors the difficulties of these two language systems during the acquisition period. Clearly, if you are destined to be dyslexic, it is preferable to learn to read a consistent and transparent orthography. In this sense the cultural effect of a writing system can have a beneficial and even remedial effect. By contrast, a complex writing system such as English will not facilitate learning, and thus the English dyslexic is in a particularly vulnerable position.

However, not all is gloom if you are destined to be dyslexic and to learn to read in English. Your dyslexia is likely to be recognised more speedily than in your Italian counterpart and, once recognised, you are likely to receive remedial teaching. Good remedial teaching in English often starts with a systematic treatment of the regularities in syllables – as would be normal in Italian. Exceptions are treated quite separately and often taught with the aid of ingenious memory tags and jingles. From the work reviewed here, it would be fair to conclude that English acts as a magnifying lens for the study of reading difficulties and their remediation. It is perhaps no coincidence that reading research has flourished in this complex and even picturesque orthography.

References

Aitchison, J. (1981). *Language Change: Progress or decay?* London: Fontana Press.

Brunswick, N., McCrory, E., Price, C.J., Frith, C.D. and Frith, U. (1999). Explicit and implicit processing of words and pseudowords by adult developmental dyslexics: A search for Wernicke's Wortschatz? *Brain* **122**: 1901-1917.

Cossu, G. (1999). The acquisition of Italian orthography. In: Harris, M. and Hatano, G. (eds), *Learning to Read and Write: A cross-linguistic perspective. Cambridge studies in cognitive and perceptual development.* Cambridge: Cambridge University Press, pp. 10-33.

Démonet, J.F., Chollet, F., Ramsay, S. et al. (1992). The anatomy of phonological and semantic processing in normal subjects. *Brain* **115**: 1753-1768.

Frith, U. (1999). Paradoxes in the definition of dyslexia. *Dyslexia: An International Journal of Research and Practice* **5**: 192-214.

Frith, U., Wimmer, H. and Landerl, K. (1998). Learning to read and phonological recoding in English and German. *Scientific Study of Reading* **2**: 31-54.

Landerl, K., Wimmer, H. and Frith, U. (1997). The impact of orthographic consistency on dyslexia: a German-English comparison. *Cognition* **63**: 315-334.

Lindgren, S.D., De Renzi, E. and Richman, L.C. (1985). Cross-national comparisons of developmental dyslexia in Italy and the United States. *Child Development* **56**: 1404-1417.

Morton, J. and Frith, U. (1995). Causal modelling: a structural approach to developmental psychopathology. In: Cicchetti, D. and Cohen, D.J. (eds), *Manual of Developmental Psychopathology*, Vol. 1. New York: John Wiley & Sons, pp. 357-390.

Paulesu, E., McCrory, E., Fazio, F. et al. (2000). A cultural effect on brain function. *Nature Neuroscience* **3**: 91-96.

Paulesu, E., Démonet, J.F., Fazio, F. et al. (2001). Dyslexia: Cultural diversity and physiological unity. *Science* **291**: 2165-2167.

Price, C.J., Wise, R.J.S. and Frackowiak, R.J. (1996). Demonstrating the implicit processing of visually presented words and pseudowords. *Cerebral Cortex* **6**: 62-70.

Price, C.J., Moore, C.J., Humphreys, G.W. and Wise, R.J.S. (1997). Segregating semantic from phonological processes during reading. *Journal of Cognitive Neuroscience* **6**: 727-733.

Wimmer, H., Landerl, K. and Frith, U. (1999). Learning to read German: Normal and impaired acquisition. In: Harris, M. and Hatano, G. (eds), *Learning to Read and Write: A cross-linguistic perspective*. Cambridge: Cambridge University Press, pp. 34-50.

CHAPTER 14

The role of genetics in understanding memory

LARS-GÖRAN NILSSON

In 1986, Ingvar Lundberg and the author published a paper on some very unique data about the inheritance of reading disability (Lundberg and Nilsson, 1986). The data were unique in the sense that they were more than 200 years old. They were collected from church examination records. After the literacy campaigns started at the end of the seventeenth century, the parish priests made great efforts to assess reading ability and some other cognitive functions at annual catechism examinations. The results of these examinations were recorded in church registers and are now readily available.

The priests used a 5-point scale to evaluate reading ability of all inhabitants in a parish. In the study reported by Lundberg and Nilsson (1986), we focused on individuals with low and high reading scores from the early nineteenth century. We were interested in exploring how the low scores were transmitted through several generations to their relatives living today. In another study of the same paper, we traced families with dyslexia today back to 1750 and explored whether the ancestors of these dyslexic people were poor readers at the time.

In the first study we found that the descendants of poor readers in 17 families showed significantly lower scores than the descendants of good readers. The transmission pattern in the family trees of poor readers was quite complex and we were unable to identify any simple genetic mechanism. In the second study, we identified a massive familial pattern of reading disability down to the eighth generation in one family. In another family, the ancestors had average and above-average reading ability as judged by the priests.

This investigation into the inheritance of reading disability was very important for the author's own choice of route for his research on memory functions. The reading disability study based on these unique church records was an important first step in entering a new and exciting field of exploration, namely the role of genetic factors for understanding cognitive functions in general, not just reading. After considerable reading in this new field, genetics and behavioural genetics, and after having started a longitudinal project, the author was ready to analyse cognitive functions in relation to different genetic factors. This longitudinal project, with the title 'Betula: A prospective study on aging, memory, and health', started in 1988 and is currently planned to continue until 2003. This chapter first describes the basic features of the Betula study, followed by a presentation of some data on behavioural genetics from the study.

Betula: objectives, methods and some findings

Four main objectives of the Betula study hint at the overall goal for the project. The objectives are: (1) to examine the development of health and memory in adulthood and old age; (2) to determine early preclinical signs of dementia; (3) to determine risk factors for dementia; and (4) to assess premorbid memory function in individuals who have accidents or acquire diseases during the course of the study.

Betula was designed on the basis of the assumption of continuous interactions between the individual and the environment in which the individual lives. The individual factors include medical and psychological parameters, in addition to age, gender and genetic markers. The environmental factors include a chain of events to which the individual is exposed, and the experiences that the individual accumulates from these exposures throughout life. These environmental factors are manifested in family history, education, occupation, residential area, previous morbidity, risk factors, socioeconomic status, social networks, lifestyles and habits, and use and availability of social and medical facilities.

There are three waves of data collection in the Betula study. The first was conducted in 1988-90, the second in 1993-95 and the third in 1998-2000. One sample of 1000 participants in the age cohorts of 35, 40, 45, ..., 80 years underwent testing in 1988-90 (100 participants for each of these 10 cohorts). This sample and two additional samples of equal size were tested in 1993-95 and in 1998-2000. A fourth sample was tested for the first time in 1998-2000.

With this design, it is possible to make cross-sectional, cross-sequential, cohort-sequential, time-sequential and longitudinal analyses, with proper control for practice effects. These analyses could be made after the third wave of data collection had been completed in 1998-2000. Thus, this design presents clear advantages when compared with traditional cross-sectional or purely longitudinal designs.

The participants in the Betula study were first of all given an extensive examination of various memory functions. In addition, a health examination including blood tests was carried out. There was also an interview about health status and activities of daily living, and questionnaires about social and economic issues and critical life events. The memory tests were conducted by psychology students, who had been given special training in administration of such tests. Professional nurses, under the supervision of a doctor, did the health examinations and the interviews, and administered the questionnaires.

Health assessments were done on one occasion for each participant and lasted 1.5–2 hours. Blood samples were taken for blood chemistry and were deep frozen for future use. The health examination was extensive in order to provide a good picture of the health of each participant. The selection of laboratory tests was aimed at disclosing unknown somatic disorders, which might be associated with cognitive impairment, and screening for abnormal laboratory values known to be associated with cognitive impairment. Examples of such tests are for levels of vitamin B_{12}, blood folate, T_4/TSH (thyroxine/thyroid-stimulating hormone), blood glucose and serum calcium.

A large-scale test battery was used for assessing memory. This battery was composed in such a way that tests were theoretically motivated, and so that a wide range of processes and memory systems (episodic memory, semantic memory, perceptual representation system, short-term memory and procedural memory) could be explored analytically. The memory tests selected and a few traditional psychometric tests were thoroughly described in Nilsson et al. (1997). A brief outline is presented here, together with some of the main results obtained from the first wave of data collection.

Episodic memory

There were eight sets of episodic memory tasks included in the battery: prospective memory, face recognition, name recognition, action memory, sentence memory, word recall with or without a distractor task, source recall and memory for activities. In the prospective memory task, participants were instructed to remind the experimenter at the end of the memory test session, when all tests had been completed, to sign a piece of paper. When the whole memory session was completed, the participant reminded the experimenter to sign a paper, or failed to do so. This is an event-based prospective memory task, which, in line with previous research (e.g. Einstein and McDaniel, 1990), revealed decreasing levels of performance as a function of age (Mäntylä and Nilsson, 1997). Those participants who failed to remember to remind the experimenter about signing the paper were cued about the task.

With regard to the recognition task for faces and names, participants were first presented with 16 colour photographs of faces and made-up, regular and frequently used Swedish names. They were told to remember the faces and the surnames for a later recognition test. At this later test, they were also asked to remember the first name of each face, which was, therefore, learnt incidentally. Data from the Betula study revealed age deficits in face recognition (Larsson et al., 2002), which is in line with previous research (e.g. Smith and Winograd, 1978; Bartlett and Leslie, 1986; Larrabee and Crook, 1993). Data also revealed age deficits in memory for names (Nilsson et al., 1997; Larsson et al., 2002) in line with previous studies (e.g. Cohen and Faulkner, 1986; Larrabee and Crook, 1993). Comparison of face and name retrieval showed that younger as well as older adults remembered faces to a greater extent than names.

Action and sentence memory tasks have been extensively used in our laboratory for a long time and play an important role in the Betula battery. In these tasks, participants were first presented with two successive lists of short sentences in imperative form (e.g. *roll the ball, break the match*) with a free recall test given immediately after each list. Each sentence, consisting of a verb and a noun, was presented visually on an index card. For one of these lists, participants were instructed to enact each imperative presented, whereas no such enactment was required for the other list of sentences. In addition to free recall, cued recall and recognition tests were also given. Age deficits were found in all these tasks (Nilsson et al., 1997; Rönnlund et al., 2001). In this context participants were also tested on source recall. The participants were asked, at the time of the cued recall test, whether each test item had been presented as an enacted or non-enacted sentence. Large age effects were obtained (Erngrund, Mäntylä and Nilsson, 1996; Nilsson et al., 1997).

An experimental paradigm developed by Baddeley et al. (1984) served as a model for the word-recall task with or without a distractor task. Four different conditions constitute this task. In each of these four conditions, participants were presented auditorily with a list of 12 common unrelated nouns with the instruction to learn these words for an immediate free recall test. The concurrent task was to sort a deck of playing cards into two piles: one red and one black. In one condition this card sorting was done during both the study and the test. In another condition the card sorting was done at the study only – not at the test. In still another condition the card sorting was done at the test but not at the study. In the fourth condition there was no card sorting, neither at the study nor at the test. The rationale for this task was to explore the extent to which participants can encode and retrieve information while being engaged in carrying out a concurrent task. Nyberg et al. (1997) showed that the age differences in memory performance were substantial under single-task conditions but, after correcting memory performance under dual-task conditions for differences in single-task performance, age did not predict performance. Thus, the results do not support the hypothesis that reduced attentional capacity in old age underlies age differences in episodic memory.

One further episodic memory task involved the study and test of made-up facts about famous people (e.g. *Astrid Lindgren collects stamps as a hobby*). Statements of this sort were presented in one of four different ways: auditorily by means of a male voice or a female voice, or visually on a yellow or a red card. At the test the information in the statements was presented again, but now in the form of questions (e.g. *What is Astrid Lindgren's hobby?*). This task is referred to as item recall of recently acquired facts. Participants were also asked about how each item was presented (i.e. source recall of recently acquired facts). The results obtained showed a substantial decrease in both item and source recall as a function of age (Erngrund et al., 1996; Nilsson et al., 1997), which is in line with the results from a similar study by McIntyre and Craik (1987).

In a final episodic memory task in Betula, participants were asked, incidentally, to report as many memory task activities as possible of all those in which they had been engaged during the whole test session. Nilsson et al. (1997) and Rönnlund et al. (2001) showed a clear age deficit in performance, which is in line with previous research (Kausler and Lichty, 1988; Kausler, 1991).

Semantic memory

Three sets of semantic memory tasks were included in the Betula battery: word fluency, word comprehension and general knowledge. In the word-fluency task, participants were asked to generate as many words as possible during a period of 1 minute. In one condition of this task, participants were instructed to generate words with the initial letter 'a'. In another condition, the task was to generate five-letter words with the initial letter 'm'. In still another word-fluency condition, participants were to generate names of professions starting with letter 'b'. In a final word-fluency task, subjects generated five-letter names of animals with the initial letter 's'. Word-fluency tasks usually produce minor age deficits. As time restrictions in responding were required, it was, however, thought that age differences may occur (e.g. Hultsch et al., 1992; Salthouse, 1993). The data from the Betula study revealed significant age deficits. However, when number of years in formal education was used as a co-variate in the analysis, the age differences were eliminated (Bäckman and Nilsson, 1996; Nilsson et al., 1997).

In the word-comprehension task, the participants were presented with a list of 30 target words and 5 other words next to each target word. Among these five words there was one synonym to each target. The subjects were instructed to underline this synonym. Seven minutes were allowed for this task. The results showed an age deficit (Bäckman and Nilson, 1996; Nilsson et al., 1997), which is in line with previous research (e.g. Berkowitz, 1953; Kausler and Puckett, 1980; Arenberg, 1989). In the same way as for word fluency, the age deficit disappeared when education was used as a co-variate. The third semantic memory task included a set of general knowledge questions. Erngrund, Mäntylä and Nilsson (1996) demonstrated that the 75 and 80 year olds showed a lower memory performance in this task than all other age cohorts.

Perceptual representation system

A name stem completion task was used for assessing the perceptual representation system or priming. In this task, participants were presented with name stems and were asked to say the first name that came to mind for each stem they saw. There were two-letter stems of the surnames previously presented in the face–name recognition task. One set of stems served as targets for one half of the participants in each cohort and the other set served as distractors. For the other half of the participants in each cohort, the target and distractor sets were reversed. The difference in completion rate between target names and distractor names is a measure of priming, which in turn is assumed to reflect one form of memory that does not require conscious recollection of a study episode. Data from the present study revealed no age deficits (Nilsson et al., 1997). Previous research has revealed a rather mixed picture regarding the effect of age on priming. Whereas some studies report age deficits in priming (e.g. Chiarello and Hoyer, 1988; Hultsch, Masson and Small, 1991), others do not (e.g. Light, Singh and Capps, 1986; Light and Singh, 1987).

At the second wave of data collection (T2), one additional priming test was added to the Betula battery. This task is called word fragment completion. A series of words is presented to the participants at one occasion during the test session, e.g. the word *assassin*. On a later occasion participants are presented with fragments of the word, _ s s _ s s _ n. The participant's task is to say the first word that comes to mind when seeing each fragment by filling in the missing letters of the word. The amount of priming for each participant is the proportion of fragments solved minus the proportion of fragments of words that have not been presented previously in the session. Currently, no analyses have been done on these data in Betula and there are no data to report.

Short-term memory

Short-term memory performance was estimated on the basis of the Tulving and Colotla (1970) lag measure. Lag for a given word of a study list is the number of words appearing after the presentation of this item plus the number of items that are recalled before this item is recalled. If this lag value is ≤ 7 for a given item, this item is regarded as having been read out from short-term memory. If the lag value of a given item is ≥ 7, this item is regarded as having been retrieved from long-term memory. No short-term memory data from Betula have been published yet. Preliminary analyses, however, suggest that there is no age deficit for short-term memory assessed in this way, which is in line with several earlier studies (compare Craik and Jennings, 1992).

Procedural memory

Procedural memory tasks require the acquisition and retention of motor skills without conscious awareness. Mirror-image drawing, learning to read transformed script and Tower of Hanoi are examples of such tasks. The fact that amnesic patients with various aetiologies manage such tests has been taken as evidence that these tests reflect these implicit procedural abilities (Cohen and Squire, 1980; Cohen, 1984; Saint-Cyr, Taylor and Lang, 1988). We included the Tower of Hanoi test at the second wave of data collection in Betula for assessing the function of procedural memory. Although Cohen (1984) has argued that the Tower of Hanoi test is a measure of procedural memory, this problem-solving task also contains features of visuospatial ability and executive function (e.g. Kotovsky, Hays and Simon, 1985; Lezak, 1995). A reasonably fair test of procedural memory would therefore seem to require two successive tests of Tower of Hanoi. Such data will be available after analysis of the third wave of data collection. Data from the second wave of data collection only, involving visuospatial ability and executive function, showed age-related deficits. Rönnlund, Lövdén and Nilsson (2001) interpreted the results obtained in Betula as supporting the notion that the age deficits in Tower of Hanoi performance reflect age-related impairment in visuospatial ability and impairments in executive functions.

Genetic markers and memory

By the time the Betula project was well under way and the author had updated his knowledge about genetics and behavioural genetics, a first study of the effects of some genetic markers on memory had been carried out. In this first genetic study within the Betula project, Nilsson et al. (1996) examined possible associations between six serum protein polymorphisms and high versus low scoring on episodic memory tasks in an attempt to identify quantitative trait loci (QTL) contributing to the heritability of memory. These serum polymorphisms were complement C3, haptoglobin, properdin factor B, orosomucoid, group-specific components and transferrin C, which were available for analysis at the time. We were eager to include genetic markers related to the immune system and assumed that complement

C3 and the acute-phase reactant haptoglobin would be of interest as immune response factors.

Based on sex differences that we had demonstrated in Betula (Herlitz, Nilsson and Backman, 1997), analyses for these polymorphisms were done separately for men and women. In Herlitz, Nilsson and Bäckman (1997), it was demonstrated that women performed at a higher level than men in all episodic memory tasks. In tasks assessing semantic memory, there were no differences between women and men.

Significant differences between the high and low performing groups for episodic memory tasks among women were found in four of six marker systems (complement C3, haptoglobin, transferrin C and group-specific component). In men a significant difference was found only in the hapto-globin system. The strongest marker associations were found with complement C3 and the acute-phase reactant haptoglobin, suggesting that immune response factors may be of importance in preserving episodic memory function. In the haptoglobin system, there was evidence of a primary pheno-typic association involving heterozygotes (Nilsson et al., 1996). This means that haptoglobin may somehow be functionally involved in the preservation of episodic memory. An association involving heterozygotes indicates that linkage disequilibrium with alleles at other loci influencing memory function is unlikely. The association with complement C3 alleles may be the result of either linkage disequilibrium or functional involvement on the protein level.

A second genetic project within the Betula study involved the role of apolipoprotein E for memory function. Apolipoprotein E, located on chromo-some 19, is responsible for transportation of lipids, primarily cholesterol. There are three genetic forms of ApoE (alleles, $\varepsilon2$, $\varepsilon3$ and $\varepsilon4$) coding for three forms of the protein (isoforms): ApoE2, ApoE3 and ApoE4. These isoforms differ in one amino acid. ApoE3 is the most common isoform occurring in about three-quarters of the population. ApoE2 and ApoE4 occur in about 10% and 15% of the population, respectively.

Previous research (e.g. Peterson et al., 1995) has shown that allele $\varepsilon4$ of ApoE is known as a strong risk factor for the development of Alzheimer's disease with late onset and a risk factor for cardiovascular disease in middle-aged people. The pathophysiological mechanism behind $\varepsilon4$ and Alzheimer's disease is still not fully understood; at least there is still no consensus among several alternative hypotheses. One general claim is that the $\varepsilon4$ allele does not protect key neuronal structures from excessive phosphorylation, thus leading to neuronal degeneration. People with the $\varepsilon2$ and $\varepsilon3$ alleles, on the other hand, receive necessary neuronal protection and are much less likely to develop Alzheimer's disease.

There is some evidence to show that the ApoE isoforms are involved in transport of lipids to cells in the continuous synthesis or repair of cellular membranes. ApoE is necessary for cellular membranes in response to neuronal damage. Stone et al. (1997, 1998) have shown that ApoE2 and ApoE3 isoforms serve a more important role in this repair work than the ApoE4 isoform.

Within the Betula study, we are currently exploring the potential role of the three different alleles of ApoE in memory performance of non-demented participants. The three alleles of ApoE, ε2, ε3, and ε4, form six genotypes – 22, 23, 24, 33, 34 and 44. In a recent study, Nilsson et al. (2002) reported cross-sectional data from Betula on this topic. To increase the power of the data analyses, we grouped those aged 35–45 years as young participants, those aged 50–60 years as middle-aged participants, and those aged 65–80 years as old participants. Moreover, we made two categories of the six genotypes of ApoE. In one category we included ApoE genotypes with at least one ε4 allele (i.e. 24, 34 and 44). In the other category, we included individuals without any ε4 allele (i.e. 22, 23 and 33).

Previous research (e.g. O'Hara, et al., 1998) has demonstrated that carriers of the ε4 allele are more likely to develop Alzheimer's disease and, thus, have a lower memory performance, because memory disorders are seen as a cardinal indicator of a developing disease. Assuming a quantitative difference between normal ageing and dementia (e.g. Bäckman and Small, 1998), rather than a qualitative difference (e.g. Weingartner, 1986; Bartlett, Halpern and Dowling, 1995), one might expect a lower memory performance for individuals with the ε4 allele than those individuals with the ε2 and ε3 alleles, even before a dementia diagnosis is determined. According to the view of a qualitative step between normal ageing and dementia, preclinical loss of memory function should not necessarily be a critical factor.

The analyses reported by Nilsson et al. (2002) were based on crosssectional data from the first wave of data collection in Betula (T1) for nondemented participants, i.e. demented people who were randomly sampled to be included in Betula were excluded from the core sample of the 1000 participants in the S1 sample before the testing started.

The data reported by Nilsson et al. (2002) did not reveal any differences between the two groups of participants with different allele compositions. If anything, the performance for participants with the ε4 allele was slightly superior to that of those who did not carry this allele. Participants with the ε4 allele performed slightly better than those without this allele in middle age for episodic memory and in both middle age and old age in semantic memory tasks. However, analyses of variance, with number of years in formal education as a co-variate, revealed significant effects of age for both episodic memory and semantic memory, but no effect of ApoE category and no interaction between age and ApoE.

Another way of analysing data on the effects of genetic markers on cognitive performance was also reported by Nilsson et al. (2002). In this analysis participants were divided into two extreme groups with respect to cognitive performance, and the relative frequencies of the ε4 allele and the non-ε4 alleles, respectively, were examined among high-performing and low-performing participants. In a first analysis, we contrasted the ε4 allele with the ε3 allele as control.

These data revealed that the relative frequencies for high- and low-performing participants in each age group were similar for both episodic memory tasks and semantic memory tasks. Thus, even based on this type of analysis, the conclusion is that ApoE alleles do not seem to predict memory performance.

In a second analysis we contrasted the ε2 allele with the ε3 allele as control. The idea for this analysis was to examine whether the ε2 allele could be seen as a protective factor for poor memory performance. It is known from previous research that ε2 is a protective factor for the development of cardiovascular disease; it has also been suggested that ε2 is a protective factor for Alzheimer's disease, but the results reported are somewhat mixed. With one exception, there were no differences between the ε3 allele and the ε2 allele with respect to performance level. The exception was that there were no carriers of the ε2 allele among young participants, who perform at a low level in semantic memory tasks. This means support for the notion that ε2 might be a protective factor against poor memory, at least in the age range 35–45 years. To our knowledge there are no data reported in the literature that show this relationship. Further research is needed to demonstrate the reliability of this finding.

Nilsson et al. (2002) also reported cross-sectional data from the first wave of data collection in Betula for participants who, by the time of the second wave of data collection 5 years later, had been diagnosed as demented. The objective of this analysis was to compare the performance of these people at T1 with that of those who had not been diagnosed as demented.

At the time of T2 (1993–1995), there were 28 participants who had become demented out of the 1000 involved at T1. One of these participants was a 55-year-old man who had been diagnosed as having cardiovascular dementia. The remaining 27 participants in the demented group belonged to the oldest age group: 8 were diagnosed as having Alzheimer's disease, 18 as having vascular dementia and one as having alcohol dementia. Thus, the comparison of interest was between these 27 people in the old age group and the total 372 participants in the same age group who had not been diagnosed as demented.

It is quite clear from the data reported by Nilsson et al. (2002) that those who developed dementia, during the 5-year period after T1, performed at a much lower level already at T1, compared with those who did not develop dementia during the same period of time. However, these data did not reveal any differences between carriers of the ε4 allele and carriers of the non-ε4 alleles, for neither episodic memory nor semantic memory.

Obviously, these results will have to be confirmed in subsequent research before firm conclusions can be reached. One opportunity to do this will be after the third wave of data collection has been completed in the Betula study. Analyses of these third wave data are currently under way.

Thus, there is some evidence in the Betula data that genetic markers related to the immune system may play an important role for determining memory performance. However, quite unexpectedly, the ApoE gene seems to play a rather minor role in determining memory performance in the cross-sectional data from the first wave of data collection in Betula. Preliminary analyses from all three waves of data collection suggest that it is possible to tease out some negative effects of the ε4 allele on memory performance when change scores from T1 to T2 to T3 are analysed, rather than cross-sectional data from a single data collection only.

A word of caution should also be mentioned with respect to the first steps taken in the Betula study in trying to relate one single genetic marker to memory performance. Plomin (1997), when relating genetic markers to intelligence, emphasised that the heritability of intelligence is more likely to be the result of many genes of varying effect size than of few genes of a major effect. It is therefore likely that multifactorial abilities such as memory and reading should also be related to multiple genes rather than to a single gene. It might also be the case that environmental factors play a critical role in determining which genetic markers are associated with memory performance. It is a challenging task to try to determine which genes are associated with memory functioning and which environmental factors may play a significant role for these associations to be revealed. Moreover, something that is perhaps even more challenging – psychology, in particular cognitive psychology – has much to contribute to under-standing how genes work. If cognitive psychologists take their competence and skill seriously, they can play an important role in uncovering the expression of genes in complex systems such as memory and reading requiring many genes and many environmental factors. In a recent paper, Plomin and Crabbe (2000) expressed the hope that, for psychologists in the future, DNA should mean 'deoxyribonucleic acid' rather than 'did not attend'. This is a real challenge for psychology in the future: for teaching, training and research.

Acknowledgement

This research was supported by grants from the Bank of Sweden Tercentenary Foundation, the Swedish Council for Research in the Humanities and the Social Sciences, the Swedish Council for Planning and Coordination of Research, and the Swedish Council for Social Research.

References

Arenberg, D. (1989). Longitudinal changes in memory performance. Poster session presented at the Fifth meeting of the International Study Group on the Pharmacology of Memory Disorders Associated with Aging.

Bäckman, L. and Nilsson, L.-G. (1996). Semantic memory functioning across the adult life span. *European Psychologist* 1: 27-33.

Bäckman, L. and Small, B.J. (1998). A continuity view of episodic memory impairment: Illustrations from Alzheimer's disease and major depression. In: Von Euler, C., Lundberg, J. and Llinás, R. (eds), *Basic Mechanisms in Cognition and Language*. New York: Pergamon, pp. 243-260.

Baddeley, A.D., Lewis, V., Eldridge, M. and Thomson, N. (1984). Attention and retrieval from long-term memory. *Journal of Experimental Psychology: General* 113: 518-540.

Bartlett, J.C. and Leslie, J.E. (1986). Aging and memory for faces versus single views of faces. *Memory and Cognition* 14: 371-381.

Bartlett, J.C., Halpern, A.R. and Dowling, W.J. (1995). Recognition of familiar and unfamiliar melodies in normal aging and Alzheimer's disease. *Memory and Cognition* 23: 531-546.

Berkowitz, B. (1953). The Wechsler–Bellevue performance of white males past 50. *Journal of Gerontology* 8: 76-80.

Chiarello, C. and Hoyer, W.J. (1988). Adult age differences in implicit and explicit memory: Time course and encoding effects. *Psychology and Aging* 3: 358-366.

Cohen, G. and Faulkner, D. (1986). Memory for proper names: Age differences in retrieval. *British Journal of Developmental Psychology* 4: 187-197.

Cohen, N.J. (1984). Preserved learning capacity in amnesia: Evidence for multiple memory systems. In: Squire, L.R. and Butters, N. (eds), *Neuropsychology of Memory*, 1st edn. New York: Guilford Press, pp. 83-103.

Cohen, N.J. and Squire, L.R. (1980). Preserved learning and retention of pattern-analyzing skill in amnesia: Dissociation of 'knowing how' and 'knowing that'. *Science* 210: 207-209.

Craik, F.I.M. and Jennings, J.M. (1992). Human memory. In: Craik, F.I.M. and Salthouse, T.A. (eds), *Handbook of the Psychology of Aging*. Hillsdale, NJ: Erlbaum, pp. 51-110.

Einstein, G.O. and McDaniel, M.A. (1990). Normal aging and prospective memory. *Journal of Experimental Psychology: Learning, Memory, and Cognition* 16: 717-726.

Erngrund, K., Mäntylä, T. and Nilsson, L.-G. (1996). Adult age differences in source recall: A population-based study. *Journal of Gerontology: Psychological Sciences* 51B: 335-345.

Herlitz, A., Nilsson, L.-G. and Bäckman, L. (1997). Gender differences in episodic memory. *Memory and Cognition* 25: 801-811.

Hultsch, D.F., Masson, M.E. and Small, B.J. (1991). Adult age differences in direct and indirect tests of memory. *Journal of Gerontology: Psychological Sciences* 46: 22-30.

Hultsch, D.F., Hertzog, C., Small, B.J., McDonald-Miszczak, L. and Dixon, R.A. (1992). Short-term longitudinal change in cognitive performance in later life. *Psychology and Aging* 7: 571-584.

Kausler, D.H. (1991). *Experimental Psychology, Cognition, and Human Aging*, 2nd edn. New York: Springer-Verlag.

Kausler, D.H. and Lichty, W. (1988). Memory for activities: Rehearsal-independence and aging. In: Howe, M.L. and Brainerd, C.J. (eds), *Cognitive Development in Adulthood: Progress in cognitive development research*. New York: Springer-Verlag, pp. 93–131.

Kausler, D.H. and Puckett, J.M. (1980). Frequency judgments and correlated cognitive abilities in young and elderly adults. *Journal of Gerontology* **35**: 376–382.

Kotovsky, K., Hayes, J.R. and Simon, H.A. (1985). Why are some problems hard? Evidence from Tower of Hanoi. *Cognitive Psychology* **17**: 248–294.

Larrabee, G.J. and Crook, T.H. (1993). Do men show more rapid age-associated decline in simulated everyday verbal memory than do women? *Psychology and Aging* **8**: 68–71.

Larsson, M., Nyberg, L., Bäckman, L. and Nilsson, L.-G. (2002). Effects on episodic memory of stimulus richness, intention to learn, and extra-study repetition: similar profiles across the adult life span. *Journal of Adult Development* in press.

Lezak, M.D. (1995). *Neuropsychological Assessment*, 3rd edn. New York: Oxford University Press.

Light, L.L. and Singh, A. (1987). Implicit and explicit memory in young and older adults. *Journal of Experimental Psychology: Learning, Memory, and Cognition* **13**: 531–541.

Light, L.L., Singh, A. and Capps, J.C. (1986). Dissociation of memory and awareness in young and old adults. *Journal of Clinical and Experimental Neuropsychology* **8**: 62–74.

Lundberg, I. and Nilsson, L.-G. (1986). What church examination records can tell us about the inheritance of reading disability. *Annals of Dyslexia* **36**: 217–236.

McIntyre, J.S. and Craik, F.I.M. (1987). Age differences in memory for item and source information. *Canadian Journal of Psychology* **41**: 175–192.

Mäntylä, T. and Nilsson, L.-G. (1997). Remembering to remember in adulthood: A population-based study on aging and prospective memory, manuscript. *Aging, Neuropsychology, and Cognition* **4**: 81–92.

Nilsson, L.-G., Sikström, C., Adolfsson, R., Erngrund, K., Nylander, P.-O. and Beckman, L. (1996). Genetic markers associated with high versus low performance on episodic memory tasks. *Behavior Genetics* **26**: 555–562.

Nilsson, L.-G., Bäckman, L., Erngrund, K. et al. (1997). The Betula prospective cohort study: Memory, health, and aging. *Aging, Neuropsychology and Cognition* **1**: 1–32.

Nilsson, L.-G., Bäckman, L., Cruts, M., Edvardsson, H., Nyberg, L., Van Broeckhoven, C. and Adolfsson, R. (2002). Memory development in adulthood and old age: The Betula prospective cohort study. In: Graf, P. and Ohta, N. (eds), *Lifespan Development of Human Memory*. Cambridge, MA: MIT Press, in press.

Nyberg, L., Bäckman, L., Erngrund, K., Olofsson, U. and Nilsson, L.-G. (1996). Age differences in episodic memory, semantic memory, and priming: Relationships to demographic, intellectual, and biological factors. *Journal of Gerontology: Psychological Sciences* **51B**: 234–240.

Nyberg, L., Nilsson, L.-G., Olofsson, U. and Bäckman, L. (1997). Effects of division of attention during encoding and retrieval on age differences in episodic memory. *Experimental Aging Research* **23**: 137–143.

O'Hara, F., Yesavage, J.A., Kraemer, H.C., Meuricio, M., Friedman, L.F. and Murphy, G.M. Jr (1998). The APOE epsilon 4 allele is associated with decline on delayed recall performance in community-dwelling older adults. *Journal of the American Geriatric Society* **46**: 1493–1498.

Peterson, R.C., Smith, G.E., Ivnik, R.J. et al. (1995). Apolipoprotein E status as a predictor of the development of Alzheimer's disease in memory-impaired individuals. *Journal of the American Medical Association* **273**: 1274–1278.

Plomin, R. (1997). Current directions in behavioral genetics: Moving into the mainstream. *Current Directions in Psychological Science* **6**: 85.

Plomin, R. and Crabbe, J. (2000). DNA. *Psychological Bulletin* **126**: 806–828.

Rönnlund, M., Nyberg, L., Bäckman, L. and Nilsson, L-G. (2001). Recall of subject-performed tasks, verbal tasks, and cognitive activities across the adult life span: parallel age-related deficits. (submitted).

Rönnlund, M., Lövdén, M. and Nilsson, L-G. (2001). Adult age differences in Tower of Hanoi performance: Influence from demographic and cognitive variables. *Aging, Neuropsychology, and Cognition* **8**: 269–283.

Saint-Cyr, J.A., Taylor, A. and Lang, A. (1988). Procedural learning and neostriatal dysfunction in man. *Brain* **111**: 941–959.

Salthouse, T.A. (1993). Speed mediation of adult age differences in cognition. *Developmental Psychology* **29**: 722–738.

Smith, A.D. and Winograd, E. (1978). Age differences in recognizing faces. *Developmental Psychology* **14**: 443–444.

Stone, D.J., Rozovsky, I., Morgan, T.E., Anderson, C.P., Hagop, H. and Finch, C.E. (1997). Astrocytes and microglia respond to estrogen with increased apoE mRNA in vivo and in vitro. *Experimental Neurology* **143**: 313–318.

Stone, D.J., Rozovsky, I., Morgan, T.E., Anderson, C.P., Hagop, H. and Finch, C.E. (1998). Increased synaptic sprouting in response to estrogen via an Apolipoprotein E-dependent mechanism: Implications for Alzheimer's disease. *Journal of Neuroscience* **18**: 3180–3185.

Tulving, E. and Colotla, V.A. (1970). Free recall of trilingual tasks. *Cognitive Psychology* **1**: 86–98.

Weingartner, H. (1986). Automatic and effort-demanding processing in depression. In: Poon, L.E. (ed.), *Clinical Memory Assessment of Older Adults*. Washington, DC: American Psychological Association, pp. 218–225.

CHAPTER 15

Twenty-five years of reading research as a basis for prediction of future development

INGVAR LUNDBERG

Reading research has been a very active field over the past 25 years: a number of new journals (such as *Reading and Writing*, *Scientific Studies of Reading*, *Dyslexia*, *Journal of Learning Disabilities*) have been established; an increasing stream of handbooks and edited volumes are published; and societies and academies (such as the Society for the Scientific Study of Reading, the International Dyslexia Association, the British Dyslexia Association, the Rodin Remediation Academy and the International Academy for Research on Learning Disability) and numerous informal networks have been formed. Specific conferences and workshops devoted to reading or reading disability are arranged with increasing frequency each year. Reading research occupies a significant part of congresses in education and psychology (such as American Educational Research Association [AERA], International Congress of Psychology [ICP], 2000). Large-scale international assessment programmes are other expressions of the remarkably strong focus on the scientific study of reading (The International Adult Literacy Survey, International Association for the Evaluation of Educational Achievement [IEA] Reading Literacy Study and Progress in International Reading Literacy Study, Organisation for Economic Co-operation and Development [OECD] Programme for International Student Assessment).

Why did reading and reading research come into such vogue during this period? What kind of *Zeitgeist* forces can be identified behind this remarkable development? As I have been active in the field for some 25 years, my personal experience might throw light on some of the factors involved. My justification for the egocentric departure is that it is almost inescapable given the subtitle of this book, but also because of my awareness that my experiences are shared by many of my colleagues from the cohort to which I belong. Thus my personal focus may imply the potential of discerning some features of the development that might otherwise have been less obvious.

By consideration of past and recent developments, we might be in a better position to anticipate the future ahead. At least we can attempt to make extrapolations of some current trends, while being aware of the great uncertainty involved in such attempts. In the porch of a new millennium it is, nevertheless, quite natural to take stock and reflect on future development.

Early activities

The first step of my research career was taken some 45 years ago under the mentorship of Carl Ivar Sandström at the Teachers College of Stockholm. We looked at gender and age differences in spatial localisation among schoolchildren. The theoretical inspiration for this work was provided by Herman Witkin and his ideas about cognitive styles (field dependence and independence). So, basically, it was a study of individual differences in personality and cognitive style as well as a study of how a specific kind of information processing changed across ages.

My next step was taken after some years as a schoolteacher in Stockholm. In 1959, under the supervision of Mats Björkman at the Department of Psychology at Stockholm University, I started to apply *psychophysical scaling* techniques to the study of memory. If a perception could be related to the physical stimulus by a power function, why could a memory magnitude not be related to the perceptual magnitude by the same type of mathematical function? It actually worked out well. It was also possible to see the functional changes over time. This idea was too good to be forgotten, and I still have a secret dream to revive the issue.

Anyway, it was quite a natural step to look closer at the nature of *perceptual learning*. How did the perception change as a function of experience? What was actually learnt in perceptual learning? Was the learning process or the increased discrimination capacity a question of cue detection and differentiation, or was a component of verbal association involved? These questions were approached in a series of experiments where the possibility of applying information theory to quantify stimulus complexity and response patterns was also explored. In hindsight, I now think of reading acquisition as a fascinating example of perceptual learning.

The fourth theme also concerned information processing and was inspired by *the new cognitive psychology* at the end of the 1960s. The theoretical issue in my focus was now the distinction between *item information* and *order information*. In a long series of experiments it was quite convincingly demonstrated that temporal order, spatial order and item information were independently processed. The recognition or identification of an item is thus different from the processes involved in temporally and spatially relating the item to other items in a sequence. This was still very basic research related to the classic problem of serial order in behaviour.

Converging forces

In the early 1970s, we felt an increasing pressure from students and society around us that people at the university should leave their ivory tower, stop breathing the thin air of theoretical abstractions, and prove the usefulness and relevance to the urgent societal problems of their research efforts. How could ordinary people benefit from what we did? Social sciences including psychology was particularly affected by this *Zeitgeist* pressure. I responded to this pressure by looking for a field in which I could fruitfully apply my insights gained from cognitive psychology.

The experiments on item and order information involved the use of alphanumerical symbols. From my time as a schoolteacher I remembered the characteristic sequencing problem observed among students with word blindness (Dyslexia was an unknown term in those days in Sweden.) These students tended to confuse order information resulting in the typical reversals in reading and spelling. Some of them also had difficulty with the order of the months of the year or even the days of the week. Obviously, there was a chance that my findings could be relevant and help bring about a deeper understanding of reading disability. In my academic teaching I had also become interested in psycholinguistics which seemed to be a very promising branch of cognitive psychology. I had the intuitive feeling that reading was primarily a language process.

Now a challenging field of enquiry seemed to be formed. My early studies of age and gender differences, my attempts to measure memory magnitudes, my exploration of the nature of perceptual learning, my studies on item and order information and my interest in the new cognitive psychology, including psycholinguistics, all converged nicely towards a field of application of highest social relevance. And the basic question was: why is learning to read such a hard task for some people?

During the 1970s, secondary education had become available to a vast majority of the population. The labour market had become more knowledge demanding as new techniques had been introduced. Civic life increased in complexity. Urbanisation, new media, information technology, the enrolment of women in the labour market, increased mobility across borders, etc. changed the living conditions for most people. A basic prerequisite for functioning in society, for success in further education and in the labour market was now a high level of literacy. Those who failed to reach a sufficient level of reading skill thus ran serious risks of staying outside. Considering the societal importance of reading and the advances in the scientific base, it was then quite natural that reading research became a rather hot topic in the mid-1970s.

In Sweden, as in many other countries, research on reading and spelling had typically and traditionally been a responsibility of education, not psychology. However, the educational departments had responded to the *Zeitgeist* pressure by turning away from the individual learner to the general system of education and society. Philosophical issues and macrosociological analyses came into vogue. The increasing diversity of the educational system also marginalised reading instruction, in the view of many educators who had to face many problems and challenges related to secondary education. An experimental psychologist with interests in cognition, psycholinguistics and learning could easily fill the empty space left by educational research.

The final converging force was related to my involvement in textbook writing together with Mats Björkman and David Magnusson in 1969. In those days publishing houses had been influenced by art directors, copy writers, designers and other people from the advertising industry. The readability of texts became a high priority, and the interaction of text and illustrations was emphasised. However, firm opinions on linguistic and visual properties of texts were seldom based on empirical evidence. Thus, I became aware of the lack of research in this field and felt that psycholinguistics could make significant contributions.

First attempts to understand the difficulties in learning to read

My psycholinguistic orientation also included contacts with researchers in phonetics, such as Björn Lindblom and Gunnar Fant, who in turn inspired me to consider the work of the Haskins group under Alvin Liberman's inspiring leadership. The work of Alvin and Isabel Liberman convinced me that a major obstacle for many beginners in learning to read is related to the elusive nature of the basic building block of the alphabetic script, namely the phoneme.

During talking a child is normally paying attention to the meaning of a message rather than its linguistic form. As the Duchess in *Alice in Wonderland* expressed it: 'Take care of the sense and the sounds will take care of themselves.' Thus, the phonological segments of speech are not spontaneously extracted and dealt with in the everyday life of a pre-school child. According to Al Liberman, the phonological system functioned as a module that did not require conscious control. In the speech stream, the phonemic units were co-articulated by complex gestures such that the physical realisation of the phonemes varied considerably depending on the context.

The crucial factor in becoming literate then involves a step from implicit to explicit control of the phonemic segments of language. The productive use of an alphabetic script requires an explicit awareness of phonemes, a conscious control of these units, such that they can be manipulated, substituted and recombined. In a chapter in a book (Lundberg, 1978) I discussed the precursors of this ability and related the basic shift of attention from content to form to the more general decentring ability that emerges in the preoperational stage of cognitive development.

Research on phonological awareness as related to reading acquisition

A distinct advantage in doing research on the relationship between phonological awareness and reading in Scandinavia is the late school start. Until recently most children did not enter school before the age of 7. Thus, one can find perfectly healthy and cognitively well-developed children who, by the age of 7, know only a few letters and cannot read a single word (except for a few logographs). The main reason for this state of affairs is the simple fact that they have not yet enjoyed the benefit of explicit reading instruction. This situation makes it possible to avoid the confounding effects of reading skill and reading instruction when the critical role of phonological awareness is examined. It is also possible to clarify the role of general cognitive development.

Reading disability can be predicted and prevented

In my research I have attempted to answer a number of questions discussed in the current literature on the interrelationship of phonological awareness, reading acquisition and dyslexia.

My group started our research programme by demonstrating a strong connection between early phonological awareness and later success in learning to read (Lundberg, Olofsson and Wall, 1980). This association is actually one of the most robust findings of developmental and cognitive psychology, repeated and replicated over and over again across languages and different tasks. What develops later in time (reading) can hardly be the cause of something preceding it. Thus, the longitudinal research brought us a step closer to an understanding of the causal relationship. The crucial question now is whether explicit training in pre-school also facilitates later reading and spelling acquisition in school.

A commonly held view is that reading instruction is necessary for the development of phonemic awareness. However, we could demonstrate that phonemic awareness can be developed among Scandinavian pre-schoolers outside the context of formal reading instruction without the use of letters or other elements of early reading instruction. Lundberg, Frost and Petersen (1988) designed a Danish programme which required daily games and exercises in group settings over a full pre-school year. The programme included listening games, rhymes and ditties, playing with sentences and words, discovering the initial sounds of words and finally carrying out full segmentation of words into phonemes. (An American version of this program is now available – Adams et al., 1998.)

The effects of this programme were very specific. There were modest or even no effects on general cognitive functions, on language comprehension, vocabulary and rhyming and on syllable segmentation, but rather dramatic effects on phonemic skills. Thus, it was concluded that phonemic awareness could be developed among pre-schoolers by training, without introducing letters or written text. A more crucial element seems to be the explicit guidance of children when they are trying to access, attend to and extract the elusive, abstract and implicit segments of language.

The pre-school children studied by Lundberg, Frost and Petersen (1988) were followed up through 4 school years, and reading and spelling were assessed on several occasions (Lundberg, 1994). The trained group outperformed the control group on each of 12 points of measurement, indicating the long-term beneficial effect of the pre-school programme.

I presented data from children in pre-school with a high risk of developing reading disability as revealed in a pre-test on phonological awareness and general language development (Lundberg, 1994). Children at risk who were involved in the training programme had fairly normal reading and spelling development, whereas the control children showed the expected poor literacy development. Thus, it seems to be possible to prevent the development of reading and spelling disabilities in school by a carefully designed pre-school programme that brings the children to a level of phonological awareness that is sufficiently high to meet the demands involved in the alphabetic system. The at-risk children who did not enjoy the benefit of such training seemed to face serious obstacles on their journey to literacy.

Already, in 1978, I had assumed that there are different components of phonological awareness corresponding to the different levels of language analysis required by the task (Lundberg, 1978). A study by Høien et al. (1995) later confirmed this view. More than 1500 children in pre-school and grade 1 were tested with a battery of tasks including rhyme recognition, syllable counting, initial phoneme identification, phoneme deletion, phoneme synthesis and phoneme counting. Three basic factors were extracted in a principal component analysis: a phoneme factor, a syllable factor and a rhyme factor. It was demonstrated that the three components of phonological awareness were separate predictors of early word-reading ability, with the syllable factor as the weakest predictor. Not unexpectedly, the phoneme factor proved to be the most powerful predictor of early reading acquisition. Among the various phonemic tasks, the phoneme identification tasks explained the highest proportion of unique variance.

The concept of dyslexia

The traditional definition of dyslexia has been based on various exclusionary criteria (see the *Diagnostic and Statistical Manual of Mental Disorders* or DSM-IV – American Psychiatric Association, 1994). Developmental dyslexia is regarded as the kind of reading and spelling problems among young children that cannot be explained as the result of poor intelligence, lack of educational opportunities or cultural deprivation. The unexpected literacy problems seem to have a genetic and constitutional background. However, the assumed discrepancy between reading ability and general intelligence has been seriously challenged in recent research (Stanovich and Siegel, 1994; Gustafsson and Samuelsson, 1999; Lundberg, 1999). The kind of reading and spelling difficulties observed do not seem to be different among children with a wide variation in IQ. Instead, the common core problem, the hallmark of dyslexia, is assumed to be a dysfunctional phonological module, a circumscribed subsystem of the cognitive–linguistic system.

The phonological weakness, which may have a genetic background and a neurobiological substrate, is manifested in unusual difficulties with the alphabetic code, resulting in slow, effortful and error-prone recognition of written words. Thus, word-decoding problems rather than comprehension difficulties are the hallmark of dyslexia. Comprehension problems are in most cases secondary consequences of poor word recognition.

As reading is a recent cultural skill in the history of humankind, acquired and developed by systematic instruction, there is no reason to conceive of dyslexia as basically a reading problem. The human brain certainly has no special arrangement that evolved for dealing with written language. However, the process of reading parasitically uses more basic capacities, some of which might be less well developed among some individuals. These minor deficiencies, although of critical importance for reading acquisition, might not have any significant role in human life outside the context of literacy.

Our line of reasoning implies that dyslexia is a rather specific weakness often expressed in reading problems. By carefully assessing an individual's phonological processing capacity it might be possible to capture the basic mechanism involved in dyslexia (see Frith, 1997; Lundberg, 1999). Although our conception of dyslexia as a basic phonological weakness is well supported by decades of research (for an overview, see Høien and Lundberg, 2000), there are some alternative models suggesting other basic mechanisms, such as temporal processing, magnocellular deficiencies, cerebellum problems and persistence of primitive reflexes.

Further research will eventually clarify the basic mechanisms involved in dyslexia. On the other hand, manifest problems with reading and writing might be caused by a large number of factors outside the phonological module, including socioemotional problems, lack of motivation, chaotic learning and instructional conditions, cultural deprivation, language problems, etc. (Svensson, Lundberg and Jacobson, 2002).

There are a number of proximal and distal factors that influence the quality of reading comprehension. First of all, the reader has to be able to recognise or identify the written words in the text. The *word recognition* must be fast, accurate and automatic, thus enabling the reader to attend to the meaning of the text, to allocate all mental resources on the comprehension work rather than trying to figure out the identity of written words. The mental work or *cognitive processes* related to comprehension involve activation of relevant prior knowledge and schemata, forming and modifying mental models or representations, making inferences, constructing causal chains, integrating knowledge and text, monitoring comprehension by metacognitive strategies, etc. This active mental work draws on accumulated experiences stored in long-term memory. The success or failure on this level is dependent partly on the *general intellectual capacity* (sometimes indicated by IQ) and partly on the active involvement in the reading task. This involvement has to do with *motivational processes*, especially intrinsic motivation such as mastery and competence, recognising the personal significance of the text, deep interest and personal involvement.

If more than 20% of the words in a text are unknown, the resulting comprehension will probably be very modest. It has been estimated that the size of the vocabulary should amount to 40 000–50 000 words to enable young people to comprehend texts in newspapers, textbooks, manuals, directories, novels, and the like. A major bottleneck for reading comprehension, over and above poor decoding, is then a limited vocabulary. On the other hand, written texts may be the main source of vocabulary acquisition. Thus, you must know the words to comprehend a text. And if you do not comprehend, you tend to avoid texts – texts that might have given you a chance to learn new words. This vicious cycle is certainly not easy to break. The poor vocabulary observed among poor readers might be the consequence of limited reading experience and lack of early verbal stimulation in a culturally deprived home environment (see Hart and Risley, 1995).

Almost a quarter of all children in Sweden today have a foreign background with one or both parents being immigrants. Many of these children speak a language at home that might be very different from Swedish. Some children have only stayed in Sweden for a short period of time, and we should not expect them to be able to read Swedish texts with good comprehension. Children with more advanced knowledge of Swedish might not have any problems with word decoding, but they still find reading comprehension difficult. These *linguistic difficulties* are then related to limited vocabulary and limited syntactic skill. Limited cultural competence might also be an obstacle for comprehension where the child is lacking relevant prior knowledge or adequate schemata for organising and interpreting the text material.

The *cultural conditions* of some children might not encourage literacy activities. Reading and writing are not particularly highly valued in some cultures. In such environments books, newspapers and magazines are rare, and reading habits and reading interests are not well developed. Young children are not read to and they have no access to adult models who show the value and importance of literacy skills. The cultural conditions may have their strongest impact on the motivational factors.

Reading is a skill that is acquired through instruction. The *quality of the education* will certainly have a strong influence on the success of learning. In Sweden, most teachers are well trained and they use adequate instructional procedures in teaching the first steps of reading. The relatively small variance of teaching behaviour makes it difficult to demonstrate the impact of teaching on students' reading achievement (Lundberg and Linnakylä, 1992). Home background has such a powerful influence that almost no variance is left for teaching to explain.

In a longitudinal study, Jacobson and Lundberg (2000) followed the reading development of 90 dyslexic pupils from grade 2 to grade 9 and analysed their growth curves; 25% of the variance of the individual slopes could be explained in a multiple regression where intelligence and phonological factors contributed significantly. This kind of analysis deserves more attention because it can answer the critical question of which factors determine individual success. Knowledge of these factors would have important implications for remedial work in special education.

Neurobiological perspectives

A step in the direction of finding a neurological correlate to the phonological problems was taken by Larsen et al. (1990) in a study of 15-year-old dyslexic adolescents in Stavanger. Brain scans (using magnetic resonance imaging or MRI) revealed that the planum temporale tended to be of equal size in the two hemispheres more often among dyslexic individuals than among normal controls. More specifically, however, all dyslexic individuals with severe phonological problems had symmetry of the plana temporale. This was a rather unique demonstration of a neurological correlate to a specific cognitive–linguistic function. We still do not know, however, how this deviation from the normal pattern in the language cortex affects the development of phonological coding and other processes necessary for fluent reading.

It would be tempting to look for a clear-cut diagnosis of dyslexia by using brain imaging and referring people with symmetrical plana to the dyslexic category. Even when the discouraging costs are disregarded, such a procedure is not feasible. It will certainly be very difficult to assess reliably the symmetry of individual cases. Individual variability is considerable. One can also find individuals with strong indications of dyslexia based on other criteria, but with perfectly normal asymmetry of the planum temporale as well as non-dyslexic individuals with symmetry.

In this context the Rodin Remediation Academy deserves mentioning. It is an international academy of scientists with interests in language impairments and dyslexia. It was founded in 1984 by a Swede, Dr Per Uddén, and has its executive council located in Stockholm. Among its 100 members there are seven Nobel laureates and an impressive row of other, highly respected scientists from various fields. The primary interest of the academy is to promote research on reading disabilities and language dysfunctions. Since its founding there have been 25 international conferences and seminars organised under the auspices of the Academy in many different countries (the 25th was held in Riken Brain Science Institute in Japan in 1999), attended by distinguished researchers from all over the world. Several of these meetings have been documented by important publications (e.g. von Euler, Lundberg and Lennerstrand, 1989; von Euler, Lundberg and Llinàs, 1998). The Academy emphasises the multidisciplinary nature of learning disabilities and has members from a range of different fields, including brain sciences, linguistics, psychology and education.

Social dimensions of reading disability

A social perspective on reading disabilities is also provided by studies of long-term unemployed people, prisoners and inmates in institutions for juvenile delinquents.

Recently, two studies have been conducted in Sweden, reporting high frequencies of dyslexic problems in different samples of prison inmates (Alm and Andersson, 1997; Jensen et al., 2002). Alm and Andersson (1997) found that 39 of 61 prison inmates (64%) exhibited reading and writing skills that were below average for grade 6 children (12 year olds); they also concluded that 19 of 61 inmates (31%) in their sample showed reading and writing deficits attributable to dyslexic problems. Jensen et al. (2002) reported similar findings. They found that 26 of 63 inmates could be diagnosed as having dyslexia (41%) and that an additional 10 cases were borderline (10%).

However, there are methodological drawbacks associated with these Swedish studies, with high attrition rates and lack of relevant control groups together with controversial assessment methods. Information to distinguish between poor reading caused by lack of educational opportunity and that caused by phonological coding deficits has not been reported.

The first step to overcome some of the problems mentioned was taken in a study by Samuelsson et al. (2000). On the basis of detailed assessments, we estimated that about 10% of the prison population suffered from dyslexic problems, i.e. just a slightly higher prevalence than in a normal population and far below earlier estimates. The extensive literacy problems observed among the inmates were interpreted as based on social, cultural and educational deprivation rather than constitutionally based dyslexia.

In a study in progress we have an even more extensive battery of tests, questionnaires and interviews with a total testing time of about 4 hours for each participant. We have also two comparison groups: one group of younger individuals matched on reading level and one group of adult readers matched on educational level and reading habits. Preliminary results based on uncompleted groups indicate that the incidence of dyslexia is about the same in the three groups.

Institutions for juvenile delinquents

Studies by Svensson, Lundberg and Jacobson (2000) have attempted to estimate the prevalence of literacy problems in the population of juvenile delinquents in Swedish institutions. The picture turned out to be more complex than had been reported earlier. Literacy problems are certainly common among the inmates, but a surprisingly large number of pupils show adequate reading and spelling skills. In the poorly achieving group (about 25%), immigrant youngsters are highly over-represented. Immigrant pupils often show adequate word-reading ability but fail in text comprehension tasks. Dyslexia in the restricted sense (word-recognition problems based on deficit phonological coding) was not more frequent among the inmates than in the normal population (6–8%).

Dyslexia and creativity

Our main focus so far has been on dyslexia as a serious handicap in current society. However, the coin might have another side. It has been suggested that dyslexic individuals sometimes show uncommon gifts, skills and talents in fields such as the creative arts, architecture, construction, handicraft, design, etc. (see West, 1997). Systematic studies of this assumption are few, however. An attempt at clarification has recently been made by Wolff and Lundberg (2000). We studied a sample of students in creative arts and photography, and compared them with a sample of students in business school. Both types of higher education have very restricted admission policies with about 10% selection rate. Among the art students close to 30% showed dyslexic tendencies. In contrast such tendencies were almost completely absent among students in the business school. Further studies on this issue are under way.

Reading research in the beginning of the new millennium

Predicting the future development of reading research is an impossible task. Research is by its very nature unpredictable. What we have seen in the past, however, is that the development of new techniques and tools has a profound impact on the direction of research. Indeed, we do not know what new techniques will be developed over the coming decades. Some modest extrapolations based on knowledge of existing technology might nevertheless be allowed.

Further development of information and communication technology with improved speech recognition and speech synthesis will certainly be very visible in Sweden as a technologically advanced society. The empowerment potential of the new techniques is indeed very promising.

Proficiency in foreign languages, especially English, has an obvious survival value in Sweden. At the same time, individuals with dyslexia normally have basic problems with foreign language acquisition, which further increases the burden for these individuals. We have reasons to expect strong efforts in Sweden and many other countries to understand these problems better and to find new teaching approaches. One step in this research direction has been taken by Miller Guron and Lundberg (2000).

The rapid development within brain science and genetics will also have a strong impact on dyslexia research in Scandinavia. One such promising example is Päivi Helenius's dissertation in Helsinki, in which she used the new magnetoencephalographic (MEG) recording technique (see Chapter 12). Another example is Torkel Klingberg's recent work in Stockholm on the structure of the white matter of the connections between Broca's and Wernicke's areas in the brain. Functional brain imaging techniques will certainly be further refined and yield detailed knowledge about the neurological substrate of reading disabilities.

Molecular genetics is also a hot topic, which will influence our understanding of learning disabilities. The relatively homogeneous populations of Scandinavia and the Swedish Twin Registry will probably facilitate the work on locating critical genes involved in learning disabilities. This work might also be important in identifying subgroups of disabilities.

The number of genes involved in dyslexia, however, may be shown to be far higher than was initially expected in early linkage studies, and the complex interactions between the critical genes may cool off some of the optimistic claims seen over the last few years.

At the psychological level, more studies related to motivation, self-concept, and attitudes are expected. Systematic evaluations of intervention programmes will probably be more frequent and more sophisticated as the public concern over literacy problems in society increases.

The scientific study of reading and reading disability has been a hot topic for only 25 years so far. During this period remarkable progress has been made. There is no indication that the next 25 years will be any the less active or yield more modest results. On the contrary, the importance of literacy in present-day society is greater than ever, and public concern and the tax payers' willingness to spend money on reading research will be higher than ever. The future is indeed exciting.

References

Adams, M.J., Foorman, B. R., Lundberg, I. and Beeler, T. (1998). *Phonemic Awareness in Young Children*. Baltimore, MD: Brookes.

Alm, J. and Andersson, J. (1997). A study of literacy in prisons in Uppsala. *Dyslexia* 3: 245-246.

American Psychiatric Association (1994). *Diagnostic and Statistical Manual of Mental Disorders*, 4th edn revised. Washington, DC: American Psychiatric Press.

Euler, C. von, Lundberg, I. and Lennerstrand, G., eds (1989). *Brain and Reading*. New York: Stockton Press.

Euler, C. von, Lundberg, I. and Llinàs, R., eds (1998). *Basic Mechanisms in Cognition and Language*. Oxford: Elsevier Science.

Frith, U. (1997). Definitions of dyslexia and their paradoxes. In: Hulme, C. and Snowling, M. (eds), *Dyslexia. Biology, cognition and intervention*. London: Whurr, pp. 1-19.

Gustafson, S. and Samuelsson, S. (1999). Intelligence and dyslexia: Implications for diagnosis and intervention. *Scandinavian Journal of Psychology* 40: 127-134.

Hart, B. and Risley, T.R. (1995). *Meaningful Differences in the Everyday Experience of Young American Children*. Baltimore, MD: Brookes.

Høien, T. and Lundberg, I. (2000). *Dyslexia. From theory to practice*. Dordrecht, The Netherlands: Kluwer Academic Publishers.

Høien, T., Lundberg, I., Bjaalid, I.K. and Stanovich, K.E. (1995). Components of phonological awareness. *Reading and Writing. An Interdisciplinary Journal* 7: 1-18.

Jacobson, C. and Lundberg, I. (2000). Early prediction of individual growth in reading. *Reading and Writing. An Interdisciplinary Journal* 13: 273-296.

Jensen, J., Lindgren, M., Wirsén-Meurling, A., Ingvar, D. and Levander, S. (2002). Dyslexia among Swedish prison inmates in relation to neuropsychology and personality. *Journal of the International Neuropsychological Society* 5: 452-461.

Larsen, J.P., Høien, T., Lundberg, I. and Ödegaard, H. (1990). MRI evaluation of the size and the symmetry of planum temporale in adolescents with developmental dyslexia. *Brain and Language* 39: 289-301.

Lundberg, I. (1978). Linguistic awareness as related to reading. In: Sinclair, A., Jarvella, R.J. and Levelt, W.J.M. (eds), *The Child's Conception of Language*. New York: Springer-Verlag, pp. 83–96.

Lundberg, I. (1994). Reading difficulties can be predicted and prevented: A Scandinavian perspective on phonological awareness and reading. In: Hulme, C. and Snowling, M. (eds), *Reading Development and Dyslexia*. London: Whurr, pp. 180–199.

Lundberg, I. (1999). Towards a sharper definition of dyslexia. In: Lundberg, I., Tönnessen, F.E. and Austad, I. (eds), *Dyslexia: Advances in theory and practice*. Dordrecht, The Netherlands: Kluwer Academic Publishers, pp. 9–29.

Lundberg, I. and Linnakylä, P. (1992). *The Teaching of Reading Around the World*. Haag: IEA.

Lundberg, I., Frost, J. and Petersen, O.-P. (1988). Effects of an extensive program for stimulating phonological awareness in preschool children. *Reading Research Quarterly* **33**: 263–284.

Lundberg, I., Olofsson, Å. and Wall, S. (1980). Reading and spelling skills in the first school years predicted from phonemic awareness skills in kindergarten. *Scandinavian Journal of Psychology* **21**: 159–173.

Miller Guron, L. and Lundberg, I. (2000). Dyslexia and second language reading. A second bite at the apple. *Reading and Writing. An Interdisciplinary Journal* **12**: 41–61.

Samuelsson, S., Gustavsson, A., Herkner, B. and Lundberg, I. (2000). Is the frequency of dyslexic problems among prison inmates higher than in a normal population? *Reading and Writing: An Interdisciplinary Journal* **13**: 297–312.

Stanovich, K.E. and Siegel, L.S. (1994). The phenotypic performance profile of reading-disabled children: A regression-based test of the phonological-core variable-difference model. *Journal of Educational Psychology* **86**: 24–53.

Svensson, I., Lundberg, I. and Jacobson, C. (2002). The prevalence of reading and spelling difficulties among inmates of institutions for compulsory care of juvenile delinquents. *Dyslexia. An International Journal of Research and Practice* **7**: 62–76.

West, T.G. (1997). *In the Mind's Eye*. New York: Prometheus Books.

Wolff, U. and Lundberg, I. (2000). Dyslexia and creativity. Poster presented at the International Dyslexia Association conference in Washington, DC, Nov 2000.

Index